To Remember Forever

GLADYS HASTY CARROLL

To Remember Forever

The Journal of a College Girl
1922=1923

Little, Brown and Company • Boston • Toronto

The author wishes to thank the following for permission to use copyrighted
material:

*Old Sturbridge, Inc. for use of a short section which originally appeared
in their publication,* THE NEW ENGLAND GALAXY.

Harcourt, Brace & World, Inc. for use of excerpts from the Preface to
MODERN AMERICAN AND BRITISH POETRY *by Louis Untermeyer, copyright,
1922, by Harcourt, Brace & World, Inc.*

The Emily Dickinson poem, "The pedigree of honey," is included in the
collection published by Little, Brown and Company entitled THE COMPLETE
POEMS OF EMILY DICKINSON, edited by T. H. Johnson.

To the Bates College class of 1925,
to all who were members of the Bates
Spofford Club in 1922-1923,
and to the Bates faculty and administration
of the time

Acknowledgments

For permission to reprint sections from Louis Untermeyer's Preface to the 1922 edition of his MODERN AMERICAN AND BRITISH POETRY (several times revised in more recent years), as then published by Harcourt, Brace and Company, the author is grateful to Mr. Untermeyer.

She also wishes to thank her sister, Jennie O. Sanborn Hasty, for the privilege of including "At Home from Church" by Sarah Orne Jewett, a poem handwritten by Miss Jewett for her friend, Miss Kate Sanborn, and now in the possession of Mrs. Hasty. Several years after Miss Jewett's death this poem was one of several privately printed for distribution among Miss Jewett's personal friends by The Merrymount Press of Boston. In 1949, on the hundredth anniversary of Miss Jewett's birth, this same little group of poems was issued by American Weave Press of Cleveland, Ohio, with a foreword by Burton W. Trafton, Jr., of South Berwick, Maine.

To Remember Forever

THIS is the summer between my freshman and sophomore years in college, and I have decided to keep a journal.

If I am right that a diary is what you write in every day, and that a journal is what you write in at length from time to time when you have thoughts and feelings that must be held onto somehow, it is a journal that I want to keep.

I shall write in it only when I am at home on vacation. If you are keeping a journal or a diary in a dormitory everyone there wants to read it. If you don't let them, they suspect you are writing about them and that they wouldn't like what you are saying. If you do let them, they are no better pleased, either because they *don't* like what you are saying about them or because you are not saying anything about them. I know from having tried it last year, when Mr. Purinton told our English class that the way to learn to write is to write and write and write. Since then anything I have written in the dormitory has been the height of imagination, unless it was in a letter which I sealed and mailed.

The purpose of this journal is to help me remember forever what went on and how I felt about it before my nineteenth birthday. I shall be nineteen next June.

What has started me off today — given me thoughts I feel I must hold onto — is the preface to *Modern American and British Poetry* which I bought at the college bookstore in June. This preface was written last January, in New York City, by Louis Untermeyer. I have read it at least a hundred times and every time it excites me.

He says:

"Modern" is, perhaps, the most misleading adjective in the dictionary . . . The present merges so swiftly into the past that today's definition of modernity may seem, after the shortest of intervals, an impertinent apology for some safely enshrined classicism . . .

It is a happy circumstance that this volume should begin with the poetry of Emily Dickinson (born 1830) whose work, printed for the first time after her death, was unknown as late as 1890 and unnoticed for several years later. For hers was a forerunner of the new spirit — free in expression, unhampered in choice of subject, keen in psychology — to which a countryful of writers has responded. No longer confined to London, Boston, or New York as literary centers, the impulse to create is everywhere. There is scarcely a state, barely a township that has not produced its local laureate . . .

It is instructive as well as interesting to see what effect, if any, climate and conditions exert on the creator's expression; how much the gaunt and quiet hills of New Hampshire manifest themselves in the New England soliloquies of Robert Frost or how the noisy energy of the Middle West booms and rattles through the high-pitched syllables of Vachel Lindsay . . .

Vers libre, that bugaboo of many of our otherwise liberal critics, has produced an incalculable quantity of trivial and tiresome exhibitions. But so, the *vers librists* might reply, has the sonnet. Any form, in the hands of the genuine artist, not only justifies but dignifies itself. Free verse (a misnomer, by the bye, for free verse instead of being "free" obeys certain well-known though flexible laws of rhythm, balance, return and cadence) is capable of many exquisite and unique effects impossible of achievement in a strict, metrical pattern . . . Its variety is as great as its exponents . . . We find it . . . rough-hewn and massive as in the iron solidity of Carl Sandburg, brilliantly glazed and riotously colorful as in the enamelled pictures of Amy Lowell, restrained and biblical as in the sonorous strophes of James Oppenheim . . .

Latter-day . . . American poetry might be described as a sudden rush of unconnected mountain torrents, valley streams, and city sluices; instead of one placidly moving body, there are a dozen rushing currents. It is as if here, in the last fifteen years, submerged springs had burst through stubborn ground.

For this reason I have included . . . not only the often quoted poems by those poets who are accepted everywhere as outstanding figures, but examples of lesser known singers who are also representative of their age. The same spirit has impelled me to reprint a liberal portion of that species which stands midway between light verse and authentic poetry. The Eugene Fields, the J. W. Rileys . . . may not occupy the same high plane as the Masefields and Frosts, but there is scarcely a person that will not be attracted by them and thus be drawn on to deeper notes and larger themes.

What a wonderful, *wonderful*, WONDERFUL time this is to be young in America! What an absolutely, positively marvelous thing to know that, if you have something you want to say and can find out how to say it, you will be one of the springs bursting up through, and part of some rushing current, and representative of your age! Even though what runs out is only a little brook and you are listed, if at all, among the lesser-known singers, still "there is scarcely a person that will not be attracted and thus be drawn on to deeper notes and larger themes."

Emily Dickinson, "a physical as well as a spiritual hermit" of the nineteenth century, turned the key in the American literary lock with the four lines of her "Pedigree":

> *The pedigree of honey*
> *Does not concern the bee;*
> *A clover, any time, to him*
> *Is aristocracy.*

In this twentieth century in America one does not have to be Sophocles, or Shakespeare, or George Eliot, or Browning, or even Melville or Hawthorne or Walt

Whitman to be read by his fellow citizens. He has only to be swept by an urge to create, to *re*-create the America — even the small piece of America — he knows, and to discover how to do it. "The gaunt and quiet hills . . . the noisy energy . . . the iron solidity . . . the enamelled pictures . . . the sonorous strophes. . . . The impulse to create is everywhere . . . scarcely a state, barely a township that has not produced its local laureate. . . ." Oh, glory hallelujah! Because my small piece of America is singing in me, waiting to burst through, and I want nothing so much as to see it spilling out; my whole ambition is to be a local laureate. Or, just between you and me, Emily, I've collected (not personally manufactured) the honey; out there are the bees, and I'm a little old all-American clover plant. Question is: Am I going to bloom?

Oh, well, I'm not going to worry about *that*. It is much too soon to tell.

But in the meantime, what shall I do with the singing of this underground spring? Where can I keep so much honey?

The honey, of course, is everything I remember, filling the honeycomb of my mind; and the singing is in my own heart, from the way I feel about everything I remember.

The time when this house my grandfather built, this yard, these outbuildings, these fields and pastures, were my whole world, peopled only by my parents, my brother, my aunt, my grandfather and me . . .

My first memory is very distinct. I was sitting in Aunt Vinnie's lap, forming letters with toothpicks on the windowsill, and the teakettle was humming on the wood stove beside us. My brother was stamping off snow on the porch. My father and grandfather were coming up the shed stairs from the barn. My mother put a pan of biscuits into the oven and lit an oil lamp. As she lifted it to go to the cellarway where the saltfish hung I saw that she was beautiful. That is all of that first memory.

But then come the hot beach rocks and sandbags in the beds; the sunrise over the mountain, the sunset over the marshes; the howling wind, the driving snow, the pelting rain, the sea turns, the brilliance of sunlight flooding a clearing among cathedral pines; the grandmother and aunts and uncles and cousins to visit and be visited by, and neighbors of all ages known to me by their first names; the family stories, the family graveyards, the songs at night around the kitchen table or on the doorstep; the hills to slide on, the river to skate on; the neighborhood church at the fork of the roads sans steeple and sans bell; the one-room school with its flag at the top of a peeled-pine pole; the gnawing hunger, the taste of radishes just pulled, of the first cucumber of the summer, of slippery elm and tough checkerberry leaves, the smell of wild meat stewing and sour-milk bread baking . . .

How many books to hold all these, and all that is associated with them?

For a long time nothing seemed to change except the weather and the seasons. Then the changes began. The going-away began.

My brother Harold went to the city of Dover to work in a belt factory as a draftsman for $1.35 a day; but at the end of the first week his pay was raised to $1.50; and he came home every weekend.

There was the brown frame Grammar School in the village, to which I went for a spring term to learn what it is like to be in the same class with others. But I came home every night with my father from the shop where he painted and hand-decorated signs, sleighs, wagons, and automobiles.

There was the stone building on Academy Hill, where I went to meet the first people I had ever known who had been to college. A picture of blind Milton dictating to his daughters covering one whole wall . . . statues of Mercury and Cicero and Virgil on marble pedestals in the corridors . . . thousands of books in the dim, quiet library with the arched window.

The freshman reception . . . Football games . . . Camp Fire Girls . . . Hare-and-hound chases to the riverbank for frankfurt roasts and doughnuts and sweet cider . . .

But because of the time essential to all these new experiences, because I was thought too young to drive a horse ten miles a day before and after school, because my mother's only sister died and my grandmother, who had been living with her, came to live with us, and now the farmhouse was overcrowded, I was at home only for vacations. I stayed in a village house in term-time, with my mother and grandmother. My father came there for his noon dinners, but I was not there at noon, except on Saturdays; sometimes he stayed overnight, but he looked out of place among the upholstered chairs and sofas of the house we had rented furnished. My grandfather came on Fridays, which was his market day, to bring our milk and eggs and butter and vegetables; but I was not there on Fridays.

In term-time I was of the Academy and of the village, waking incredulously every morning before dawn to the clop-clop of horses' feet on the pavement, the rattle of milk bottles, and the running footsteps of the milkman across a neighbor's dark porch; drifting back to sleep to be awakened again by storekeepers opening their doors, sweeping off the sidewalk, putting out their newspaper racks and bins of fruit and vegetables, calling to one another, "Fine morning," or "Looks like rain," or "Quite a fire down at the Point last night."

There were the church bells, the factory whistle, the Town Clock, the streetlights at night. It was a world filled with people, with man-made sights and sounds and teeming activity. Yet it was a small world which I could see across, hear its every sound, feel into.

Remember the hot air rushing up through registers in the stores and in the Academy main room, making my accordion-pleated skirt stand out like a wheel. The sad, sweet face of the principal's wife, who was also my English and Latin teacher and my Camp Fire Guardian. The minister's son, who had a front tooth on a pivot and could take it out at will and make us laugh by smiling at us from behind his hand in class. The Academy library, a gathering place every Wednesday and Saturday evening though no one ever spoke aloud there and we all walked on tiptoe. The Academy motto, *Dei Timor Initium Sapientiae,* and our class motto, *Non Vespere Sed Mane.* The smell of the powder with which the post office floor was cleaned. The girls' class at the Baptist Sunday School. The play rehearsals. The Chautauqua programs. The pickle barrel in the meat market and the cats sleeping in grocery store windows. The bobsledding on Landing Hill.

Remember the war.

The tall black headlines, *ENGLAND'S BACK TO THE WALL.* The great posters everywhere, with Uncle Sam's piercing eyes looking straight into yours and his long finger pointing at you. Preparedness Parades. The call-up songs — "Joan of Arc," "America, Here's My Boy." Everybody's older brother glancing around the supper table and saying quietly, "I signed up today." Harold waiting until after supper one Saturday night, sitting beside my mother on the sofa, putting his arm around her, and saying, "I decided on the Signal Corps. I'll only be going to school, at first. At the University of Vermont. I go up there Tuesday." He stayed with us until Tuesday. Tuesday he went back to Dover to get the last of his things from his boardinghouse, return a library book, deposit some money at the bank. I was dismissed early from school to go with him. My father took us to the railroad station, but when we were ready to come back there was no train and Harold hired a man at

the livery stable to drive us. It was very cold and the
sky was gray. He held my mittened hand hard under
the fur robe on the back seat of the sleigh.

I remember the next hour in the village house, the
last hour before he went away. Five of us sitting
in the kitchen, the only room where there was a fire.
My mother's eyelids swollen from crying in the night.
My father and Harold clearing their throats before
they spoke.

"I'll get me some khaki yarn," said Grammy, "and
start knitting you some heavy socks. Right away."

I watched the clock. Half of the hour was all I
could bear. I went upstairs to a chamber where there
had been no heat all winter. The strange yellow
furniture standing all around. The straw matting on
the floor.

Once when I was small I asked, "Will Hal ever be
a soldier?"

My mother said then, "Of course not. The country
is free and united. We won't have any more wars."

But Auntie said, "You never can tell ahead."

I knelt and prayed:

*Dear God, let it be time for him to go. When he
has gone, we can think what to do. It's the going-to-go
I can't stand. . . .*

Remember the service flags in the windows; the fat
letters with service insignia in the corners lighting
the long rows of post office boxes; the training songs,
"You Can't Get 'Em Up," "Pack Up Your Troubles
in Your Old Kit Bag," "Good-morning, Mr. Zip-Zip-
Zip"; the thinking-of-home songs, "There's a Long,

Long Trail A-Winding," "Smile the While," "My In-
diana Home"; the on-to-war songs, "Good-bye Broad-
way, Hello France," "How You Goin' to Keep 'Em
Down on the Farm," "It's A Long Way to Tip-
perary" . . . The casualty lists. The headlines. The
epidemics. The meatless days, the wheatless days, the
sweetless days. "Buy a Bond, buy a Bond, buy a
Bond." People calling on the streets, "There's sugar
at the A and P!", the long lines waiting while the
grocer handed out pound bags, one to a family, and
children late for school from taking home the precious little packages to be saved for time of sickness
or a soldier's leave. Buses carrying women to work
at the Navy Yard, and bringing them back after a
ten-hour day; their proud, tired eyes at the small, high
windows. The knitting, knitting, knitting, everywhere, even in church; and the bandage-rolling at
kitchen tables after supper every night. . . . *Did you
hear — Carleton! Carleton Nowell is missing in action! Only six months after he left home . . . They
just got a telegram — Ernest! Ernest is wounded! . . .
Have you heard — Henry! The ship he was on was
torpedoed, and he was twelve days at sea in an open
boat! But he was rescued. They say he'll be decorated.*
(Henry was the mischievous one in Auntie's district
school, the one who hated to wear shoes, who said,
"Here I stand before Miss Blodgett," who brought
her in a saltbag the Scotch rose which still blooms
by our kitchen door.)

The bad news and the good belonged to us all. No
war was ever more everybody's war than that one. It
was in every hour of every day and night. We thought:

When this is finished, if the Kaiser is overcome, if the world is again safe for democracy, if Harold comes home, the ordinary troubles of life will hardly trouble us at all, for God sends them to us and we wrestle with them on the soft blanket of His wisdom and mercy. The causes of war are of Satan, who works through men and nations to wipe good from the face of the earth. Satan is the cunning, the awful adversary, now marching, rolling, rumbling across Europe, plowing beneath the seas, even piercing the skies, and we cannot rest until he is stopped.

Yet through it all our personal lives went on: The moving-picture theater upstairs over the drugstore, where a piano played and a space was cleared for dancing in the dark . . . Camp Fire meetings, Valentine parties, singing in the choir.

At the village house there were always money problems. My father had not had rent to pay for many years, until then, and his creditors were slow to meet their obligations in wartime. Grammy was trying to get a pension as the widow of my mother's father, who died soon after he returned from the Civil War, but the fact that she was now the widow of a second husband complicated the effort. My mother advertised to do fine mending and did great quantities of it on lisle stockings, handkerchief-linen underwear, lace, and silk dresses. When I was paid a dollar for giving a recitation on a Knights of Pythias program, we used it, a quarter a week, to buy sweet pickles to eat with our suppers of potatoes hash-browned in pork fat and steamed gems of barley flour; that recitation brightened a month of evening meals. At

Christmas, when two new coats were needed and only one could be bought, my mother told my father to get one for me and I told him to get one for her. I won, and my mother wept. She wept again a few months later when I was asked to carry the flag in a Buy Bonds parade, and did so, wearing my threadbare plaid mackinaw; but I was proud, both of my old coat and of the symbol of democracy which I carried. Every month a check came to me from Harold's pay, for he had named me his dependent. He had written to my mother, "What you don't need for current expenses of Gladie's education, I wish you would use to buy her a piano and give her music lessons. If anything should happen that I'm not there to help her through college, she will have my life insurance of ten thousand dollars. It is made out to her." We made the payments on the piano and I took the lessons. The rest of each check was put in the bank in Harold's name.

"He will need clothes when he comes out of uniform," said my mother.

Home was another world, in those years, to which I went for Christmas and Easter vacations, and to which we all went for the summer and early fall while Grammy made visits to her sister, brother, and nieces. At home there were still the familiar hollows in the pine floors, the braided and hooked rugs, the good homemade couches, willow and wicker rockers, and Windsor straight chairs my great-grandfather had brought there. At the kitchen table the food was much as it had always been, since it was mostly from the farm and Auntie favored molasses and maple syrup as sweeteners and cornmeal to white flour. The same faces and figures were in the same places, except that Harold had sat beside me at the end of the table until he went away and now I sat alone there. But the water from the well had the same flavor, the three maples and the ash tree stood in a row in the yard, growing bigger and mossier each year; a little beyond were the apple trees; sweetfern and yellow evening primroses still covered the banks of the lane in summer. The sun rose over the mountain and set over the marshes. We went to church on Sunday, and now I played the organ for my mother and Grammy and her sister Em to lead the singing.

I shall always be glad that on the day the Armistice was signed we had not yet gone back to the village. We had stayed at home very late that fall. It was a bright day, and I was taking clothes off the line for my mother. The wind was from the west. A crow was cawing. A hen in the barn cellar was announcing that she had laid an egg. I stood with my arms raised, holding a towel against the wind, blinking before the sun, when I heard a long, low whistle.

My first thought was, "It isn't noon!"

The next instant I shrieked, "MAMA!"

The whistle kept on, and was joined by whistles from every factory and sawmill in all the towns around, and by then the church bells were ringing everywhere. My mother and Auntie came out onto the porch and stood there with shawls over their heads, the shawls uneven and clutched at the neck.

My grandfather came from the cider cellar and stood in the shed door.

I remember their eyes. My mother's wide, wondering, prayerful, their purplish-blue turned almost to black; Auntie's round, bright hazel, beginning to dance; my grandfather's steel-blue slits under his shaggy gray brows as if he were adding long, four-column figures in his head.

"Take it war's over," my grandfather said finally.

He could recall the end of the Civil War, but for the rest of us this was our first — and last. This was the war to end war. This was the war to make the world safe.

Safe . . .

"He'll be coming home soon," my mother said to Auntie, tears raining unnoticed down her thin cheeks.

"Maybe before we can get anything better than melted chocolate drops to frost him a cake with," Auntie answered gaily.

After a while the others went back inside, but I stayed out listening to the bells and whistles until they stopped. And that was the best time. The stillness. The whole world suddenly gone as still and warm and sweet as church on a summer Sunday when the organ has just stopped playing and the Elder has not begun to speak but stands in the pulpit looking tenderly down upon his children, his young children and his old children, thinking — you see it in his face — "Of all the beautiful things I know, which beautiful thing shall I tell them?"

Harold came home, to return to his work at the

belt factory, to be with us weekends, to be baptized with me, to join the Baptist church with me, to sing duets with me at Young People's meetings Sunday nights and then to walk home with Jennie Sanborn, the girl who had been valedictorian of their class at the Academy, graduated Phi Beta Kappa from Colby College, and now teaching English at Sanborn Seminary. The boy who walked home with me from Young People's was the handsomest boy I have ever seen; he sold sandwiches and tonic on trains running between Portland and Boston; I have a picture of him standing in his starched white coat, wth his basket on his arm, on the station platform at Portsmouth. The boy I rode to school with from the farm, in late spring and early fall, had thick black hair and black eyes and a beautiful singing voice. He often sang as we rode — because his horse's name was Max — "Ma-axwelton's braes are bonny — get *up*, Max!"

The boy who took me to school parties and sliding on Landing Hill was the minister's son with the pivot tooth; he had a sister who was a student at Bates College.

Remember, oh, remember forever how the bewildering, challenging, inexorable process of going-away quickened in my last year at the Academy.

Uncle George Webber died in the fall. My great-uncle, Joe Brown, died in the spring, one early morning as he sat in a chair between the tent with the fly and the screened-in "skeeterette" and the "cookhouse" which he and his wife had put on the spot, now three miles deep in the woods, where he was born, and where they spent the pleasant months, calling it "Camp Happy-go-lucky." . . . Harold and Jennie were engaged. . . . As my mother and grandmother were going to spend the day with Jennie's mother in the old Dr. Sanborn house, my mother slipped and fell, tearing the ligaments in her shoulder. She had no use of her arm for many weeks. Before she did, Grammy had a series of strokes; her right side has been paralyzed ever since. . . . Whatever my mother could not do with one hand was now mine to do. . . . I never missed a full day of school, though I was often very tardy. As a Camp Fire Torchbearer, I had a leading part in an Indian play, and afterward Dr. Eastman, an Academy trustee down from Boston, talked long with me, telling me that he was an honorary member of a Western Indian tribe. This was important, as time proved. . . .

Though no one from our family or community had ever been to college, Harold had long been determined that I should go.

"How will it be paid for?" asked my mother.

"I will help her," Harold promised, as often before.

"You are going to be married soon," she pointed out. "You will have new responsibilities. You must live your own life."

"Go as far as you can," Auntie advised me. "The Lord works in mysterious ways —"

All those catalogues my teachers gave me to ponder on! How little effect they had on me! The nearest institution of higher learning was New Hampshire State, and I did not want to go there because I did not want to leave my home state. I decided against the University of Maine when it supplied us with a substitute teacher who came in lipstick and a black silk dress. None of the women teachers I respected wore lipstick to school, and all of them wore tailored blouses and wool skirts. The other two coeducational colleges in Maine are Colby and Bates. My favorite teacher — she of English, Latin, Camp Fire, and sad, sweet face — was a Colby graduate. I also wanted to teach Latin and English and have a Camp Fire group; but I did not want to go to Colby, because my sister-in-law-to-be had won high scholastic honors there quite recently and I was sure that, wherever I went, I would not be an honor student. I applied for admission to Bates, not only because I had no reason not to, but also because I had a reason to. I assumed that the minister's son would go where his sister had been. (How mistaken I was! He went to Bowdoin!)

I was now a paid correspondent for the South Berwick weekly, the *Independent*. I was also selling short stories to the *Eliot Weekly Post* (where I had won first prize — a silver spoon — in a short story contest when I was eleven) at five dollars each. This was my college fund. My mother had always made all my clothes, was making me a blue organdy dress for Class Day and a white seed voile for Graduation.

I was the secretary of our class, and its Class Prophet, and wrote the class poem which the minister's son was to deliver on Class Day.

"I suggest you apply to the Board of Trustees for a scholarship," said Mrs. Gray, my Camp Fire Guardian.

I stared at her. There were several in my class

with grades higher than mine, and all of them were going to college. She read my thoughts.

"It will do no harm to apply," she said. "You, too, have received notice of admission. Not all of those who have been admitted will apply, for some of them have no financial need. Some years the trustees have more funds than others. Just write your letter, and then forget about it."

This was easy to do. Auntie came to town with my father one Saturday and we rode to Dover together on the electrics. She went boldly through the big white door of the Pacific Mills, and I followed. She asked to see the Agent. The switchboard operator rang his private office and waited. I watched her doing amazing things with long rubber tubes and switches in response to flashing red and white lights.

"Mr. Minnick will see you," she said. "That door there."

The private office door was open and Auntie went through it in her écru muslin printed with blue roses, brown velvet shoulder cape and wide-rimmed brown straw hat, like a schooner under full sail, I the dory bobbing behind.

The Agent rose from his big desk. He was a heavily built, partially bald man, impeccably dressed, with a gold chain across the front of his vest.

"How do you do, Vinnie," he said in a deep, surprised voice.

"How do you do, John," replied Auntie, extending her hand. "You remember Gladys?"

He looked at me. I quailed.

"Certainly. Please sit down."

"Thank you. I want you to understand at once that this is not a family matter and that I have not come to ask a favor. Gladys is graduating this month and plans to go to college in the fall. She will be available for summer work. If you happen to have an opening in your office for the summer months, perhaps you would like to consider her for it. She has not taken a secretarial course, but she writes a good hand, is quick to learn, is reliable and accurate."

The Agent turned his head and stared through the window into the mill yard. After what seemed a long time he slowly opened a drawer of his desk, withdrew a folder, and spread out papers from it to study. Finally he handed me a form sheet.

"This is an application. You may take it to the wicket window to fill out," he said. "Miss King at the switchboard will give you a pen. When you have finished, you may bring it back to me, and I will put it on file."

I don't know what they talked about while I was gone. Perhaps they considered that the business had been concluded, and Auntie felt free to inquire of John for the health of his wife Florence, who was her second cousin once removed, and to ask how the Minnick children — Dorothy, Hamilton, William, and Elizabeth — were coming on in school. Perhaps he inquired for "Cousin George," for that is what he and his wife always called my grandfather, and Auntie said he was fairly well but complained of loss of strength in his legs, and John said, "We'll bring over a bottle of a good tonic for him the next time we come." For the Minnicks came often on Sunday afternoons, and Auntie and I had visited them in the Agent's house and slept in an all-white bedroom where President Lincoln had once slept. But Auntie would not for a minute have considered mentioning, in either our house or theirs, a possible position for me in the Pacific Mills office. For that it had been necessary that she come into town and take me on the electric car to the mills.

A week later I received in the mail a formal letter stating that for the vacation season beginning in late June and ending Labor Day the position of switchboard operator at the Pacific Mills was open, at wages of fifteen dollars a week. Would I accept it? Fifteen dollars every week! My mother hurried out to a pay station to telephone her Uncle Ezra and Aunt Mollie Goodwin, in Dover, to ask if I could board with them for the summer. They said I could, for three dollars a week, if I would take care of my own room and help with the supper dishes.

"You must be very careful not to make any trouble for Aunt Mollie," my mother told me. "Help her in any way you can. Do whatever they ask you to do. It is very good of them to have you."

"That is high pay for a girl your age," said Auntie. "Be sure you earn it. Never be late. Don't leave until your day's work is done. While you are there, work as if you expected to stay for years and hoped to be promoted."

I heard them vaguely. They were ahead of me. I was still climbing Academy Hill every morning, and going back afternoons and evenings for rehearsals of class parts, of processionals, and recessionals, of the

Senior Dance grand march which the class officers
would lead. . . .

Remember the June afternoon, after hours of work
on the intricate movements of the march, when Doris
and Ralph and Ted and I walked down to Great
Works and borrowed the Goodwin boat to row along
the river. In a shady cove we pushed the boat ashore
and sat under the pines, looked at one another, and
tried to understand that the time was close when we
would not be together every day, in school or church
or post office or drugstore, when we would be among
strangers; Ted at Bowdoin, Ralph at Northeastern,
Doris at secretarial school, I at Bates, places which
were so far only names to us, for we had never seen
them.

Somebody said, "It's hard to imagine . . ."

"Guess when you finish one thing, all you can do is
go on to the next."

"I'll certainly never feel about any other school
the way I feel about B. A. To me college is just where
you go to learn a profession."

"Know what you want to be?"

"Gosh, no."

I said, "I know. I think. I want to be a teacher like
Mrs. Gray."

"Not many like her."

"I mean I want to try."

We walked together on Sunday afternoon down a
church aisle and back, for Baccalaureate exercises.
Wednesday was Class Day. Thursday was Alumni
Day, and we seniors were guests of the Alumni at a

dinner and ball. Friday afternoon was Commencement, and on the platform, below the school colors of
a banner we had made by sewing the white letters of
"Dei Timor Initium Sapientiae" to blue cambric, behind a hedge of blue and white flowers we had picked
in village gardens that morning, we girls sat in white
dresses and the boys in blue serge suits. When Marjorie had given the salutatory, Armand the honor
essay, a college president the address, and Ruth —
who would be my roommate at Bates — the vale-
dictory, the awards were announced. There were
prize books for undergraduates, a gold medal for the
valedictorian, a key for the highest ranking student
in the secretarial course, a four-year-scholarship for the
salutatorian; and then (I could not believe my ears):

*"A scholarship relinquished by a member of the
Class of 1919, who did not return to college after
her freshman year, is therefore now a three-year
scholarship and is awarded to Miss Gladys Winifred
Hasty. . . ."*

"Stand up!" someone whispered. "You have to
stand up! Marjorie did!"

I stood up, looking helplessly down into the auditorium at the row in which my parents and my
brother sat with my two aunts. My mother was dressed
all in white, Aunt Vinnie in pink mousseline and a
white hat with pink roses, Aunt Hattie in widow's
black silk.

They were all looking at me, except Aunt Hattie.
She was looking at my mother, shaking her arm and
whispering to her. My mother's eyes on me were like

twin purplish-blue stars. I did not think she heard what Aunt Hattie was saying, but she did, for she told me later.

"Hattie said, 'I knew it, Frankie! I knew it all the time! When I got there early, on the electrics, the auditorium wasn't open so they took me into the principal's office to wait and it was all written out on his desk. I saw Gladie's name. But I didn't tell you. I knew you'd be surprised!'"

And Mrs. Gray told me later, "Dr. Eastman asked me to see that you applied for a scholarship. I had told him of your writing and no doubt that seemed to him reason to work for you. You know Miss Sarah Orne Jewett was his aunt. He would like for South Berwick to have another writer."

But I shall always believe I was awarded the scholarship chiefly because Dr. Eastman was an honorary member of a Western Indian tribe.

That is the only time I have ever enjoyed hearing my given names. I have always wished I had been named Sarah for my two grandmothers, née Sarah Jane Brown and Sarah Louisa Brooks. It would have been very distinctive, for absolutely nobody of my age is named Sarah. Still, my grandmothers could not have liked the name, for the one always preferred to be called Say Jane and the other would answer to nothing but Louise. My mother herself, named for her two Aunt Emmas and her Aunt Frances, has always been called Frankie. But she named me Gladys because she was so glad I was a girl; Aunt Vinnie added Winifred because she hoped I would be winsome. It is not easy to alter names like that.

But that Commencement day it was right that they should hear the names they had given me read out for all to hear.

At supper that night, Auntie said to my grandfather:

"Gladie was awarded a scholarship of three hundred dollars at her graduation today. If she goes to college she will get a hundred dollars each year for three years."

He looked at me and then back to Auntie. It was the first time anyone had mentioned college to him.

"That so? Cover the cost, will it?"

"I don't suppose it will. But if she doesn't go, she will lose the three hundred."

After a minute he said, "Well, then . . . Likely, amongst us, we'll have to put enough with it so's t' she can go. But mind she earns as much as she can to help herself as she goes along."

"She will," said Auntie. "She is going to be the switchboard operator at the Pacific Mills this summer, and get fifteen dollars a week."

"Good pay . . . That where John Minnick works?"

"Yes. But her letter came from a Mr. Henderson who is in charge of the office. She's been hired because they need her there."

I am not at all sure of this last, but it was necessary to Auntie to believe so. Certainly the Agent and I were punctiliously correct all summer. He never more than nodded and said "Good morning" to me, nor I to him, except over the wire; and during a nerve-wracking first week at the switchboard I was far more

appalled when I pulled the wrong switch and buzzed
in *his* ear than when I did it to anyone else.

Remember that Sunday Uncle Ezra and Aunt Mollie came for me in the Maxwell. . . . Unpacking my
suitcase in Aunt Mollie's upstairs sewing room with
the white iron bed and the painted blue bureau. The
electric lights to snap on and off wherever I went.
. . . The next morning, when I walked along the
path through a hilly pasture, crossed the railroad
tracks, came up to Washington Street, went on to
Central Avenue, and was admitted at the big white
office door while hundreds of men and women
swarmed through the mill gate. . . . How, gradually,
I came to know most of them, and they me; for of the
office staff only the switchboard operator came to work
at the same time as the carders, the weavers, the ship-
pers, the mechanics, and their foremen. . . . That first
week of discovering the meaning of my lights, tubes,
switches, headphones, and beginning fearfully to use
them; of learning to take from the foremen's books
the amount each mill-worker had earned that week
and copy it on the corner of a small brown pay envelope where the millworker's name had been typed.
What if I wrote a 7 where a 9 should be? What if I
wrote Thomas A. Smith's earnings on Thomas J.
Smith's envelope? . . . But gradually it became easier, slowly it became natural, and then how lovely it
was! That half-mile walk across pasture, railroad
tracks, and down the sidewalks in the early morning.
Sometimes I was so early the gates had not yet been
opened, and I sat with the gatekeeper on his sidewalk

bench and talked with other early arrivals. Many of
them were Armenian, with names like Bagdikian
and Ablahadian. As soon as the gates were open, a
foreman opened my door to me — "Hi, sweetheart!
Say, now, that's a pretty dress! Mama make it?" —
and I was in the cool, dark lobby, letting myself into
the long, dim office with its rows of neat, polished
desks, their covered typewriters, yesterday's tea-rose in
the cut-glass vase at the corner of Mr. Henderson's
blotter; rose-growing was Mr. Henderson's hobby.

I opened the switchboard, and perhaps a light came
on, the overseer of Number Two mill asking to be
connected with Number Three. But I was never busy
until the Agent and my fellow office workers came in at
eight. I watched the big trucks and wagons drawn by
two pairs of horses pass my window, hauling bales of
cotton through the gates, and the janitor stopped by
the wicket to ask if I went to the carnival last night.
His name was Mr. Macdonald, and I have a snapshot
of him in my album. I could tell him I had been to
the carnival and that I rode on the Ferris wheel and
the whip.

"I'll bet you squealed. By golly, I'd like to heard
the way you squealed. Who was the lucky boy?"

"His name is Fred. He lives next door to my aunt's.
We rolled balls and won a teacup and saucer. Japanese. Fred let me have it. He said what did he want
of a teacup and saucer."

Mr. Macdonald went off guffawing. Mr. Henderson came in and put fresh water in the cut-glass vase,
exchanging yesterday's rose for today's. Sometimes he
had several roses, and then there was one for me to

put in a paper cup from the washroom, others for the
other girls — Lena, Stubby, Bessie, Leone. Mr. El-
well, the bookkeeper, came, and opened the safe, the
files. The Agent passed the wicket on his way to the
office, and his light flashed on.

"Get Lawrence on the wire." Lawrence was the parent mill.

The day had begun.

I usually walked back to Aunt Mollie's for lunch. If
I had a dental appointment, it was during the noon
hour and I carried a sandwich to work. I had never
visited a dentist before that summer, but Bates required of all entering students a dentist's bill of
health. I had four extractions in those noon hours.
"Six-year molars," said the dentist, cheerfully. "Most
people lose them early. You don't need them. The
other teeth soon move over and fill the spaces." I also
had many fillings. One tooth ached all afternoon and
I went back to the dentist at 5:30. The other office
workers left at five, but the switchboard operator
stayed whenever a long-distance call had not yet been
completed. The dentist said, "The nerve may be dying. There is nothing I can do." It did not want to die
— does anything? — but succumbed in time to give
me two hours' sleep before my alarm rang the next
morning.

I was always back at Aunt Mollie's for six o'clock
supper. After the dishes were done, unless I was sewing upstairs (I was now making my own dresses of material I bought with my own earnings) we usually sat
on the porch and talked. Uncle Ezra is much interested in the stars and taught me to find and name all

the constellations. Sometimes I went to an early movie with Fred. Sometimes we went to call on neighbors, or Uncle Ezra drove us to visit Aunt Mollie's relatives in nearby towns. One evening I did not want to go with them, for it was hot and I was tired. I told Aunt Mollie so.

"I don't like to leave you alone," she said. "Once in a while a tramp comes over from the railroad."

"I'll ask Fred to come down."

"Call him, then. To be sure."

I called him while Uncle Ezra was backing out the car, and he said he would be there as soon as he had fed his dog.

"Don't ask him in," said Aunt Mollie. "It wouldn't look right. Stay on the lawn or the porch."

I promised. Why would anyone stay in, on such a hot night?

Fred and I were sitting on the porch in wicker chairs when they came home at half-past nine. Uncle Ezra walked between us into the house without a word.

"You'd better go," I told Fred. "I have to hem a skirt before I go to bed."

I went into the house and Aunt Mollie was starting the oatmeal for breakfast.

"Where's Uncle Ezra?"

"He went right upstairs."

"I thought he looked strange. Is anything wrong?"

"He's very upset because Fred came over when we weren't here. He says your mother would be, too."

"She wouldn't. I don't see why —"

"I don't either. But he's mad with both of us."

We smiled at the absurdity of men, then began to laugh, and went upstairs muffling our laughter like two schoolgirls.

If I did anything wicked that summer it was something Uncle Ezra could know nothing about. One evening Aunt Mollie's nephew, whose wife and children spent the school vacation at a lake cottage where he joined them on weekends, stopped by and asked us all to ride to Hampton Beach in his new car. Uncle Ezra had no wish to ride so far at night or with another's hands on the steering wheel. (Had he but known what was to transpire, doubtless he would have gone at whatever cost to his own comfort and personal safety.)

"Won't it be cold?" asked Aunt Mollie. "And a fog is rising."

But we all knew she meant to go. Aunt Mollie loves a good time and runs to meet the unexpected. I, who had never been to Hampton Beach, nor to any other beach that summer, waited, as the saying is, with my heart in my mouth — which, as it happened, was where it stayed for a long time.

"By no means cold," Paul assured her. "My side curtains are all buttoned down. And they will keep out the fog, too."

So off we went, Aunt Mollie in front with Paul, I alone on the back seat. I had never until then ridden with curtains down, and before we reached the beach I was nearly deafened by the roar of the engine in the motionless dark air. As Paul had been somewhat deaf since he was my age, I felt I was suddenly gaining a new understanding of him, a new sympathy with him.

Aunt Mollie talked all the way at the top of her voice,
but Paul and I caught only a few of the words. *Paul
and I . . .*

As we approached the blackness which was the
ocean, Aunt Mollie said something.

"What?" asked Paul.

I strained to hear the repetition.

"I said," shouted Aunt Mollie, "there's the Casino!"

She pointed and we saw it, a ring of light like a
bright island on the blackness.

We stepped out onto the boardwalk and smelled
the sea air.

"There's music!" cried Aunt Mollie. "It must be
dance night. Oh, Paul, let's go watch them!"

"Well, whatever you say, Aunt Mame." (All her
relatives call her "Mame." Uncle Ezra and his relatives call her "Mollie.")

We crossed the street through the fog. I could hear
the waves slapping behind us. I wondered if Paul
could. I wondered if he recognized at the same instant
I did the dance tune the band was playing.

The Casino was like bandstands I had seen on several village greens (though our town does not have
one) and at Short Sands in York, but enormously en-
larged. Aunt Mollie pushed me ahead of her, through
the crowd of onlookers, until we reached the trellis-
like fence around the dance floor. I clung to it, not to
be pushed aside, dabbing the fog from my face with
my folded handkerchief. I could feel Aunt Mollie
at my back. I did not know what had become of
Paul. I twisted my head to look for him. He was just

behind Aunt Mollie, lighting his pipe. He caught my eye, smiled, and — winked! At least, I thought he winked. . . .

"Look at them!" cried Aunt Mollie, squeezing my shoulder. "Did you ever see such going-it as that?"

I looked at the dancers and shook my head. I never had seen such going-it as that. At the Academy we did only waltzes and fox-trots. When my brother went there they did two-steps and schottisches, and he had taught them to me. But here, the floor was filled with couples going forward and back, swooping, separating and returning, the men spinning the girls by a high-held hand.

"Do you know what dance that is, Paul?" Aunt Mollie shouted. "Has it got a name?"

I heard him answer, "It's tango music, Aunt Mame. Some of them are doing the tango, and some of them just think they are."

"Must be the latest thing," said Aunt Mollie happily. "Must be fun! Wish I was young enough! Have you tried it, Paul?"

"I've tried it," I heard him admit.

"Well, show Gladys how," Aunt Mollie ordered instantly. "Likely they'll all be doing it at college when she gets there this fall. Take her on and show her."

My heart rose higher. I could hardly breathe. She must have moved back and pushed him forward, for now he was behind me.

"What do you say?" he asked in his low, slow voice. "Want to try it?" He had stooped to my ear and was still stooped to hear my answer.

Oh, I did . . . but I didn't.

Twisting my damp handkerchief, I whispered, "I guess . . . No . . . I never —"

"Go *on*," urged Aunt Mollie. "Don't be shy. Nobody knows you here. How'll you ever learn if you don't try?"

"Might as well give in to her," Paul said gently in my ear. "Don't worry. I'll steer you through."

His hand was on my elbow. I moved beside him. In a daze, I watched him pay our admission. Dazed I felt his arm around me, my hand taken in his. Lost in the crowd, we were going forward and back, separating and returning, spinning . . .

The music stopped.

"That was all right," Paul said, smiling his slow smile down at me. "You learn fast. Want to do it again?"

Aunt Mollie loomed across the fence. She was applauding harder than any of the dancers, beaming and nodding vehemently.

"Go ahead! Go ahead!" I could see her say.

But I shook my head.

"No . . . no. It must be — getting late."

"And six o'clock comes early," Paul agreed.

We pushed through the crowd to Aunt Mollie, and only half-heard her expostulations all the way back to the car, above the crashing of the waves.

"If I'd had a chance when I was your age, I'd have danced all night!"

Aunt Mollie was married at sixteen to a man who had a grown son and daughter. My Aunt Hattie Webber was married at sixteen, too.

I was just turned seventeen.

I did not say a word, riding back, but sat covering my handkerchief with both hands. At the house I left Aunt Mollie thanking Paul and saying "Good night" to him. I ran up to my room, put my handkerchief under the pillow, undressed in the dark, and crept into bed. I was sleepless for hours, every now and then drying my eyes with the precious handkerchief, which only made me cry harder because it smelled of Paul's tobacco.

I was in love with a married man! It must be love, I thought, because I had never felt like this before. Well, I had felt a *little* like this when our local war hero, Henry Earle, came home after being decorated for bravery and talked at my YP meeting at church about his experience when his ship was torpedoed and he was twelve days and nights in an open boat. But even at the time I had been able to convince myself that most of what I felt about Henry was hero-worship combined with sisterly pride and affection, for he had been our next-door neighbor. For the feeling I had for Paul there was no explanation but that I had fallen in love with him. Chase was just a boy I liked to ride to school with and to hear sing. Ted was just a boy I liked to watch play basketball, and to go sliding with, and to find holding the red-paper heart at the end of a mile of string I had been unwinding at a Valentine party. One of the Freds was to walk home with me from YP (except the night Henry was there) and to send me boxes of Armstrong chocolates from the railroad-station lunch counter; the other Fred was to go with to movies and the carnival. But Paul . . .

"I love him," I sobbed into the fog-and-tear-damp-
ened, tobacco-scented handkerchief. "I love him; I
love him; but he is married and a father and I *must
never see him again.*"

I never have; and this required elaborate tech-
niques of watchfulness and timely withdrawals all
summer, not because Paul made any effort to see me
— he never gave any indication of desire to see me or
not to see me, and it probably did not matter in the
least to him whether he did or not — but because he
worked as a bookkeeper across the street from the Pacific Mills, and because he often called on his Aunt
Mame in the evening.

Perhaps that ride to Hampton Beach was not important enough to put into my journal. Perhaps it
was. I don't know. . . . I don't know yet which experiences will prove important and which unimpor-
tant in my life. I only know I wish I could remember
every one of them vividly as long as I live. I only
know that I never washed that handkerchief while I
could even pretend convincingly that it still had a
tobacco scent, that I have never yet felt about anyone
else as I felt about Paul, and that I have never since
wanted to go out with a boy for the sake of being
with him, only sometimes to get where I wanted to go.

Perhaps I never shall. Perhaps I really was in love
with Paul and can never love another man. It is a
sobering thought. Since I was a little girl, I have never
wanted to remain unmarried as Aunt Vinnie did. I
wanted to be a teacher like her and like the principal's wife, first; but after that I wanted to be a mother
like mine. . . . Now I don't know what I want. . . .

Yes, I do. I want *more than anything* to feel about a man who isn't married the way I felt about Paul last summer. I try but I can't. For one reason, I don't seem to *know* any men who aren't married. College boys are — just college boys. And the men I know who are married are — just men who are married. For which I am thankful. I certainly don't want *that* over again!

I went home every weekend, and the weekends were heavenly. Every Saturday noon I hurried up Central Avenue to the open electric in the Upper Square, climbing the steps which ran the whole length of the car and finding a place on one of the varnished wooden seats which ran crossway. If it rained, canvas curtains were pulled down. Rain or shine, the conductor swung hand-over-hand along the side, collecting money, making change from a metal coin-holder attached to his belt, as we bounced across the fields while the motorman kept his hand on the throttle, the trolley on the wire, and the wheels on the rails. Sometimes Harold rode with me; but if he did, when we got off in the village he went down Main Street to the Dr. Sanborn house and I went up Portland Street to my father's paintshop for the ride home behind Pony, the big white workhorse who pulled all our workloads and was our only means of conveyance since first my grandfather's Old Belle and then her once fleetfooted daughter Bess had been turned out to pasture.

All the way along the sandy road, past Clara Warren's little house and big flower garden riotous in late

June with huge Oriental poppies, David Hanson's
milk farm, and Woodlawn Cemetery; through Old
Swamps, across the railroad tracks of the Boston and
Maine Eastern Division, over Agamenticus Bridge, on
to Ed Goodwin's hill; past Witchtrot Road, Nason's
pump, the district schoolhouse; down Nason's hill,
through the woods, over White's Marsh Bridge; past
Dorr's Gate, the Boston place, the old Min Joy place,
we talked. I told him where I had been and what I
had done; he told me what had happened while I was
away — how far along the haying was, what vegetables were at their prime, who had come to spend the
day. By the time we turned up the lane and into the
dooryard I was reoriented. It was as if I had been gone
only for an hour or two, except that everything now
stood out for me, every smallest thing three-dimen-
sional, like a separate piece of sculpture; every sound,
however soft or low, distinct from every other; and
the smells — oh, the good, familiar smells of sweet-
fern and pines, of mountain-brook water, of sweet-
grass cut and drying with the hay, yes, of pigpen and
cattle stanchions and sweating countryman and beast.
It was in every way another world from that of the
city, even of a small city.

Remember running up the porch steps; seeing the
dish towels on the line above the railing boxes full
of house plants taking their summer outing; hugging
and kissing my grandfather, who sat there in visored
cap and a wool jacket over his gingham shirt — because now he felt cold even on warm days unless he
moved about — with the knotty pine stick he used as
a cane resting between his swollen knees; feeling the

softness of his gray side-whiskers and mustache; trying to give him part of whatever I had that he was
growing short of.

"Well, Gladie," he always said. "Home again, be
ye?"

Yes. Yes, I was home again.

Remember going through the small entry, seeing
the high hooks and the low hooks (though there were
no children now to use the low hooks), and on into
the kitchen where my mother and Aunt Vinnie were
sewing or mending, each by her own back window,
unless one of them was starting the fire in the kitchen
stove for supper or my mother had gone into the parlor to do for Grammy. Auntie had given up the parlor
to Grammy when we came home in the spring and
now slept in what had been Harold's chamber. Whenever I was here I slept with Grammy, so that I could
give her the care she needed at night and my mother
could have uninterrupted sleep. When Harold was
here he slept on the sitting-room couch.

Remember all their faces — Mother's, Auntie's,
Grammy's — and their dark percale dresses, their
bright percale aprons. Though she could go only to
her platform rocker by the window which looked out
upon the lane, Grammy would never have left her
bedside without an apron on.

Remember how clean the house was — a cleanli-
ness impossible where there are many things, especially many rugs, cushions, and pieces of upholstered
furniture. In the kitchen a dining table, six straight

chairs, a dropleaf table with a tidy newspaper and the mending basket on it, a wooden couch padded with a folded quilt and covered with a flowered cretonne "throw"; a clock on the mantel; a scrubbed pine floor; on the wall a Currier and Ives print, and a comb case under a small mirror. In the sitting room the sewing machine, the Windsor chairs, a willow rocker, a horsehair-covered couch which could be opened into a bed, the Larkin desk with two shelves of books, three small braided rugs on an oiled floor, and on the mantel over the small fireplace the luster pitcher, the blue glass basket, and perhaps a mug full of sweet peas. In my grandfather's room his four-poster with the corn-husk mattress and the dotted blue calico spread, his chest of drawers, and on his shelf the tall green bottle from which he drank night and morning a swallow of the herb tonic he made himself; nothing else; he will not have even a strip of straw matting on the floor. No curtains in any of these rooms; only rolled green shades to pull down against strong sunlight if need be.

Nobody was ever surprised to see me. I was never surprised to be there. The surprising thing always was, and is, to become conscious that I am somewhere else — that I, the person who was here, am in another place.

The smell of those rooms, in summer, is always of the summer fields and woods which stretch out farther than the eye can see from all their open doors and windows. If there is any other smell it is of naphtha soap, flowers brought close, new cloth, wood burning, bread baking or other food cooking; and these are soon gone, lost in the currents of air from fields and woods which sweep them away.

But the room at the end of the long front hall, which used to be the parlor and Auntie's room and now was Grammy's, had its own smell. The parlor furniture was stored in the shed chamber, and she had by her (except for the piano) only what she used: her bed, her platform rocker, her commode, her table piled with books and magazines, her windowsill lined with bottles of medicine, and two or three chairs for visitors. But the flowered, ingrain carpet was still on the floor, and the carpet sweeper could not pick up every fleck of dust from many feet between the biennial sweepings with wet shredded newspaper or sawdust. The lace curtains, though too old for many more launderings, were still at the windows because she liked them; I suppose they added to her feeling of elegance. My proud little grandmother, now stooped to less than her own five feet in height and with one of her tiny, slim-fingered hands useless, reads avidly every mention of Queen Mary of England and greatly loves both princes. So it was age Grammy's room smelled of, for she never wanted a window open, said she had enough air from the door. Lady, bed quilts, carpets, curtains, books; all as clean as what is old can be. Age, and medicines. The black pills she took until she asked Dr. Ross to give her white pills, and white pills she still had when she told Dr. Ross she thought the brown pills he gave her first had done her more good. The yellow liquid she had been taking until she asked him to change it; the new liquid was pink; but she still kept what was left of the green he had given her in the spring to bring back her strength after a winter cold.

She let me kiss her cheek.

"I was in hopes," she said, "you'd get here in time to wash my hair."

"I'll do it in the morning, Grammy."

"If it's warm enough. Only I don't like to do such things of a Sunday."

"It won't take long. God will understand. He'd want you neat when people come to call on you after church."

"See what I took out of my Sunshine Bag today?"

The neighbors had filled a big cretonne knitting bag with surprise packages for her to open, one after breakfast every day. A pin for her collar, a thin old silver teaspoon for her tea, a colored picture of Queen Mary cut from a magazine, the copied words of an old song, a package of flower seed, a tumbler with lilies of the valley etched on it, a box of Canada mints . . .

At suppertime I tucked a white linen napkin under her soft little double chin and took in her tray covered with a fringed white linen cloth set with my mother's best china. She put aside her Bible and bowed her head to say grace. Grammy is a little queen on a little throne and bows only to God.

We commoners eat in the kitchen. At the table my grandfather's swollen knees are obscured, and he still eats well as he always has, using both knife and fork to carry the food to his mouth, leaving the plate so clean it is difficult to see that it has been used, and drinking his well water poured from an ironstone pitcher into a thick glass. My father sits beside him, tall and handsome, very straight; his grandmother was of a family known as the Brace-back Warrens. His reddish brown hair is thinning, but he has it cut in a special way and combs it carefully to cover the bare spot at the top; it hasn't a thread of gray. My mother's pompadour is pure white now, above her low forehead and her small, shell-like ears — it turned quickly during the weeks after Grammy's stroke when we were caring for her with only three hands between us — but her back hair and the smooth, thick coil on top are still purplish-black like Harold's. The white frame makes her eyes less purple, more blue than they used to be, but it is a very deep blue with a purplish tinge. Her face is heart-shaped, and her skin is very fine-textured, translucent. My mother is beautiful. I look like my father, and his features are more becoming to him than to me. A man should have a Roman nose, I think. A woman should have a slender, straight one like my mother's.

But during those Saturday night suppers I often looked past my mother to Auntie, who was beside her, opposite my grandfather as my parents were opposite each other; I sat at the end of the table, at a leaf which was raised when the table was set and put down when it was cleared.

Auntie was not beautiful. She was a tall, large-boned woman with a round face, the Warren nose, and the Warren high forehead. But Grammy says, "Pretty is as pretty does," and any smart woman can make herself look pretty. Everything Auntie did was prettily done, everything she wore was pretty; and she was a smart woman. She softened her hairline with curly bangs; she always wore earrings, for her ears had been pierced as long ago as she was a little girl living for a year with her Aunt Annie in Lawrence, Massachusetts; and her step was the lightest in the household. Still, no artist would have longed to paint Auntie as surely he would long to have my mother sit for him. But I am not an artist. I wanted to paint Auntie; not her features or even her expression, but what it was inside that made her glow like a lamp that will never go out because its supply of oil is limitless, and its wick has been treated with a magic potion so that it will never burn unevenly or char, and so will never need the trimming, which shortens a wick's life.

She is the first person recorded in my memory. I was sitting in her lap one winter day, learning to make an A with toothpicks on the windowsill . . . She was Warmth. She was Strength. She was Wisdom. She was Security.

I never knew her to show fear or even doubt. I never saw her hands tremble or even hesitate. I never saw her hurry, yet I never knew her to be late. She spoke briefly, and every word counted. She never appeared to be tired, nor indicated that anything she undertook to do would be difficult. I cannot remember her ever being sick, though I have been told that she resigned her position as the teacher of the district school because of a persistent cough which she concluded might endanger her pupils; and though I spent my Christmas holidays with her, in my first year at the Academy, just two weeks before she entered the

Homeopathic Hospital in Boston for major surgery. I
do remember that she was still in the hospital two
months later when Harold went into the service,
and that she was convalescing with her sister, my
Aunt Hattie Webber, in Eliot, until midsummer —
but by the time I was free to visit them, she was frol-
icking with Aunt Hattie like a young girl and I joined
in like an indulgent elder. With her own family Aunt
Hattie has never been more than sixteen, the age she
was when she married. I loved to hear Auntie's hospital stories of the "pinkies" and the "blueys" and the
graduate nurses in white uniforms and caps, and of
the long-stemmed greenhouse roses which were sent
to her there. She is the only person I know who has
ever been a hospital patient except my playmate,
Bernice, who had a mastoid infection, and my grandfather's brother, Uncle Gran, who at past seventy was
to have a tumor removed from under his arm. As he
was about to take the ether, the surgeon said, "Please
remove your teeth, Mr. Hasty," and Uncle Gran,
flashing a broad smile, replied, "If you want my teeth
removed, doctor, you will have to call a dentist."

I looked at Auntie those Saturday nights last summer and wondered how she learned that whatever is,
is right — so well that she had sent off in apparent
equanimity a man who loved her and whom others
thought it would not be difficult to love, but whom
she did not love, and, when he returned years later,
sent him off again; so well that when her cough was
cured and she found herself not needed at home she
had gone happily to keep a fine house for a widower,
and when he was to marry again came happily home

for a long visit, laughing a little that a man his age would marry on Valentine's Day; so well that when she might have taught again she had chosen to be housekeeper and companion for Madame Brooks of Bolt Hill, in Eliot, a regal old lady with a black velvet bow on the top of her head and a long gray curl behind each ear; and to join Mrs. Brooks in welcoming home to the great house each summer the son from Washington, D. C. and his wife, the son who was a college president and had married a Southern belle whose name was Belle, and all the charming granddaughters and tall grandsons who were graduates of fine Eastern colleges. It seemed a small miracle that nothing had called Auntie home as long as Mrs. Brooks lived, but that she was here to keep house for her father when it was time for us to go into town for the winter months. But I suppose if she had not been here, we should not have gone.

After supper Auntie and I always did the dishes together in the sinkroom, while my mother was helping Grammy to bed, my grandfather lay on the kitchen couch, and my father sat by the big pink lamp at the kitchen table reading the paper. Auntie wanted to hear about my week, and my grandfather listened, too, but my father didn't because he had heard it all on the way home. When everyone else had gone to bed, my mother had her first freedom of the day and we went out to the swing-chairs under the maples to talk for a while, and, when everything had been said, to sing together for a while; then we went inside to make up the sitting-room couch for Harold. We never saw him until Sunday morning, he came home so late, but sometimes I was just going to sleep after being up with Grammy when he came walking up the dark lane, whistling softly.

"Here comes Harold," Grammy would say. "Boy must be tired to death."

"He'll sleep late," I could promise her drowsily.

Once more, for tonight, we were all together. . . . Everything was as it should be.

Remember the lovely, slow waking Sunday mornings in the big bed beside Grammy, and the talk; the sound of Auntie moving about the kitchen and the smell of her browning potatoes and barley biscuits; my mother singing as she poured through cheesecloth into pans the milk my father had just brought up from the barn . . . all the coming and going through the sitting room never woke Harold. It took my mother and me, by turns, to do that; so by turns we sat on the edge of his couch and talked with him. He had breakfast later than the rest of us, and then worked until dinnertime in Mother's flower garden, which is always larger than she can keep as she wants it kept. After she has planted all she has room for, neighbors bring her bulbs, slips, and bushes from their thinning-out.

It seems to me there is almost constant talk at our house, yet it is a very quiet house. No one ever speaks loudly or dramatically. No one interrupts anyone else. There is always time for a thoughtful silence between one remark or another, and mostly conversations are between two people. If others are in the room they are more likely to listen than to take part, but each most likely to continue with his own thoughts. It is a small, crowded house, yet two can easily be alone, and often are.

Alone with my father in the wagon or the barn; alone with my grandfather on the porch or in the yard; alone with Grammy in her room; alone with Auntie at the dishes; alone with my mother in the swing-chairs; alone with Harold in the sitting room.

I don't know when I learned — it seems as if I have always known — that I could, even should, speak of different experiences or of the same experiences differently to each member of my family. My mother, who has a full share of her family melancholy, is the perfect audience to hear of happy times I have had and little compliments which have been paid me; she listens hungrily as I begin, then appreciatively, and at last contentedly — as the wise enjoy a Thanksgiving dinner, or the first greens from the brooks and fields. My father, warm, kind, stable, is a safe repository for whatever ill fate has befallen me. I can look at him with trouble in my eyes and find none in his, only a friendly twinkle, an alert attentiveness. My sadness, anxiety, or uncertainty are as contagious for my mother as my happiness; my father is immune to all. My mother feels whatever I feel, if she knows of it, more than I do. My father feels only his own feelings, which are generally comfortable, and what he feels for me is affection and interest. . . . When I talk to Grammy she is thinking up a quotation with which to respond. Most often it is a Biblical quotation which she can identify by chapter and verse. Other quotations may be from Shakespeare, Milton, Benjamin Franklin, old songs, or school copybooks; she does not know which and it does not matter. These are to her truths in nutshells, pearls of wisdom, simple, incontrovertible facts.

"It's a long lane that has no turning, my girl."
"Procrastination is the thief of time, they say."
"Pride goeth before a fall."
"Truly, there is a tide in the affairs of men."
"A stitch in time saves nine."
"If wishes were horses, beggars might ride. We can't always have our druthers."
"There's nothing new under the sun."
"Use it up, wear it out; make it do, or do without."
"There's no accounting for tastes."
"How are the mighty fallen!"
"We have to work out our own salvation."

Though Grammy is the most likely to repeat quotations, we all try to live by them, perhaps especially the last one I have listed. I suppose that is why I have had so much less family advice than most people I know of my age. My mother enjoys my happiness. My father sympathizes calmly with me in trouble. Grammy tosses off quotations which I must interpret and apply as best I can. Auntie has always liked best to hear what I have learned, overcome, accomplished. My grandfather is most pleased by such evidence as I can present of my diligence, frugality, capability, and self-reliance. It is only with my brother that I talk over unsolved problems. Even he gives me little advice; but he listens to me groping for a solution as

closely as the others do to a fait accompli, and his "I
see what you mean," or "Don't hurry it; take your
time," are just the encouragement I need.

After dinner on Sundays my father took Mother,
Auntie, and me to church. My grandfather no longer
felt able to go; besides, we had a new minister who
was a stranger to him. Harold stayed to visit with
Grammy, since he and Jennie would go to evening
service in the village. Auntie sat alone in the Hasty
pew; Mother, with her Aunt Em and others of her
family, in the singing seats. I played the organ, and
the same old breezes came through the open windows
to ruffle the hymnbook pages and stir the air, which
smelled of Sunday School books, varnish, and the oil
in the lamps. Most of the same people who had been
there when I was a child were facing me when they
rose to sing, but older now, browner now, with deeper
lines. I thought, "How can I tell them, or show them,
how much I love them, before it is too late?" I found
no way. I've found none yet. I am still looking for it.
When big gray Pony pulled us back up the lane
from church and into the dooryard, Uncle Ezra's
Maxwell was usually already there.
My first thought on seeing it was always as it would
have been on a Sunday afternoon in earlier summers,
"Why, Uncle Ezra and Aunt Mollie are here!" I was
never expecting them, had never made any preparation for going back to Dover. I lived each of my weekends as if it would have no end.
But there they were, sitting with Grammy — the

man we called Uncle Ezra was a cousin of her second husband, my mother's stepfather — and *they had
come for me.*

"Get your things together right away," Auntie always said. "Not to keep them waiting when they're
ready to go. They're good to come for you every Sunday."

Within an hour Harold and I were kissing everybody good-bye, saying "We'll be back Saturday," riding down the lane, back down the sandy road past the
old Min Joy place, the Boston place, Dorr's gate, over
White's Marsh Bridge, through the woods, up Nason's
hill, past the schoolhouse and Nason's pump and the
end of Witchtrot Road, on to Ed Goodwin's hill,
across Agamenticus Bridge and over the railroad
tracks, through Old Swamps and past the Woodlawn
Cemetery, David Hanson's, Clara Warren's . . . Harold was talking with Uncle Ezra about his work. Harold was happy, on his way — and quickly — to the
girl he loved and would marry. He left us when we
reached the village square. I was quiet, seeing all I
knew best and loved most slip behind me.

But as soon as we crossed the state line into New
Hampshire I was a person waking in another world to
another life. I asked if they had gone to Hedding
Camp Ground the day before, as they had planned.
I told Aunt Mollie I would buy material tomorrow to
make a blouse. We rode into Dover and down Central Avenue, and I blew a kiss at the white door in the
brick wall of the Pacific Mills. We went on up Washington Street and down Prospect past Fred's house
to Uncle Ezra's. As I was taking my bag upstairs the

telephone often rang and, if it did, it would be Fred asking if I wanted to walk down to the drugstore for an ice-cream soda after supper.

But on Labor Day I went back to Dover for my last week of days at the switchboard, of nights in Aunt Mollie's sewing room. The last walks through the pasture, across the railroad, and down Washington Street; the last early-morning visit on the gatekeeper's bench; the last opening of the white door, greeting the janitor, opening the switchboard, seeing the still office come alive, watching for red lights, taking the calls, making the connections, and disconnecting. Remember the weight of the head-phone, the lightness when I took it off, the pull of the rubber tube when I drew it out, the click when I let it snap back, the voices which had become familiar over the wire though I had never seen the people to whom they belonged. On my desk were seven roses which Mr. Henderson had brought to me, with a stiff little smile, saying, "The last roses of the summer." In my drawer were a silver pin Mr. Macdonald had taken from his pocket, saying he had found it in the street on his way home yesterday — but it looked quite new — and little gifts from Lena, Leone, Bessie, Stubby; an embroidered towel, a verse in a blue frame — *God's in His heaven, All's right with the world* — a handkerchief with a tatted edge, and an Eversharp pencil.

I was going away, and I did not know why I was going away. My work here had become familiar and easy and I enjoyed it; I was well paid and had few expenses; Uncle Ezra and Aunt Mollie, Fred, the people in the office and the mills had become a second family to me. Why was I leaving all this to undertake what perhaps I could not do, where I had never been, in an effort to get where I might not want to be?

"Good-bye, good-bye, good-bye." . . . *"Come back next summer."* . . . *"Oh, I will, I will!"* . . . *"Write to us!"* . . . *"Of course I will!"*

I went out of the white door that Saturday noon half-blinded by tears, carrying roses and loosely wrapped packages, wearing the silver pin. Only the fact that I was going home kept my feet moving toward the Maxwell, where Uncle Ezra and Aunt Mollie waited with my suitcases on the back seat.

And home was waiting for me. That weekend was like all the other weekends of the summer, except that Sunday afternoon I did not have to leave when Harold did. I walked to the end of the lane with him. Goldenrod and wild blue asters were beginning to bloom among the sweetfern. It was coming back-to-school time, but I was not going back anywhere. I was heading out into a stiff breeze, and the cables, one by one, were being slipped.

Harold stopped and smiled down, put his hands on my shoulders.

"Well, good luck, little sister," he said. "Let me know if you need anything. I'll take care of the first term bill when it comes. You'll have a great time."

I nodded. We kissed. I watched him almost out of sight. He turned and waved. I turned and walked in the opposite direction.

When I got home, my father had brought down the

dome-covered wood-and-steel trunk from the shed chamber, and he and my mother were scrubbing it with brushes. I watched my father carry it, when it was clean, into the sitting room. It stood there empty, with the cover raised, and all the next two days we were adding to the heap around it. The great heap of things they thought I would need at college . . . A bed pillow, patchwork quilts, the Indian blanket my father had won by paying ten cents for a number which turned out to be the lucky one; the winter coat to keep me warm, the shoes and rubbers to keep my feet dry, the graduation dresses, the skirts and blouses, the sweaters, the bureau scarf, the toilet things, the fountain pen on the black ribbon which would hang around my neck so I would not lose it, the towels and facecloths, the family photographs, the underwear.

"It will *never* all go in the trunk!" I cried, despairing.

"In the trunk and your valise. I think it will," my mother told me. "When it's all together I'll show you how."

She showed me by doing it the night before I was to go, after everyone but us had gone to bed. She knelt and I passed her things carefully folded. She fitted them together like a jigsaw puzzle. I had never before seen a trunk packed. When she rose to rest and sat on the couch I rubbed her back and brought her a cup of tea. For her to finish the packing, I placed a cushion for her knees. She smiled up at me as she knelt before the trunk which had gone with her to Rochester before I was born, and I smiled back; but we could not see each other very well.

It was a warm night, and after a while we went out and sat in the swing-chairs, but we did not sing and we did not talk much. I heard the frogs croaking in the marshes. I saw the black roof of the barn blotting out the stars.

The next morning they called me early. I bathed at the big flowered china bowl and put on a suit my mother had made over from a suit once worn by a friend of hers who lived in Pasadena, California, and who often sent us boxes. The suit, a tan blouse I had made, the pendant Harold had given me at Christmas, the ribbed tan stockings and the new brown, laced oxfords. . . . Grammy lay watching me. I went along the hall carrying my valise, my pocketbook, my brown cotton gloves, and the brown velvet hat which had been Jennie's.

"I got the trunk locked," said my father, "and it's loaded into the wagon. Here's the key. Put it where you won't lose it."

I sat at the breakfast table. It was all a blur. Mother was not there. She had gone in to help Grammy.

"Better get started," my father said. "Trains don't wait."

I went into the parlor and kissed Grammy and my mother good-bye.

"Act like a lady," said Grammy, "wherever you go."

My mother did not say anything. She was crying. She held me as if she could not let me go.

I went out alone into the sitting room and put on my hat and gloves.

My grandfather was still at the kitchen table. He

was staring into the distance. I kissed his cheek. Then he looked at me. I saw how old his eyes were.

"Well," he said. "Well — come home when you can."

"Where is Auntie?" I asked.

He shook his head.

The door was open into the shedroom. I went out there. She was building a fire in the stove. I don't know why. I doubt if she did. I stood watching her shake the oil over the wood from a bottle with a quill in the cork. She dropped in a match and replaced the cover.

"I suppose you're all ready to set sail," she said.

There was a faint smell of kerosene and wood smoke in the air.

"Now don't cry," she said. "You wanted to go and you're going. Remember what you wrote in your class poem?"

I couldn't remember a word of it.

"The last verse," she said, and repeated it:

> *"So for us the sun is rising*
> *Sending forth red glowing rays,*
> *Omens of a gleaming future,*
> *Prophets of successful days.*
> *And about us brightly smiling*
> *Is the fairness of the morn,*
> *For to us, all bravely ready,*
> *'Tis not evening — but dawn."*

"It's not a very good poem," I said.

"No," Auntie agreed. "Whatever else you may be going to be, I don't think you're going to be a poet.

But the idea is good. Your sun *is* rising. You've got
your day ahead of you. Now see what you can do with
it."

She gave me a quick kiss and went around the stove
to the woodbox.

"Let us hear from you," she said, stooping until I
could not see her face.

"I'll — write every day," I promised. And fled.

Down the lane. Past the old Min Joy place, Boston's, Dorr's gate. Over White's Marsh Bridge,
through the woods, up Nason's hill, past the schoolhouse, down Goodwin's hill, across the tracks of the
Eastern Division of the Boston and Maine. Through
Old Swamps, past Woodlawn Cemetery; then to Powder House Hill, my father's paintshop, down Portland
Street into the village square, and along Main Street
to the New Hampshire line and the Salmon Falls railroad station . . .

Away, away, away.

My father and I, though we had come so far behind
a slow horse, were the first arrivals. He bought my
ticket and checked my trunk. I watched it being lifted
to a cart on the platform. I had taken off a glove and
was stroking Pony's nose.

"Guess you'll have more of a load before traintime," my father said to the freight agent. "A number
of 'em setting off Down East to school today."

"More goes every year, seems like," the agent answered, taking his pipe from the pocket in the bib of
his blue overalls. "Keeps on, don't know who'll be left
to haul their baggage."

They both grinned.

"There's a lot of different kinds of work in the world," said my father. "A good deal of it books can't do."

They were together, apart from me. I was alone. Why had I chosen books?

But then the Nutter automobile drove up, and Ruth and her parents and two girls who had been in our class — Gertrude and Camille — got out. Ruth and I said "Hi" to each other. Her mother began reminding her of many things she must not forget. My father helped Dr. Nutter take out Ruth's trunk, and my father and the freight agent put it on the cart while Dr. Nutter went into the station to buy tickets. The minister and his son came walking up the hill. Hoyt's high wagon was close behind them, coming for the mail, and Ted's trunk was in the back.

"Have to get this over to you for another paint job, Verd," said Dr. Nutter, "as soon as I can spare it."

"Still looks pretty fair," said my father, "except in spots." He put his hand on a mudguard. "I could give these a coat, and you could get it back in a couple of days. Last you till winter, when I suppose you could leave it longer. Couldn't use it much then anyway."

The train whistled in the distance. The platform I was standing on began to throb. The station agent was trucking away the three trunks.

"Good-bye, Pony," I whispered, putting my cheek against his nose. "I love you. I don't want to leave you. Good-bye, Pony. Good-bye."

The train roared in and came to a stop.

"Take care of yourself," said my father as I climbed

the steps behind Ruth. He passed up my valise to me. Our hands touched. It was not the valise which I wanted to take and keep, but his hand.

Now Ted was between us, climbing the steps. In the coach he reversed a seat, and sat down facing Ruth and me. We looked out of the window at his father talking to Camille and Gertrude, and at my father unhitching Pony from the post.

"All-l-l aboard!" called the conductor. "All aboard!"

The train began to move. We waved from our enclosure. Mr. Miller and the girls waved back from the sunny platform. We left them behind.

"We're off, the captain shouted," Ted said, "as he staggered down the stairs."

Ruth, beside me, smiled at him — her quick, sweet smile.

The quote, I thought, was inaccurate. It should be:

> "We are lost!" the captain shouted,
> As he staggered down the stairs.
> But his little daughter whispered,
> As she took his icy hand,
> "Isn't God upon the ocean,
> Just the same as on the land?"

I felt as if we were spinning through space, but now I was comforted. Like the captain, I was reminded that God was on trains and on college campuses as well as at home. We three, all just turned seventeen, would not be entirely alone.

Ruth was taking off her gloves. I took off mine. Ted showed us a farewell letter he had received from a girl who liked him better than he liked her. By the time

we reached Portland, left the train on which Ted
would go on to Brunswick, and climbed the steps of
the Lewiston train on the Bangor and Aroostook line,
we felt near the end of the high wire between the
past and the future.

Ted stood at the end of the coach we had left,
grinned, and shouted, "Rah, Bowdoin!"

We looked across at him from the end of the new
coach in which we had claimed seats with our valises,
and called back, "Rah, Bates!"

Dr. and Mrs. Nutter had ridden all the way to Portland, in a seat across the aisle from us, to be sure that
we found the train to Lewiston, but they had seemed
to me like the other passengers, all strangers. I think
Ruth, too, was hardly aware of their being there. We
had left home.

*I*T took me over a month of writing time to make a rough outline of what I remember from before I went to college. Now that I read it over, how very rough it is! And how little I have set down of all that should be there! If I were to begin again, I should put in much that is now left out, for *I must not forget it, any of it.* I spent so much time telling what happened, yet so little happened; and how it was when nothing was happening is what I want most to remember. The sound of two streams of milk striking the bottom of a tin pail; the way the sound changes as the pail gradually fills; the film which covers a man's eyes as he sits on a stool with his pail between his knees and fits his cheek to his cow's warm, silky side (I think the eyes of a nursing baby must be like that, though I have never seen a baby at his mother's breast). . . . The smell of the air the morning after the first hard frost, when the leaves on the squash and pumpkin vines begin to curl and darken in the October sunlight. . . . The indescribably delicate flavor of checkerberries, the toughness of their fibrous green leaves between the teeth, the bite of pink ivory pips to the tongue. . . . The colors of Mount Agamenticus as first seen when you reach the top of Goodwin's hill on your way home; never twice the same but changing with the season, the time of day, and the depth of color — or lack of color — in the sky. I have seen it crowned with gold, and obscured by dark or fog as by black velvet or gray gauze; or a mass of a dozen blended shades of green; or rimmed in snow against blue; or pink and purple from the sunset. I look at it and long to go there, as to the Promised Land. But whenever I have gone, I have been drawn irresistibly to the one place on the one ledge from which, with the naked eye, can be seen the white box of the George Hasty house snuggled against the big red George Hasty barn. . . . Remember the feel of bark, and boards just brought home from the mill, and prickly cucumbers, and blackberries, and mud to bare feet, and pulling off bloodsuckers, and drinking brook water from your hand or a birchback cup; the taste of marsh ice and spruce gum and hazelnuts; the sound of peepers like the creaking of gypsy wagons in the dark. . . . I must remember it all as it was when it was *all I knew*.

Now that I am home again for the summer, sometimes I can forget that I have been away. But not often, and never for long. I can no longer lose myself in it as I used to after a week in Dover. I want to.

I try to. But now I have lived for months at a time another way, and shall again. Perhaps many other ways. . . . And even here, there have been changes which I can not overlook. Once I went to sleep every night cuddling the thought that, with my powerful, invulnerable grandfather in his bed belowstairs, his flintlock musket on the pegs above the shed door, and his lash whip in the socket of his democrat wagon or his pung in the barn, no danger or even fear could come nigh me. Musket and whip are still in their places, but dusty; my grandfather moves this summer only from his bed to the table to the kitchen couch and back to his bed; he does this with difficulty.

I am not sure what holds up the roof of George Hasty's house now that he is so feeble. Aunt Vinnie is not here. And Harold has a home of his own in Dover. I look at my father (whom my grandfather has always introduced as "my boy") and my frail, lovely mother, and feel that they are not sure, either. It is not yet their place or time to support this roof, nor is it mine. We, like the roof, are upheld by invisible threads of which we dare not test the strength, though tested they will one day be for all our going a-tiptoe.

There is no tiptoeing in my college world.

It thunders across the playing field, races along the cinder walks, strides into class or chapel, snake-dances in parade, tramps up and downstairs, whirls over the dance floor, skims around the skating rink, leaves snowshoe tracks and ski trails on hills and fields. It never tiptoes, for no one is afraid; there is no one to be frightened, and when one sleeps all sleep to be ready for the thundering, racing, snakedancing, tramping, and whirling which will begin again when Hathorn bell is rung at six-thirty o'clock in the morning.

I have never been in such an exciting place. Since the first moment of my arrival on the campus I have been all but consumed by the fires of my own responses to what surrounds me.

There is the campus, only a mile east of the business centers of the Twin Cities of Lewiston and Auburn, which are separated by the Androscoggin River and joined by a trolley-car line known as the Figure Eight. Only a mile upriver from mills, factories, stores, public schools and churches of all faiths, the college campus is a small, independent state, a monarchy under President Gray, a benevolent system dedicated to youth and learning and established in Civil War time by a few Baptist ministers and their families. Dr. Gray is our third president, following the lifelong service of Presidents Cheney and Chase; his secretary is President Chase's daughter Elizabeth.

The home in which President Cheney lived is now Cheney House, a women's dormitory. Another women's dormitory is Chase House, and Chase Hall is our social center, housing the bookstore and the alumni office as well as the auditorium with the fireplace over which hangs a portrait of President Chase. Last year dancing was for the first time permitted on the campus, and we are not certain that President Chase, looking down upon it, wholly approves. (But the rules require that the dancers be separated by at least four inches from their partners.) Before the first Bates dance the faculty members took dancing lessons in the Women's Gymnasium, and the girls who sneaked into the dark balcony and watched say they never saw anything so funny in their lives. I wish I had seen it!

The administrative offices are in Roger Williams Hall. The Stanton Elm at the corner of the campus, near the chapel where attendance is required every morning, is named for one of the early professors; he was a nature and bird lover, so we have a Stanton Bird Club which he organized, and the first social gathering of each freshman class is the Stanton Ride to Lake Auburn for a picnic. ("Uncle Johnny" used to take his freshmen there in half-filled haycarts; now we go on the Figure Eight.) Our Jordan Scientific Society is named for the college's first professor of science; Professor Jordan, who died only two years ago, was a brother of the Reverend B. D. Jordan, a missionary whose work was long supported by most of the Baptist churches in Maine; large caps in the campus newspaper still read *KEEP THE JORDANS IN CHINA*. The honorary literary society is called the Spofford Club, for an early, much loved professor of English.

The dormitory in which I lived last year is Milliken House. Many Millikens have been Bates students. One, Carl, married a daughter of President Chase, and he became the Governor of Maine. Their daughter Nelly will be a senior this year, and is president of our Women's Student Government; she goes with the president of her class. The governor's daughter,

Vivian, will be a junior this year; Viv goes with the president of the Outing Club. Nelly is dark and Viv is fair. They are both brilliant and have soft voices.

Ruth and I had the front corner room on the second floor of Milliken House. It is the room Nelly and her roommate, Bunny Lombard, had when they were freshmen; Bunny is president of the Christian Association and goes with a track star. Viv and her roommate, Louise Bryant, had the same room when they were freshmen; Louise is one of the prettiest girls I ever saw, and goes with the son of the Bates librarian.

I don't know how Ruth and I were lucky enough to be assigned to this room. I am sure we shall never have another I shall like as much.

It has the same furniture as all the other dormitory rooms — two cots, two chiffoniers, two straight chairs, one rocker, and one study table. I never had a chiffonier before, nor any bureau all to myself until now; it has five drawers. But in two ways this room is different from any other dormitory room. First, it is at the top of the stairs to the second floor and at the foot of the stairs to the third floor, so if you leave your door open you see everyone who comes and goes, and most of them come in. Second, it has two windows facing in two different directions. One looks into the windows of the other freshman dormitory — Whittier House — and you can lean out and talk to the girls over there. But the other . . . !

The other window looks across Campus Avenue (along which the Figure Eight runs, zinging, on its wires) into the green (or snow-covered) lawns, the black cinder walks, and the great elms of the campus itself, backed at a generous distance by the stone chapel, the old rosy red brick walls of Parker Hall (a men's dormitory) and Hathorn Hall where the classes in languages and history are held and where the Little Theater is, the newer brick of Hedge Laboratory and Carnegie Science, and the stone library with the pillared entrance which is the stage for the Greek play given there every year at Commencement time. The college began with Parker and Hathorn as its only buildings. There were no women students then. The men in Parker studied by oil lamps, kept warm by stoves in which they burned wood they had cut in their home pastures, and cooked and ate there the vegetables they had raised in the summer, the fruit they had picked in their farm orchards, and the ham their fathers had smoked.

Now every room in every dormitory is heated by a steam radiator and an electric light bulb swings from the ceiling above every study table. The men have their meals at the Commons in John Bertram Hall, and the women are served in the dining room at Rand Hall where all the senior women live.

But through that window in the front corner on the second floor of Milliken . . . ! If you are awake that early you hear the rub of rope against wood which precedes the ringing of the six-thirty bell from the tower of Hathorn. You turn over drowsily, thinking of the bellringer, a boy who is paying for his room in Hathorn basement by climbing the stairs to ring the rising bell, ringing again at seven-forty for the first class, and after that at the end of each class hour and the beginning of the next all day. There are five minutes between classes. . . . All day, whenever you are in the room, you can see from the window the last-minute rush to meals and classes; boys in dark red freshman caps, bareheaded boys, girls with puffs of hair over their ears, in pleated skirts, plaid or suede jackets, and — in wet or snowy weather — overshoes unbuckled and slapping against each other; faculty moving more sedately, carrying small leather satchels or green Harvard bags. Or you hear the call of "Ground, sticks — OFF" and see girls in full black bloomers and blue or white middy blouses racing up the field at the end of Rand Hall with their hockey sticks. You hear the music of the chapel organ and of choir practice. You see weather sweep across the campus; the sun rising behind the chapel and hanging overhead, its light sifting down through the elm leaves, or heavy rain pushed by the wind into a gray slant, or snow falling silently, turning the roofs white, covering grass and walks, clinging to branches, brick, and stone, filling the air. But whatever the weather, the movement on the campus never stops as long as anyone is still awake. The campus is more than anything alive. . . . Lying in the dark — freshman lights go off at ten o'clock at night — the last you know is the starlight, the smell of burned leaves or of river water, or of icy cold, or of flowers blooming along the chapel walk or in the President's garden, the zinging of the Figure Eight and a shower of sparks from its wire, and one, two, or three young men's voices singing in the distance. Sometimes they are singing the Alma Mater, sometimes a measure or two of what will be sung in chapel in the morning. More often it is, "Oh, oh, oh, my sweet Hortense," or "Yes, we have no bananas," or "Ain't we got fun?" Your eyes close. . . . The rope rubs against wood, and Hathorn bell rings out the beginning of another day.

There are many of us there together, all near the same age, all getting ready. For what? The bookstore sells printed cards, which many of us have bought to put up in our rooms. They say, AFTER BATES, WHAT? Few of us know, specifically. We only know we must be ready.

Most of us grew up on Maine farms or in small Maine towns, but every class has several members who are the sons or daughters of missionaries and who had their early education in missionary schools in the Orient. Most of our fathers are ministers, teachers, doctors, village storekeepers, postmasters, local newspaper editors; but quite a few are Aroostook potato growers and racehorse breeders, and the Aroostook girls are invariably beautiful. We also have Jewish classmates, usually from Massachusetts and New York, Negro classmates from the South, and Chinese and Japanese classmates who have come from the other side of the world to study with us. Bates is famous for debating and some of our best debaters have been Negro men; the one we have now is Theodore Pinckney; people still talk about Benjamin Mays, who was graduated in 1920. Kohe Nagakura is one of our most artistic students, and George Tsung Se Yeh is the best speaker in my section of Public Speaking.

I think I am the only one who has the distinction

of having a father who is a carriage and sign painter. As far as I know I am also the only one who was not at very least the salutatorian at his or her high school graduation. Those who were salutatorians seem to have been kept from the top position by classmates who came with them to Bates.

At the dinner table our first night on campus, after Ruth was led to admit that she had been valedictorian of our Academy class, someone turned to me and asked, "Salutatorian?"

"No. A girl named Marjorie Groah was."

"Third, then?" my friendly interlocutor persisted hopefully.

"No. Armand Toussaint was. But a girl named Gertrude McNally was very close to him."

Oh, I had by then no expectation of completing a year in this challenging company. I stared in speechless admiration at the array of seniors, one at the head of each white linen-covered table, and at the upperclass waitresses who had survived at least two, probably four, perhaps even six semesters, and thought, "I can stay until February. I have enough money for my books. Harold has promised to pay my first college bill. And how can they be sure until the end of the semester that I am not going to pass?" Five months was a long, long time and I intended to make the most of every minute of it.

I did, too. (And I stayed all year, and am going back!)

My subjects were English, Latin, French, Greek, Ancient History, Public Speaking, and Physiology. My English instructor was Mr. Purinton, son of the

professor of Biblical Literature. I had Greek with
Professor Chase, son of President Chase; Latin with
Professor Knapp, French with Professor Brown, Public Speaking with Professor Robinson, and Physiology
with the Dean of Women. All of these but Professors
Brown and Robinson are Bates alumni. We call Professor Chase "Goosie," Professor Knapp "Freddie,"
Professor Brown "La-La," Professor Robinson "Prof.
Rob." There are other professors we call "Monie"
and "Doc" and "Sammy" and "Birdie" and "Railroad" and "Pa" and "Pom."

Of course all the presidents have been called
"Prexy," and we call Miss Elizabeth Chase "Aunt
Bessie" because Nelly and Viv Milliken do. But
everyone calls the Dean of Women "Dean Niles";
she is quite young — tall and dark, with a lovely
face and a low, even voice; her office is always quiet,
and it is restful to go in there.

Actually, all the faculty offices and the classrooms
are very restful. The faculty are restful people. When
I am with them, I know that they are taking charge,
leading the way quietly and confidently, guiding us
in the way we should go. They all love us all. They
really do. We aren't going to make any mistakes they
can prevent. No harm is going to come to us if they
can help it. While we are with them we are safe, as
we were with our parents when we were children.

But we are not children now. We are almost grown
up, and so must make many decisions every day for
ourselves, take responsibilities, and find our own
solutions. We work and play together all day, and

at night we do not go home to talk over with older people what has happened; we go back to our dormitories where we are associated with no one who is older than we are, and wrestle with our problems together or alone. This is good. Hard sometimes, but good. Sooner or later *we* are going to be the parents, the teachers, the ministers, the doctors, the newspaper editors who make and keep safe, quiet corners for younger people to rest in. We have to get ready.

Bates women are very proud that their conduct in their dormitories is regulated entirely by themselves, and that each girl is left on her honor to keep the rules we make. We have no house mothers, no watch-and-ward committees. In Milliken House we were all freshmen except for the junior proctor, whose only duties were to collect used linen and pass out clean, change light bulbs and fuses, blink the lights at the end of calling hours, ring the bell at the beginning and end of study hours, and lock the outside doors at bedtime. Our athletic director, Miss Davies, had a room there, but she had — and took — no responsibility for us. Once a week our house senior came to tell us of any changes in the regulations proposed by our representatives on the Student Government Board. For the breaking of any rule — such as forgetting to sign out in the evening, or coming in late — we give ourselves two demerits. If we accumulate as many as six demerits during a semester, we report this fact to our house senior, and if we get eight she reports it at the next meeting of the board, where a penalty is assigned. The penalties are routine — campusing for twenty-four hours, or returning to the dormitory an hour early the next Saturday night. There is no girl who would not scorn to spy on another. Dean Niles attends the weekly board meetings but says nothing unless her advice is asked, and votes only to break a tie. The board members are the president, vice president, secretary, and treasurer (one officer from each class), four representatives of the four classes, a representative of girls living off-campus, and five house seniors; we elect them all.

Such guidance as we get is mostly indirect and impersonal. Chapel attendance is required six days a week, and church attendance on Sunday. The faculty and our student leaders tell us that we are doing well, that we are going to do better, and the better we do the more privileges we shall gain.

The editorials in the *Bates Student* last year said:

There have been serious objections to introducing dancing to our campus. It has not been a matter of personal whims and prejudices, but a question of the best interests of the college . . . It is now in the hands of the students to demonstrate whether the governing bodies of the college have acted wisely . . .

He may not own a textbook.
He never sits near the front.
He never volunteers to answer a question.
Whenever anyone else is occupying the attention of the instructor, you can hear his low growl of disgust, snort of ridicule, or contemptuous grunt.
He is a pest to the instructor and a nuisance to the class.

He gets nothing out of the course, he says.
No wonder! You can't "get" unless you "put."

One of the cherished traditions of Bates is that of democracy — fair play, equal opportunity, justice to every
man regardless of creed, color, or race. . . .

Congratulations, Dean Niles! Your appointment to the
office in which you have already served as acting head,
and served so ably, meets the unanimous and hearty ap-
proval of the student body, both men and women. . . .

Another victory for our debaters! Fifty-three debates in
our history and only eleven defeats! . . .

This is the day of the best seller . . . largely books
that flourish and fade in a day. . . . The reader who
wants to find the best in literature and make it his own
must decide in advance that he will avoid the surface
scum and seek the pure water. The two do not mix. . . .

The Thirtieth of May is a day on which we may well
consider what Americanism means, for it commemorates
the deeds of men who died to keep America free and true
to its principles. One fitting way in which to use a few
moments of Memorial Day is to read over the Gettysburg
Address. . . .

If we are to choose between the two philosophies —
that of the untried college graduate with his boundless
enthusiasm, energy, and hope, or that of the wearied,
cynical, disgruntled scoffer — we choose the idealist every
time. If there is anything the world needs today, it is
idealism — combined, of course, with common sense. . . .

What town or city in New England does not have a
teacher, superintendent, or professor whose Alma Mater is
Bates? What college in New England has a larger number, in proportion to its enrollment, of student volun-

teers to Christian service? In many fields of business, in all the professions, Bates has representatives upholding its traditions. May each new class grasp that vision of responsibility!

A sampling of last year's *Student* headlines are:

BATES OPENS HOCKEY SEASON WITH 1-0 WIN OVER BOWDOIN

BATES BOWS TO MAINE IN HARD-FOUGHT BATTLE

FAUST PROGRAM PRESENTED BY DEUTSCHE VEREIN AND MACFARLAND

OUTING CLUB PLANS CARNIVAL

BATES LITERARY MAGAZINE WILL BE PRINTED

SENIOR GIRLS WIN BASKETBALL CHAMPIONSHIP

PHIL-HELLENIC PLAY A SUCCESS

MISS LEAHY AND E. D. CANHAM WIN FRESHMAN DECS

JORDAN SCIENTIFIC EXHIBITION TONIGHT

WOMEN'S ATHLETIC ASSOCIATION HOLDS BANQUET

SOPHOMORE PRIZE DEBATE NEXT WEDNESDAY

PHI BETA KAPPA INITIATION

DELTA SIGMA RHO ELECTS

BUKER SHOWS HEELS TO COUNTRY'S BEST TWO-MILERS AT PENN GAMES

CAMPAIGN FOR MILLION DOLLAR FUND BEGUN

BATES WINS NATIONAL DEBATE CHAMPIONSHIP

GARNET DEFEATS NEW HAMPSHIRE STATE

ANNUAL HIKE TO MT. WASHINGTON

SPOFFORD LITERARY CLUB UNIQUE IN CAMPUS LIFE

DANCE AT CHASE HALL TOMORROW NIGHT

PHIL-HELLENES SPEND EVENING WITH SOPHOCLES

SOPHOMORE ORIGINAL PLAYS A SUCCESS

FIRST IVY HOP

JUNIOR EXHIBITION BEST IN YEARS; THEODORE PINCKNEY AND ALTA HARRIS WINNERS

In one issue the front page carries a boxed statement by the Dean of Men:

The recent discussion of "Loyalty to Training Ideals" is a step in the right direction. Most cases of remissness on the part of college students are thoughtless rather than purposeful. . . . Our athletes, as well as the athletes of other institutions, need encouragement that they may better meet the obligations placed upon them. . . . I know of no institution where conditions are superior to those on the Bates campus. However . . . where we know that WE are remiss, let's all take hold!

FRED E. POMEROY

I brought all my *Students* home with me. What I like about them is that they are all about what we do ourselves, and every week we do so many things to make headlines and fill up the paper. What my mother likes about them is that I am a reporter, and a few of the items are mine, though they are not signed. Last year, in one of her letters, she said: "I am very much pleased with your rank in English. Sometime you are going to help the old world move along, I believe."

I suppose that is what we are all trying to get ready to do, but there is no way, yet, to tell who is going to do it — or where, or in what direction.

When she wrote me that, I had just received a

copy of the *Student* in which one of my items appeared, and I read the item over to see if I was proud of it.

It had a small headline: SHOWER PARTY GIVEN TO MISS KISK.

It said:

Miss Esther Christine Kisk of Worcester, Mass., a sophomore at Bates College and a member of St. Michael's Club, was given a very pretty shower party recently at the home of Mrs. Risby W. Whitehorne, 55 College St., Lewiston, in honor of her engagement recently announced to Dr. Robert H. Goddard, head of the physics department at Clark University. Beside the members of the St. Michael's Club, Miss Elsie Roberts and Miss Elizabeth Files, both Bates girls, were guests. A large pink and blue maybasket filled with gifts was presented the guest of honor by Miss Janice Hoitt and Miss Mary Gifford, classmates of Miss Kisk. Dainty refreshments were served by the hostess in the dining room, attractive with spring flowers.

It sounded to me very much like items I had written, while in the Academy, for the South Berwick *Independent*. I could not see that I had improved as a news writer. But it is a comfort to believe — as I *do* — that even if I don't "help the world move," Esther or Elsie or Elizabeth or Janice or Mary surely will; and that all we do together on the campus is pushing ahead the one or ones who will accomplish the most, as well as making each of us more ready for the opportunities coming to her.

We feel apart from the world outside while we are in college, as in a different way most of us always have in our homes on farms or in small Maine towns; but we know from speakers who come to the campus that there is great need out there of what we ought to be able to do. It is in a frightening condition now.

My copy of the April 21, 1922, issue of the *Student* has a front-page story of a talk in chapel by Dean Brown of the Yale Divinity School.

He said: "The world we live in is torn to pieces politically, industrially, and morally. . . . Boundaries have been shifted about. Geographies of ten years ago are nothing but scraps of paper today."

(Geography was my hardest subject in district school, too; except for English grammar — I simply could not diagram sentences. A diagrammed sentence looks to me exactly like long division with words. I almost failed both. Funny! I always get A's in composition and I am an A-B student in languages. And now that geography I wrestled with is "but scraps of paper"!)

"Capital and labor must be set back into their proper channels. The cause of the last eight years of perdition was the absolute lack of personal character. The end is not yet. . . . If our present-day civilization is not to bring up with a fearful smash we must have better methods in the workaday world. Business and industry must be made a profession. The doctor, minister, and teacher each has his code of moral ethics, his ideals. . . . To bring about this better type of life we need college and university-trained men and women. . . . May God save this nation from becoming absolutely amusement-mad,

dance-crazy, and self-indulgent. Let us wake up to the
fact that our country is the Messianic nation and that by
following the faith of Washington and Lincoln we can
rebuild the world."

I don't understand *why* the world is so different
from small Maine towns and from Bates College, and
sometimes I wonder if we are going to be able to
influence people who have let the world become such
a strange and frightening place. Why haven't earlier
generations of Bates students prevented it from getting into this condition? The only explanation I can
think of is that too many of them became foreign
missionaries, not realizing how much they were needed
in their own country. I hope not many of us will become foreign missionaries. I don't think we should
go to China while America goes to perdition. There
should be several of us together in each of the other
forty-seven states. (I am sure Maine can manage without us, since it already has so many of our parents
and the Bates faculty.) Ten of us in a state surely
could do far more than ten times as much as one
alone, we are so used to working together.

Also, Bates women of our day should have more
influence — or at least a wider influence — than those
of earlier days. Of course they influenced their hus-
bands and children and neighbors, and their pupils
if they taught. We intend to do that, but we shall be
active in politics too, and in civic improvement of all
kinds. Those of us who don't marry can give our
whole lives to public service. In preparation for that
we are all required to take public speaking. My

trouble is that I only like to recite poetry and give scenes from plays. More than anything in the world I would like to be an actress. But I suppose I must strive to overcome this urge. Everyone says that whatever is bad in the world the theater has, to the nth degree. *I* should think that whatever is *good* in the world the theater would also have, or could develop, to the nth degree. But I may be mistaken. Anyway, I'm probably not tall enough — 5′ 2″! Am I even tall enough to teach? My roommate doubts it. (She is 5′ 9″!) All of a sudden I have a tremendously exciting idea! What if we should form a company of Bates Players and tour the country, giving plays we had written ourselves? Dot could write religious plays, Erwin political plays, Ken comedies, I homey ones about Maine characters, Eleanor quite sophisticated ones, Grace and Florence fantastic ones; Erwin and Ken and Eleanor could direct; George could be our business manager; Alice would play all the leading roles which required height, beauty, and an angel's singing voice; Gladys Leahey could both dance and act; the two Hazels and Ruth Garner are interpretative dancers; and I *hope* there would be parts written to fit me. For leading men we have Carl and Pete to sing, and Harold and Kirby and Tracy and several others for the kind of good looks no stage should be without. Every one of these is in our own class! Could we move the world along that way? Can you set a world right and have fun at the same time? . . . If nobody else wrote a part for me, I could write one for myself. I'd like to do a little old Maine woman with Frank for my little old Maine husband. . . .

Anyway, my freshman year was full of excitement. I suppose this was mostly because of my own reaction to a way of life, an environment, totally new to me. Everything — but *everything!* — was almost unbearably exciting, every single day, from the moment of waking in the morning to falling asleep at night.

The nickname "Sonny" which had been given to me in the Pacific Mills office was changed to "Sunny." In varying degrees and at various times I loved all the girls in Milliken, in Whit, the marvelous seniors in Rand, our junior sisters, even the sophomores who hazed us. All the time I loved every professor, every building, every tree and shrub and blade of grass, the bells, the lights, the pillars, the chapel seats and stained glass windows, the plain brown classrooms, the stacks in the library, the bookstore, the bulletin boards, the fireplaces, the cinder walks. I loved going to football games — Ruth's parents brought my mother to one; she sat beside me on the bleachers and I held her hand hard even when I was jumping up to scream, "Block that kick!" — and basketball games and track meets. (I don't understand baseball and doubt that I ever shall.) Trying to earn my class numerals, I hiked an hour every day, and went on long hikes to Taylor Pond, Sabattus, and Greene; at Sabattus (a twelve-mile hike) there is a store where we buy crackers, cheese, and chocolate; at Greene (a twenty-mile hike) there is a cider mill where we get sweet cider. I went out for hockey in the fall, basketball in the winter, and soccer in the spring; and made the second team in every one. (Ruth always makes

first.) I worked in the kitchen at Rand washing dishes
and in the dining room waiting on tables whenever
it was my turn. We are paid three dollars a week for
this work and so many of us want to earn it that a list
of applicants is kept and each of us is allowed to work
only two weeks at a time; we go for our meals a half-
hour before the dining room opens and serve ourselves at one long table; I loved it. I worked at least
two afternoons a week for a doctor's family downtown. I also worked at the alumni office, pasting clip-
pings into scrapbooks; and toward the end of the year
the Alumni Secretary, Mr. Rowe, who is also the
Bursar, let me write news items of Bates students to
send to their home-town newspapers. But my Big
Achievements of the year were not failing any subject, and being chosen one of twelve to compete in
Freshman Prize Speaking.

About this last I wrote my mother in a sequence
of letters she has kept:

". . . Everyone has to go to Hathorn and give a
recitation from the stage this week. Prof. Rob listens
and selects twenty-five to be in the preliminaries on
Saturday when the prize division will be chosen. I
went up to the senior assistant for my last rehearsal
yesterday. She asked me when I was to speak, and
said she was coming over to hear me. And, Mother,
she did! Wasn't that queer? Mil Stanley, who sat near
her, said she clapped her hands to herself when I finished. Somebody else said Prof. Rob wrote down my
name, but I don't believe it. . . ."

"I've made the semifinals!! Oh, I'm *so* pleased and surprised! The list was posted on Hathorn bulletin board just before six o'clock. I didn't go up, but just as I was getting dressed for dinner we heard Al Gordon come running into the hall and Ruth went to the head of the stairs and asked, 'Is the list posted?' 'Yes,' shouted Al, 'and Sunny made it! Sunny made it!' Two other girls from Milliken made it, too. Oh, but the other girls were darling about it! They aren't the least bit mean or small about anything. They hugged and kissed and congratulated us. I shall wear my blue serge dress and do my very best, but of course I've gone as far as I possibly can. . . ."

"I've made it! I've made it! I've made it! How do you suppose I ever did? Just two campus girls were chosen — Mil Stanley and me. It still seems as if there must be some mistake. Tomorrow afternoon I'll sit up there in my gray silk, and tremble in my gray suède pumps and truly speak in the prize division. Oh, I just can't believe it!!! . . ."

"Well, the prize speaking is over. Of course I didn't get a prize; that was a foregone conclusion. Erwin Canham got it for the men, and Gladys Leahey for the women. She is a cunning little blue-eyed girl with a curly Dutch cut. Saturday morning somebody asked Ruth if she was going and she said, 'Oh, no, of course not!' meaning 'Do you think I'd miss it?' She and our closest friends sat together down front and smiled at me encouragingly like an own family. I was frightened but I guess I didn't show it and I did the very

best I could. Erwin was wonderful and so was George
Tsung Se Yeh. Helen Lovelace's date told her today
that George told him he thought I was the best of the
girls. . . . I began this morning waiting on tables in
the dining room at Rand! Oh, but I was scared, and
still am. I have two tables of eight people each. I
rush about in feverish haste, my eyes wild, and actually panting. I hope I get over this some time. . . . It
is harder than doing dishes in the kitchen, but it isn't
such drudgery. . . . Here is the Freshman Public
Speaking program. I sent one to Jennie, and I have
one for my Memory Book, so this is yours. . . ."

I think the social occasion I enjoyed most of all was
our Original Freshman Banquet held in the DeWitt
Hotel downtown after the initiation period. It was
formal (faculty chaperones, of course) with speeches.
Kirby was toastmaster. I was the girl chosen to speak.
Eleanor had put up my hair (there is so much of it
I can't manage it at all) and I felt simply gorgeous.
. . . When we got to the hotel we found that the
sophomores had been in and left a mock program on
every plate — handsome programs printed on pale
blue. They said, "The Babies' Banquet: — We honor
the class of Twenty-four, and to them bow our heads
before." They said we would be served "After-dinner
milk," and told us not to take the silver or the nap-
kins, and listed among the speakers, "Miss G. Whiz-
shes Hasty." Sometimes I think the sophomores are
younger than we are. Our own program was quite
dignified. I talked on "Bates Spirit." Erwin Canham
was the speaker for the men and his subject was "The

Million-Dollar Drive"; that is the fund alumni and students are trying to raise for the college; we have been giving plays, bazaars, auctions, and talent shows for it all year. Eleanor wrote a play to give outdoors on the campus one afternoon. The name of it was *How Fulvia Quiritina Raised a Million for Batesina.* I was Fulvia.

I don't have any one, inseparable friend at college; but then I never have had one since Bernice and I were growing up together on adjoining farms. At Grammar School I had Eva and Beatrice and Malvena. At the Academy it was sometimes Lois and Chase and Christie, sometimes Eunice and Edith and Marjorie, sometimes Doris and Ted and Ralph, sometimes Margaret and Julia. At college last year it was Ruth and Florence Cook and Ruth Marsh; but as I've said, I liked everybody and had good times whoever I was with.

One funny thing — rather — was that Ted Miller, who went to Bowdoin the day Ruth and I went to Bates, and who used to take me to parties and home from games the four years we were at the Academy, began last fall coming up from Brunswick to see — not me, but Ruth! He brought his roommate, a boy named Webster Browne, who took Florence out. In the winter they invited Ruth and Florence to a weekend fraternity house party at Bowdoin. (Florence is one of those Aroostook County girls!) It was quite a surprise to me when the first letter in Ted's familiar handwriting came addressed to Ruth and she told me he was asking to come up to see her. But when he came I saw him as a stranger, as if I had never seen him before; he was different from Bates men, and though there is no Bates man I like better than several others, they are now my friends and my standard.

COLLEGE is one of the two small planets which I inhabit by turns. The other, of course, is HOME. Whichever I am in, I feel rooted to; but sometimes I look across space toward the other.

Twice last year I looked both longingly and helplessly toward HOME.

The first time was on October first. I had been in COLLEGE only about two weeks, concentrating during every waking hour on learning my way about the campus, studying the Blue Book of rules, buying my books, remembering my schedule of classes, doing my assignments, taking physical examinations, making friends, dressing for dinner, putting away my things (Ruth is a *very* tidy person), going to meetings, practicing the college songs, making my freshman bib and remembering to wear it. . . .

My mother was writing me every day about what was happening at home, and I had known before I left that Harold was to be married on his bride-to-be's birthday . . . but I think I had the impression that HOME and COLLEGE were on different times, that the days passed more slowly there.

When she wrote, "Harold and Jennie will be married Saturday at 12:30. They have decided on a home wedding. Will you try to come?" I sat and stared at the page. It was already Wednesday. I had classes every day, including Saturday, until noon. I knew I was allowed cuts, but I had not known anyone to take one. I had very little money left and did not know how much a railroad ticket would cost, for I had never bought one; and I did not know when trains went, how they made connections in Portland, or where I could find out. I thought that if I decided to cut my Saturday classes, walked to the depot Friday afternoon and found there was a train connecting in Portland with a train which stopped at Salmon Falls it would be dark by the time I reached there and there would be no one to meet me for I could not let them know I was coming. I could not telephone, for HOME has no telephone; my grandfather will not consent to its installation.

I was completely cut off from HOME except by mail, and I could not send myself in a letter.

So I wrote my mother that I was sorry I could not come, as I had classes all Saturday morning.

That Saturday noon I did not go to lunch. I climbed Mount David, our steep little wooded hill back of Rand, found a hiding-place among the rocks at the top, and cried.

The next week my mother sent me a clipping from the *Independent:*

SANBORN–HASTY

A pretty home wedding was solemnized at the residence of Mrs. Ida M. Sanborn on Saturday, Oct. 1, at 12:30 P.M. when her daughter, Jennie Odelle, became the wife of Harold C. Hasty, son of Mr. and Mrs. Warren V. Hasty. The house was beautifully decorated with autumnal flowers and foliage. . . . The bride wore a gown of white crepe with an embroidered veil, and carried a shower bouquet of bride's roses. . . . Following the ceremony a reception was held, after which the wedded couple left for a camping trip through the White Mountains. . . . The bride is a graduate of Colby College and has been a very successful teacher at Kingston Academy, Berwick High School, and Dover High School. The groom was graduated from Berwick Academy in 1914, and is assistant superintendent in the factory of I. B. Williams Sons, leather belt manufacturers in Dover, N. H. . . . They will be at home after November 26 at 65 Silver Street, Dover.

I pasted the clipping into my big Memory Book under the heading, *Homesick Sometimes.* I was in College.

But at Thanksgiving, at Christmas, and again at Easter, College gave a great bounce and tossed us all off to go spinning Home-ward. We crowded the trains to speed north or south, playing ukeleles, singing, eating saltwater taffy sold on the coaches by a man in a white coat with a basket over his arm. With every station we came to, there were more vacant seats, fewer voices to sing . . . only one ukelele strumming now . . . candy bags empty and crumpled on the sooty windowsills. We were a long way from College, and very close to Home.

I'll never forget last Thanksgiving Eve: the coaches less than half-filled rushing through the dark, the conductor opening the door at the end and calling, "No-orth *Ber*wick! *No'th* Ber'ick!"

Ruth and I did not leave the train until he called, "Sal-mon *Falls! Sal*monfalls!" But between North Berwick and Salmon Falls the trains pass near enough to our house so that from the sink-room window you can see the smoke and hear the whistle at the crossings. It was too dark then for my mother and Aunt Vinnie to see the smoke of my train, but I knew they and my grandparents would be listening for its whistle. . . . And when I went down the iron steps my father reached up for my valise and carried it to the wagon where Pony was waiting. All the way past the cemetery, through Old Swamps, across the bridge, up Goodwin's hill, past Witchtrot Road, down Nason's hill, and out of the woods to where I could see the lamp in the kitchen window, the red-globed lantern bobbed before us on the corner of the dashboard.

Those times at home were so short that I hardly ever went farther from the house than the barn or the yard. Except that of course I had to see where Harold and Jennie are living. They have one side of a beautiful old house — a big kitchen, dining room, and living room, downstairs; two bedrooms and a bath upstairs. There is an open fireplace in their dining room, and another in their bedroom, and they keep fires burning in both. They have a big brass bed and a beautiful Indian blanket folded on the foot. My mother made them braided rugs for their room. If I am ever married, I want a house just like theirs, and especially a bedroom just like theirs. It is such fun to be there with them — everybody young and well and happy, and nobody having to study at night! Sometimes after supper they walk down the street to the drugstore and have ice-cream sodas for dessert. They are learning to make chocolate creams! They cook the fondant, and when it is hard enough roll it

into balls and dip it into hot chocolate. *Mmm —
good!* Jennie is a wonderful cook — especially cakes.
Most especially sponge cake and a chocolate cake she
makes fudge frosting for. *Mmmm—mm!*

During my Easter holidays I stayed at Harold's
and Jennie's overnight to go to something they
thought was going to be very exciting at City Hall.
Posters were up advertising a demonstration of radio.
Harold tried to explain to me what it is and how it
works, but I am stupid about things like that, and all
I understood was that we were going to hear music
that was being played and maybe speeches people
were making as far away as Boston or New York. It
wouldn't come in over wires at all, Harold said; just
over airwaves. Radio doesn't have any wires; in England, he said, people call it "the wireless." It runs by
batteries, like the clock my father won as a prize once.

So we went to City Hall, which was full of people,
and all there was on the stage was a box on a table.
A man explained to us what Harold had explained to
me, and told us we were going to hear an opera
broadcast from New York. He turned some buttons
on the front of the box, and there was a great snapping and crackling, but that was all. He explained
that that was "static" and he would try to "clear it
up." But the more he turned the buttons the louder
the snaps and crackles grew. I thought the box might
explode. At first everybody waited politely for the
opera. Then some of them began to laugh. It seemed
to me a few wires might have helped. Finally we left.
I should think the man would have been embarrassed,
after his advertising getting so many people out of

their comfortable houses. It was a cold, wet night, too.
I don't think any singing done in New York will ever
be heard in Dover except on Victrola records, but
Harold says of course it will. He is thinking of building a radio set himself. If anyone can build one that
will work, he can. . . . My mother treasures a copy
she made of a letter of recommendation Elder Knight
wrote for him when he applied for a position as a
draftsman after completing an International Corre-
spondence School course in drafting. It says, "The
applicant belongs to one of the best families in town.
He has had a fine home training, has no bad habits
whatever, is courteous and upright in all his ways,
studious and deeply interested in the line of work
he has chosen. I most heartily recommend him for the
position he seeks."

It seems strange that all I remember specifically
about my Easter vacation is that night I went to
Dover City Hall with Harold and Jennie. The rest
of the time I was at home here and did not notice
anything different from the way it was at Thanksgiving and Christmas. I have been trying for months to
recall any sign of change, but I can't. Everything was
in its usual place, and everyone looked and did as he
had when I was there before. One visit blends into
another so smoothly that I cannot separate them.

But I had hardly been back at college a week when
I was called to the Milliken House telephone one
evening, and it was Harold.

He said, "I have some bad news for you, Gladie.
Be a brave girl now. . . . Aunt Vinnie hasn't been

feeling well for two or three days, and she died this morning."

I didn't say anything.

"Gladie? Did you hear what I said?"

"Yes."

I had heard it, but I didn't believe it.

"It was a very short sickness. She was dressed and downstairs every day."

Of course she was, I thought. Auntie never stays in bed after seven o'clock in the morning. Usually she is up earlier.

"The funeral will be day after tomorrow. Do you want to come?"

I didn't say anything.

"I've talked it over with the folks. We didn't know just how you would feel about coming. They told me to tell you to do whatever you think would be best for you. . . . If you decide to come and don't have money for the fare, probably you can borrow it there, and when you get here I'll give you what you need to pay it back. . . ."

"How is Grandpa?"

"He seemed about the same today. Aunt Hattie was up. I don't think he realizes yet what has happened, really. He has to make so much effort to keep around that his mind has to be mostly on himself."

Grandpa just didn't believe it. Grandpa and I didn't believe it. Auntie couldn't die.

"How is Mama managing?"

"All right. Grace has taken Grammy to stay with her until after the funeral; Billie and I got her into our car and drove her over today. As I said, Aunt

Hattie is there, and Aunt Lou is coming. Billie and I are helping what we can. Everybody is sending in food. Mama needs a new hat for the funeral and Dad will bring her over to get it tomorrow; we'll have them here for lunch. . . . If you decide to come, come through to Dover station. You know the way up here. If we happen to be out, the key will be under the porch rug."

"Billie" is his name for Jennie.

"I don't think I'll come."

"What did you say?"

"I said I don't think I'll come. If they don't need me."

"They said to tell you it was up to you. They know how busy you are."

Busy . . .

"Auntie wouldn't want anything to interrupt your education."

There was great sadness in Harold's voice. Anger began to rise in me. Anger has always been my defense against sadness.

I wanted to shout into the telephone: "She *doesn't* want my education interrupted; certainly not by some *funeral,* when *nobody has died!*"

But I said, "Give my love to Grandpa and — everybody."

"I sure will, Gladie. Billie and I will get flowers for Auntie and put your name on the card with ours. I'll write to you in a few days, and so will Mama."

I didn't say anything. I suppose I am very hard to understand; they are all very patient with me. They are so *good.*

"You'll go to bed now, won't you? And sleep? . . . Don't feel bad."

"I won't."

"Good night, little sister."

"Good night — dear."

The next day — and the next — I went back to my hiding place on Mount David. But I did not cry. The first day I convinced myself that Auntie was not at home and would never be there again, not in her chair at the table, not in her rocker by the back window, not stirring something at the stove, not in the garden, not in her room. All she could ever teach me she had already taught me. Or had she? Was there a reason why she had gone away? I tried to think what reason, what purpose she could have in going, and whether it was associated with me. I thought perhaps it was to help me grow up faster, and to give me experiences which would make me write better.

The next day I took a notebook with me to Mount David, and wrote an essay which was later published in the *Garnet*, the college literary magazine.

This summer my mother has told me in detail exactly what happened about a week after my Easter holidays.

She says she heard Aunt Vinnie moving around her room in the night, and the next morning she did not come downstairs until nearly nine o'clock. Auntie said she had had a pain in her stomach and it was gone now, but she was pale, and she had only part of a cup of tea for her breakfast. She sat for a while in her rocker, but went back to her room before dinner. My mother called her when it was ready, but she

said, "Go ahead. I'll be down later." She did not
come down until about four o'clock and stayed for
supper but ate only a taste of dried-apple sauce,
though it was warm, for my mother had just made
it. Then she said, "I'd better go to bed and sleep
this off."

But the next morning when she had not come
down at nine o'clock my mother went to her room
with a cup of tea and some toast. For some reason,
she says, she was afraid to knock on the door.

But Auntie said, "Come in, Frank. . . . Oh, you
didn't need to bring that tray up here. You have
enough to do, with nobody to help, without waiting
on me. I was coming down in a few minutes."

My mother says her color had changed again. It
was grayish now. And her eyes were big and dark.

"I thought you ought to have something to give
you a little strength. You didn't eat anything all day
yesterday."

"Well, I'll try. Put it on the stand. I don't know
why, I don't have any appetite."

"Have you had that pain again?"

"Off and on. It's better now."

"It's hung on so long I think I'd better run up to
Pearl's and ask Dr. Ross to come up."

"No! Don't you do any such thing. I don't need
a doctor. This is wearing off. It has to run its course."

She came downstairs after dinner, in a clean dress
and with her hair pinned up smooth. She had started
with her tray but had to leave it on the top stair
because, she said, she had a dizzy feeling and did not
want to risk breaking her favorite cup and saucer.

When my mother went up for the tray, she could not see that Auntie had touched it.

Auntie was stirring something in a cup.

She said, "Father thinks a little Jamaica ginger would make him feel better."

She took it to him and he sat up on the side of the couch.

"You got over what ailed ye, Vinnie?" he asked.

"I'm getting over it."

"I was thinking, wish you could make me a bowl of porridge for my supper. Nobody else's porridge tastes like yours."

"You'll have your porridge."

She sat down in a rocker, and took one of his socks from her mending basket. She asked my mother to thread a needle, and then drew it back and forth across the place where the darner showed through. But she did it very slowly, and before the hole was closed in, she let sock and darner lie still in her lap. She was looking out of the window. There was still snow on the ground.

"Be good to see green grass again, won't it, Father?"

He sighed.

"If I live till then," he said.

Grammy rang her bell and my mother went to her in the parlor. When she came back, Aunt Vinnie had made the porridge. Grandpa was asleep.

"Be ready whenever he wants it," Auntie told my mother. "Flavor'll be the better if it sets awhile. . . . I guess I'll go up and lie down. Seems foolish, but that little tuckered me out."

"I wish you'd let me have the doctor up, Vinnie."

"No. I don't need the doctor."

"Can't you drink some of the porridge?"

"I kept tasting it while I was making it. Probably drank a cupful."

"Why don't you rest on the sitting room couch, and not climb those stairs?"

"I never could rest on a couch."

She did not come downstairs again. That night my mother ran up across the field to Pearl's and telephoned Aunt Hattie. She told her how Auntie looked and seemed and that she would not have a doctor. Aunt Hattie said she would be up on the morning train from Kittery Depot and for my father to meet her at the Junction.

My mother did not sleep all night for listening, but she heard nothing.

As soon as my father left to meet Aunt Hattie's train, she went upstairs with a thin china dish of oatmeal she had cooked with raisins, and a thin china pitcher of cream.

"You know how Vinnie always loved cream," my mother told me.

Auntie's door was ajar.

She opened her eyes and said, "You're up early."

"It's after eight o'clock, Vinnie. How do you feel?"

"Pretty well."

"Hungry?"

"No."

"See what I brought you. All hot."

"Put it down. Till it's cool. Has the mailman come?"

"Not yet."

"Expecting a letter from Gladie?"

"Today or tomorrow."

"I hope it comes today."

She closed her eyes. My mother sat down beside her and took her hand.

After a while Auntie asked without opening her eyes, "Harold come home?"

"Not yet."

"No. Not time yet, is it? He'll get here. Don't worry."

"No. I'm not worried, Vinnie."

Later Auntie said, "Must water my — Star of Bethlehem."

"That's so. We will."

When through the window by the bed my mother saw Pony coming into the yard, she said softly, "Why — here's Hattie driving in!"

Auntie opened her eyes, and said, "Oh — say not one word!"

She meant, What a time for company to come, with me lying here and you with everything to see to!

My mother said, "It's all right. We'll manage."

Aunt Hattie was already climbing the stairs. She came into the room with her hat and coat still on. She stood beside the bed, suddenly stooped between my mother and Auntie and lifted Auntie a little, holding Auntie against her shoulder.

Aunt Hattie turned toward my mother and said low, "Don't look, Frankie. Don't look."

A minute or two later she eased Auntie's head back to the pillow, and told my mother, "It's over, Frankie. She's gone."

I have heard about this two or three times. My mother seems to need to tell me how it was.

But every week or two I still have the same dream I have had for months. It is the only dream I have ever had so often that I know what is going to happen as soon as it begins. That dream is as real as anything that ever happened to me.

I dream that someone says, "I heard your Aunt Vinnie died. How did that story ever get started? She is living in Kittery." (Sometimes it is Portsmouth or Rochester or Biddeford.) "I saw her just last week."

Then I go running and get on an electric car that takes me to Kittery. Or Portsmouth, or Rochester, or Biddeford. When I get there I knock at doors and ask, "Does Miss Vinnie Hasty live here?" Strangers say no, and shake their heads. But finally a woman says, "Not here. She lives in that house across the street." So I run to that house as fast as I can. It is a very beautiful house. Sometimes I see Auntie before I get there — sitting on the porch, or cutting roses in the garden, or sewing by the window. If she is inside with the door closed, she opens it to me. And the minute I am near enough I throw my arms around her and hug her until she tells me to stop.

"Goodness gracious sakes alive!" she says, laughing. "What is all this for?"

I am laughing and crying and I tell her, "People keep saying you have *died*. I didn't believe it, of course. But when I got home you weren't there, and nobody knew where you had gone."

"They should have known," she says, calmly. "I

had been planning to come here, and I always carry out my plans. Now sit down and catch your breath and then tell me everything you have been doing since I saw you. Every single thing."

And I do. Only each time I begin where I left off the time before. And each time I am happier than I have ever been.

This summer I have taken care of Grammy and Grandpa several weekends while my mother went on little trips with Harold and Jennie. She would not go if my father were not here to meet any emergency with Grandpa, and Grace nearby to help with Grammy if I should need her. (Grace is Grammy's niece and almost as close to her as a daughter, for when their children were small, Grammy and her sister Em lived in the same house.) But while they are as well as usual I can take care of them and I like to. It is easier for me than for my mother, because I know the routine of what she does for them and am young enough to add to it. What I add is show of affection. It seems to be hard for middle-aged people to express love for old people; also hard for old people to express theirs for middle-aged people. But a girl can curl her grandmother's hair over her finger and say what pretty ears she has and pat her soft cheek, and her grandmother can say, "You're an old flatterer but I declare you do me good"; and neither of them feels silly. They feel smart, as if they had just discovered a secret, and are only sorry everyone doesn't know it; it isn't a secret you can *tell*.

A girl can sit on the edge of the kitchen couch where her grandfather lies, put her arm across him, burrow her chin gently into his soft whiskers — how *soft* grandparents are! — and his sunken eyes will brighten. He can say, "Kind of like Grandpa, do ye?" And she can tell him, "You're the best-loved grandfather in the whole world." It isn't hard. It's easy. And it makes them both feel better.

But the things I want most to say to my grandfather I can't. I don't think they would mean to him what they mean to me.

When Grandpa says to me out of a long silence, with a puzzled and hurt look on his face, "Never thought Vinnie would go first. Never thought I'd have to make do without her," I want to say, "She isn't far away, Grandpa. She only went ahead to help your Say Jane get a home ready for you. She wanted to be there to open the door, and say, 'Well, Father, you took your time about getting here. Mother was beginning to lose her patience.' "

But I don't. I only squeeze his hand or pat his shoulder and say, "Anyway, you've got *me*."

I don't say what I want to say, partly because he might ask, "What makes you think so?" And if I told him of my dream he would shake his head and say, "Never took much stock in dreams. They don't mean anything." Besides, the kind of house I see Auntie in is not a house he would want to live in. But I know it will be when he gets there.

I don't say this, mostly because to him it would mean that I think he is going to die.

They all seem to accept death as a fact. I don't see
how they can. When I first heard of it I denied it.
Every time it has reared its ugly head I've fought it
down. I *know* there is no such thing, and I know
Aunt Vinnie knew it too. It must be that she taught
me the truth, though I don't remember her doing it
exactly; it is not in any book I have studied. But I
know a person cannot die. At least, not if he is much
of a person. Not if he is as much of a person as Aunt
Vinnie and my grandfather. Their qualities, unique
because peculiarly their own, are part of the source
of power that turns the wheels of the universe, and
without them the earth would wobble on its axis,
the sun would lose its way, and the stars would crash
into one another. God did not make them to be can-
celed out. In time they go beyond our sight, but
they are not beyond our reach unless we think so. I
feel so thankful to know that, and so *distressed* that
nobody else I know seems to! But I doubt if anything I — or maybe anyone — could say would convince them. I don't believe Aunt Vinnie ever put it
into words to me. I think the only way is to live it,
to demonstrate it, and, after you go, to come back in
dreams to those who are left — if they will let you.

September 7, 1922

$\mathcal{M}$ Y father and I brought down my trunk to-night from the shed chamber to the shedroom, which is now the temporary storage place for things which are soon to be moved again, either in or out. It used to be our summer kitchen, and a fire was built in the cookstove there for special work in fall and winter. When the string hammock was brought in from the yard at summer's end, it was always hung across a corner of this big room with unpainted board walls, and bundled in leggings and sweaters I often swung there watching Auntie "try out" fat from pork scraps to fill lard pails, or Papa "tapping" our shoes or mending harness, or Grandpa sitting astride a tub shelling field corn. But this room is too far from my mother's patients for her to be able to do more than run into it now and then. Also, three stoves are more than enough for her to keep going; beside the kitchen stove there is one in the sitting room my grandfather goes through to get to his bedroom, and one in the parlor for my grandmother. If my father resoles shoes or mends harness in cold weather, he does it in the kitchen where my grandfather can watch him; but he does not shell field corn, for he does not grow it. We keep only two cows, a horse, and a few hens now; and have only a small vegetable garden. The hay is cut by a neighbor at the halves. One man alone cannot do much farming in the half-light hours before and after a day's work at a paintshop in town.

For the next few days I shall be filling my trunk with belongings I used last year at college and know I shall use again. To these will be added the one dress I found time to make this summer, and other dresses, skirts, and a leather jacket I have bought. I also have a new brown felt hat which my father says looks like an upside down kettle; but it is the latest thing and I feel very stylish in it.

I could buy these things this summer, and my college bills will be paid this year (as my second semester bill was last year) from money Aunt Vinnie had saved and put in the bank. According to Maine law, two thirds of her little property was inherited by her father, the remaining third by her brother and sister. My father and grandfather agreed that Auntie would want it used toward my education, and so what they inherited has been set aside for me. With what I can earn, it should take me through two more years, even if I stay at home again next summer to help my mother.

In the bottom of the trunk I have put a hooked rug

which my Grandmother Hasty made. The blue in it
is from her father's and brother Joe's Civil War uniforms. It has a brown dog in the center. It has never
yet been walked on. Auntie always kept it in moth-
balls in Uncle Joe's sea chest. But I need a rug beside my bed, and I shall be very careful of it.

My dormitory this year is Frye Street House, farther from the main campus than Milliken but nearer
to Mount David. Ruth and I are to room together
again, and our room is on the second floor. All of us
there will be sophomores, including the two proctors.
Dean Niles has a bedroom and sitting room on the
first floor.

I find myself wishing that this year on campus
would be exactly like last year, but I know it won't.
No day, even, is exactly like any other day, to say
nothing of a whole year like any other year.

My subjects are to be English, Latin, French, Greek
Literature, Psychology, and Advanced Public Speaking. How lucky I am that Bates requires no mathematics of Liberal Arts majors, and only one year of
science, which for me will be a semester of Geology
and one of Astronomy (junior year)! All I really want
is languages, to read all I can and write all I can, and
to get on a stage (any platform is a stage to me) as
often as I can. I am taking Psychology this year as
preparation for the two years of courses in Education
which I must have in order to be certified for teaching. I am not sure that I want to teach, but I am not
sure that I don't, and so it is best to be certified. . . .
My English this first semester is the course in Argumentation which is required of all Bates students.

The instructor is Professor Baird, the debate coach, a *world-famous* debate coach. Though I was on the Berwick Academy debating team, I am absolutely terrified at the prospect of even giving a definition of terms, in his class! . . . But I suppose I shall get through it somehow — and second semester? Oh, second semester my English courses will be in poetry appreciation and in writing short stories and plays! Glorious, glorious, glorious! Oddly enough, Professor Baird is the instructor in the creative writing course too.

I have made up my mind secretly that for the next two years I shall work hard at what I want most to achieve for my senior year. Other girls may want to be elected to Phi Beta Kappa or be president of Stu. G. or Athletic Board or the Christian Association. I want to be an English assistant, and a member of Spofford Literary Club.

Right now I should go to bed, for there is much to do tomorrow. But how can I sleep? I am sad and happy and excited and scared, all stirred in together. It feels the way Grammy's bread used to look when it was rising in the big pan which she kept warm behind the stove with a piece of homespun wool blanket covering it. She would turn back the blanket to see if it was ready to be made into loaves, and I always wondered if it would keep on swelling until it exploded.

℩OMORROW is Thanksgiving Day, so this is Thanksgiving Eve, and unlike any other there has ever been
in this house.

It was dark when Ruth and I came down the train
steps at Salmon Falls; my father was there to meet me,
and Pony brought us home. Everything was just as it
was last year, until we were coming up the lane toward the home lights.

Then my father said quietly, "Your grandfather
has not felt well enough to get up the last few days.
He seems to get weaker all the time."

My mother had written me that he was growing
weaker and she did wish he would have the doctor
but he never had and said he never would. Aunt Hattie had been up to see him, and she and my father
had agreed that he had a right to decide for himself.
"He always has," my mother wrote.

"It must be very hard for him to stay in bed," I said.

"No strength," my father answered. "No strength at all."

When I went into the kitchen it was warm and smelled of mincemeat, but no one was there. My mother was speaking to my grandfather in his room.

"He'll be here in a minute, Father," she said. "He went to the depot to meet Gladie. She's come home for Thanksgiving. They just drove into the yard."

I put my valise on the kitchen couch where my grandfather always used to lie for a while after supper, when his day's work was done. I took off my coat and hat and gloves and laid them on the head of the couch, under which my grandfather keeps the York County Atlas. I did not want to go through the sitting room to hang my things in the front hall closet, because my grandfather's bedroom door was open into the sitting room. I looked at the table, set for supper with only three places.

My father came in from the shed and my mother called, "Verd? Father wants you."

He hung his cap and jacket on pegs behind the stove, rubbed his hands close to the heat, and went through the sitting room.

My mother came out then and we hugged and kissed. When she drew away from me there were tears in her eyes. She looked very tired.

She said, "It's worth all the gold in Alaska just to see you, dear. You must be hungry. I guess we'll have something to eat here pretty soon. I can't even remember what I've started for supper."

"I'll help, Mama."

"Well, I'll have to find you an apron first. You run in and see your grandmother a minute. She's been alone most of the day."

I went into the parlor and said, "Hi, Grammy!"

She had lit the lamp on the stand beside her and was reading one of the worn paper-covered novels by Mrs. E. D. E. N. Southworth which she always has by her, along with her Bible. She took off her steel-rimmed glasses and held out her left hand, which is the only one she can move. I bent to slide inside her arm and pull her against me.

"My, your nose is cold," she said. "Must have had a cold ride. Not very warm in here, either. Fire's getting down. Put in one of them birch sticks, will you?"

I opened the door of the little round stove and put in a birch stick. The flames curled up around it.

"Come for Thanksgiving, have you?" she said. "Poor young-one, I don't know how much Thanksgiving there'll be here."

"I smell mincemeat in the kitchen."

"Yes, your mother managed to make some. I don't know how. None of it has got into a pie yet. Hattie brought a fruit cake. She was here today. Come on the morning train, and Roland drove up for her after work." She glanced at the closed door between the parlor and my grandfather's bedroom. "Been in to see your grandfather yet?"

I shook my head.

"Don't put it off. Sounds to me as if he may go any time. One or the other of 'em sets with him day and night."

"Papa's with him now."

"Won't have a doctor."

"No."

"Your mother's all tired out."

"I know. I'll go help her get supper. And then I'll bring you yours."

She was putting on her glasses.

"You can bring it as soon as it's ready," she said. "It's an hour past time now."

As I went into the hall she was opening her book.

My father was coming out of the bedroom when I reached the sitting room. He had a cup in his hand. There was a spoon in the cup.

He said, "Go in and see him. He knows you've come. I'll be back in a minute."

I did not want to go in alone. I remembered that Aunt Hattie had told my mother, "Don't look, Frankie. Don't look."

"Soon as I put a little hot water on a cracker," said my father, "and spread some butter and sugar on it."

This was what they had brought me when I had measles.

There was a lighted lamp on the bureau beside Grandpa's bed. Still the small room was full of shadows.

I bent over the bed and said, "Hi, Grandpa, dear."

A low voice which I had never heard before said from a great distance, "I'm 'bout gone, Gladie. I'm 'bout gone."

"You'll feel better," I told him, "in the morning — you'll feel better."

"Awful — weak."

"It's late. You're tired."

There was no answer.

After a minute I knelt beside his bed and put my cheek against his hand, which was closed over the edge of the corn-husk mattress. . . .

When my father came back, I got up and went to the kitchen. Grammy's tray was ready, and I took it in to her. Mama and I sat in two of the three chairs drawn up to the table, and when my father came out to his, my mother took another swallow of tea and then went into the bedroom. Later, while my father was with Grandpa, and my mother was getting Grammy ready for bed, I did the dishes and put my hat and coat in the front hall closet.

I took my valise to Grammy's room, but Mama said: "You'd better sleep in Vinnie's room tonight. It will be quieter. Your father and I will be going downstairs and up, by turns, all night."

But they aren't going to have to. About nine o'clock there was a knock at the door and it was George Albert Earle, a neighbor only a few years younger than my grandfather. They have been neighbors and friends ever since my grandfather built this house, and he said he had come to sit with my grandfather so that my father and mother could go to bed and get some sleep.

"Oh, what a blessing if you can!" my mother said. "Just let me speak to him."

She went to the bedroom door.

"Verd, George Albert's here. Does Father feel like seeing him?"

Grandpa answered for himself.

"George Albert? . . . She say he's here?" And then suddenly in a strong, clear voice, "Zounds, tell him to come in. Get him a better chair from the setting room. And put another piller under my head."

My mother came back and took George Albert's cap and jacket and mittens. He went in, and my father came out looking amazed.

"Seems as if having George Albert here has given him a new lease on life," he told us.

He sat down by the table and peeled and cored an apple, passing a quarter to my mother and one to me.

The two men in the bedroom were talking about harvest and stock as they might have ten years ago. Whenever Grandpa spoke we looked at one another and smiled.

"Sounds just like himself," my mother whispered.

Then he called her.

"Frank! You gone to bed?"

She went to the door, open between the sitting room and the bedroom.

"No, Father. We're right there in the kitchen. You want something?"

"I was just a-thinking. George Albert says he's going to stay ontil I get sleepy. I don't feel a mite sleepy. Do feel kind of gnawing, as if I was hungry. Have you got any beans baked? Any brown bread?"

"Well, now, I'll have to see —"

She came back to us, wide-eyed.

"Verd! Did you hear? He wants *baked beans!* And brown bread!"

"Have you got any?"

"Yes. There's beans frozen in the pot in the shedroom, left from Saturday night. And there's an end of a loaf of brown bread in the cellarway; pretty dry."

"We'd better warm them up."

"My soul and body," murmured my mother. "I don't know —"

But my father brought the beans and heated them in the spider. I brought the steamer from the sink-room cupboard and we warmed the brown bread.

"Smells good," called Grandpa. "Bring in a plate-ful for George Albert, too. He can eat a bite with me."

My father took in Grandpa's tray and my mother took George Albert's. I stood in the doorway and looked at them, two old men, Grandpa with gray and George Albert with snow-white hair, Grandpa propped high in his bed and George Albert in the willow rocker facing him.

"You don't need to stay," Grandpa told us, waving his spoon. "I can feed myself. Go 'long to bed. When we're through, George Albert can take out the dishes."

So we all went upstairs. I think — I hope — my mother and father have been asleep two hours. But I am still here at Aunt Vinnie's sewing table, beside her lacy lamp with the square foot and the red wick; and Grandpa and George Albert are still talking. I can hear them quite clearly because the register is open in the sitting room ceiling to let up some warmth from the stove into my room. They are talk-ing about lumber lots now, their boundaries and where the corners are, who used to own them and who they were sold to, when they were cut, how many thousand feet were sawed out at what price per thousand. Sometimes they disagree and argue, and when they do Grandpa's voice rises. It is wonderful to hear. It is like music. It is like Christmas. It is like a miracle.

There is so much I meant to write in this book tonight, for *so much* has happened to me since September. But I can't think about it now. I just want to listen to Grandpa. I'm going to put out Auntie's light and slip into Auntie's bed and listen, listen, listen. I won't go to sleep. As long as Grandpa is talking, I'm not going to sleep.

I MUST have, though. I lay listening to the two voices using the same accents, the familiar words and phrases, George Albert's higher-pitched than Grandpa's, Grandpa's deep and strong. They seemed to speak faster and faster, as if the night might be over before they finished, the dawn come before they had settled all the boundaries to the satisfaction of both and reminded each other of the location of the Indian spring, the bear's den, the three-cornered rock, and all the other landmarks of the woods in which they had spent so much of their boyhood and manhood. . . . And suddenly I opened my eyes to stillness. It was a stillness I recognized, for it had come to me before; several times before. There is no other like it. Days when not a leaf stirs, houses where everyone is asleep and all the clocks have stopped are noisy by comparison.

Aunt Vinnie's clock had not stopped. It said ten minutes past eight, and gray light was streaming in the window.

I washed in the flowered china bowl, dressed in the stillness, and went down the back stairs to the kitchen.

My mother was just putting in a chicken to bake. There were two pies, smoking hot, on the back of the stove. She closed the oven door and looked around at me. She had been crying. I put my arm around her.

"Why didn't you call me, Mama?"

"We thought you needed your rest. And your father said it was just as well if . . . Your grandfather died in his sleep about daybreak. George Albert called us, but he had already gone. George Albert said they talked until after four o'clock, then your grandfather dropped asleep; just natural. George Albert sat there in the rocker, thinking to stay until we got up. But about half-past five, your grandfather — just stopped breathing. Nobody could have gone easier, George Albert said."

"I listened to them talking a long time. Where's Papa?"

"The undertaker has been here, and your father followed the hearse to the village. He'll pick out the coffin down there, and call Hattie and Harold to tell them the funeral will be Saturday. On the way back he'll see Lafayette and the boys about digging the grave. I doubt if he gets back much before dinnertime. Now eat your breakfast, for we have a lot to do."

We have been very busy all day. This morning we cleaned the sitting room, brought Grammy and all her daytime things out there, and opened doors and windows to air the bedroom and parlor. We packed Grandpa's best suit and white shirt in a box, with some underwear and socks and a black tie which he had never worn. After we ate our Thanksgiving dinner, my father went back to the village to take them to the undertaker, and Grace and Pearl came to help us clean the bedroom and the parlor. My father had already taken Grandpa's bed apart and carried it to the shed chamber, and put into boxes all that was in the cupboard, closet, and bureau drawers. When he came back from the village he helped us move Grammy's bed and all she uses at night into the bedroom. This is so that the parlor will be ready for the funeral. I have never before been in this house — or any other — when it was being made ready for a funeral.

I don't know what I think about it. I don't know what I feel. I don't know what anyone else feels. Except that I was glad there was so much to do.

Now it is done, and everyone has gone to bed early. But I am not tired. I am to sleep on the bed-couch here in the sitting room, to be near Grammy. There is still a good fire in the stove and I am sitting at my mother's Larkin desk to write.

What a strange night to try to tell the story of the way my sophomore year at college began! But I must do something. I had planned to do this during these few days at home. And Auntie tells me in my dream, "I always carry out my plans." I am sure that the night after his Say Jane died, Grandpa fed his hens, picked up his eggs, milked his cows, and fed and bedded down his horse. You *go on.* I know that is true and necessary and important. From wherever you are, whatever happens, *you go on.* . . .

I want to remember the way the college dormitories look and smell when we first go into them after the summer vacation. Every floor, all the stairs, and the woodwork in the halls has just been varnished; so have all the desks and chairs. Many of the rooms have just had a fresh coat of paint. Everything gleams. And it smells clean, pure, new — as if everything that ever happened under that roof had been erased, and everything that has happened to you, too. All that remains of the past, for a freshman, is that it brought him to where he is now accepted. All that remains of the past, for an upperclassman, is that it was of an order which allows him to return. No more detailed record, either good or bad, comes in with him. It has all been left behind. All that matters lies ahead. He is a welcome stranger in a bright new home, a challenging new world full of an endless variety of new truths to learn, new friends to make, new opportunities to seize, new problems to solve, new goals to reach, new qualities to develop. He feels new-born. . . .

I think it is like that for Aunt Vinnie every day. I think it is like that for Grandpa, tonight.

Most of the girls living in Frye Street House this year lived together last year in Milliken, as most of those in Chase House, farther up the street, came over from Whittier. For various reasons, we do not all have the same roommates as last year. I am glad I do. Ruth and I are on the second floor with the Stanley sisters and Ruth Marsh. Florence (we call her Cookie) lives on the third floor with Dott Hoyt, and Eleanor with Ruth Garner. These are the girls we are with most — talk with, study with, hike with, go to classes and gym and meals with — though we like everyone in the house and do many things with all of them.

Of this close but not tight group "my" Ruth, Eleanor and Mildred Stanley, are top-ranking students; Mil is also a very gifted musician. Ruth Garner is a wonderful dancer, also very pretty and one of the best-dressed girls in the class. The other two Ruths, Eleanor, Cookie, Mil, and Dott are among our best athletes. Doris Stanley is noted for her disposition — always warm toward others, interested, responsive, generous, and happy. I am very proud of my friends.

And this year I have a new one. Her name is Dorothy Clarke.

How we happened to become friends is a true story that I can hardly believe even yet.

Dorothy is sensationally talented. I knew her last year only as a tall, dark Townie (our term for a girl who lives with her family in one of the Twin Cities), who was a fine musician, a star athlete, and who was in my Greek class and could not only translate a passage of Greek better than anyone else but could translate Greek poetry into English poetry. I heard that she had been the valedictorian of her class at Cony High School in Augusta, was an only child; that her parents had moved to Lewiston so that she could live at home while a college student, that they were a deeply religious family, and that she would certainly receive at Commencement the scholarship awarded to the highest-ranking freshman girl.

Until this September I had never been nearer to her than the opposite side of Goosie Chase's Greek classroom. I no more expected ever to be her friend than I expected to be President Gray's!

But at an early meeting of "Birdie" Baird's Argumentation (where I was doing my best to keep hidden behind the tallest boy in it) he asked Miss Clarke and Miss Hasty to stop after class.

I hoped I had heard wrong.

"Did he say — me?" I asked the girl in the next chair.

She nodded, picked up her looseleaf notebook, and left.

When nearly everyone had gone but us, I stole a look at Dorothy. She was already on her way down to "Birdie's" desk, completely composed. My heart was pounding so hard it shook my new camel's hair sweater.

"All right for *you*, Miss Clarke," I thought. "He is probably going to suggest that *you* take a test and go into the *Advanced* Argumentation class. But me — *I* know I'm not going to pass this one. Only how did *he* find out so soon?"

As it turned out, he hadn't.

"Birdie" is indescribable. If I can ever describe "Birdie," I'll write a novel that will become a classic. I'll be another Tolstoy. He is quite young. He is dark. He is handsome. He is terribly *alive*. In one quick, dark glance (I guess that's why we call him

"Birdie") he seems to look straight through you and *see something good you didn't know you had.* At least, that is how I felt that day when I reached his desk, and how I've felt every time since when he has glanced at me. I don't know what it is he sees, or whether it is the same good thing he saw before or a different one, but I feel he has seen it and that he is telling me to hurry up and find out what it is and start using it.

He said — Oh, I still can hardly believe it! — that our freshman English instructors had recommended us to serve as assistants in the English department, to read, correct, and grade freshman papers; that we would be paid twenty-five dollars each semester for this work, and that if we wished to do it we were to meet with the new English instructor, Mr. Woodward, and his senior assistant, in the library at four o'clock that afternoon.

Dorothy said serenely that she would be glad to. She asked where in the library Mr. Woodward would be, and "Birdie" told her.

I just stood there. Dorothy Clarke — and *me?* Dorothy, of course. But why me? Mr. Purinton had given me A's on my papers, but I knew several who had A's on their papers. I think now Mr. Purinton suspected that of those who got A's on their papers, I was the one who most needed fifty dollars. But I didn't think of that then. I was stunned. I can't remember leaving that classroom at all. I was standing there in a state of shock — and then I was out in the sunshine on the steps of Libbey Forum, with Dorothy Clarke!

"Well, see you at four o'clock then," she said. "I suppose we are in for a lot of work; but I think it will be sort of fun, don't you? Have you seen Mr. Woodward? I have. He's terribly good-looking. His first name is Evan."

She smiled at me and went between Parker and the chapel on her way toward Hathorn, swinging the green cloth bag in which she carries her books.

I felt dazed all the rest of the day, but at four o'clock I was at the appointed place. Still I was the last to arrive. Dorothy was already sitting at a long, shining table with two men. I did not know which of the two men was Mr. Woodward. They looked about the same age and were about the same size. One was dark, like Dorothy, and one had a fair complexion about like mine.

It was the fair one who began to talk as soon as I slipped into a chair at the long table. He told us, in general, what he expected of his assistants; that we must have Woolley always at hand for reference on rules and symbols; when and where the papers were to be picked up and sorted each week, and how soon they must be returned. He said that one week he and Miss Clarke would grade the papers of one of his two sections, and the next week they would grade the other section. There were two stacks of papers on the table in front of him. He put one into his briefcase and asked Dorothy to come with him to his office.

"You, as my senior assistant, and Miss Hasty will take Section Two this week," he told the dark man. "If she has any questions, I am sure you can help her."

Mr. Woodward and Dorothy went out.

"First, we count these, and each take half," said the senior assistant. "Then maybe we should read one together, correct and grade it."

This took quite a while, because he waited for me to find the errors first, and if I didn't he explained them and we discussed them. I don't believe any student paper ever had more careful attention.

Finally we agreed on the grade, and he said he thought I was all set now to take my half of Section Two. He added that if I wished, he would meet me an hour before the papers were to be handed to Mr. Woodward and run through what I had done. I said that would make me feel much better about the whole thing.

Then he asked me if I was interested in writing.

I said I was, very much.

He asked me if I had heard of Spofford Club.

I said indeed I had.

He said he belonged to it, and explained that it could have a maximum of fifteen members, most of whom were seniors. He was not sure there were any openings for this year, but in case there were did I have one or more examples of my work — poetry, short stories, or essays — which he might take to read, and possibly to recommend to the consideration of the club as a whole?

I had begun to come out of my daze. Now I was going back into it again.

"I don't have *anything* I've written," I answered helplessly. "Not *anything*."

"Your English papers from last year must be in the files," he said. "Let's look."

He had a key to the files. He opened them. He looked. I watched him scanning page after page in my handwriting.

After a while he said, "I think I'll take these three along. You don't mind? You would like to belong to Spofford, wouldn't you?"

Would I like to be presented to the Queen? Would I like to be in the Hall of Fame? Would I like to travel the seven seas on a tramp steamer with Shakespeare, the Brownings, Hawthorne, Melville, Ibsen, Conrad, Willa Cather, and Sarah Orne Jewett?

"But — would they consider — a sophomore?"

"Probably not," he answered cheerfully. "Once in a while they have. But at least they will know your name. It may help later."

We left the library together. He went to the right toward Roger Williams Hall and I went left toward Frye Street.

"What is that great stack of papers?" Ruth asked when I dropped them on my bed.

"Freshman English. I'm supposed to grade them. I'm one of Mr. Woodward's assistants."

"You *are?*" And she went down the hall calling to girls hopping out of tubs, doing up their hair, pulling on dinner dresses, "Know what? Gladys is an English assistant!"

I was astonished by the pride in my roommate's voice. If Ruth was proud of me, what would my mother be, and what was Aunt Vinnie? I wondered if being intoxicated was a feeling anything like this. What had happened to me, was happening to me? I didn't want to go to sleep that night. I wanted to stay awake and try to understand it, to *realize* it. Not only the totally unexpected and inexplicable thing which had taken place that day, but that something else which was even now going on. I knew it was, but I did not know what it was. It was like knowing that someone is talking, when you hear the sound clearly but cannot distinguish the words. All I could figure was that somewhere that senior assistant (now more and more confused in my mind with "Birdie" — they *are* in many ways alike, not only in appearance, but in their effect on me, and in their *indescribability*) was reading and for his purposes grading my fresh-man English papers, and that on his conclusions a great deal depended, perhaps even the future course of my life.

The next afternoon when I came in from my last class the girl at the telephone (we all have assigned telephone hours so that there is no time during the day or evening when its first ring is unanswered) gave me a message from Mrs. Warren Shaw who lives on the next street to Frye. She wanted me to come at 6:00 P.M. to give her little boy his supper, put him to bed, and stay until she and her husband returned, but said they would be home early. This meant that I need not bring my pajamas and toothbrush. Sometimes I stay all night there, because unless a Bates girl can be back in her dormitory at its closing hour, she stays in the home to which she has signed out. We may sign out for overnight only to homes which are approved.

That evening I was back at Frye Street House before the bell which announces the night's quiet hours, and the reception room was deserted, so I sat down at the piano and played "Star of the East," which is the only selection I can do from memory, and "The Gypsy Trail" from sheet music Cookie had left there; it had her name on it. I felt suddenly relaxed and happy, as when a period of uncertainty is over and something has been settled, decided. I still did not know what it was.

When I went up to my room, Ruth had gone to bed, but was propped up with pillows, reading.

I said, "Hi."

She said, "Hi. Amy Blaisdell has been here. She left a note for you. It's on the desk."

Amy Blaisdell is a senior.

I opened the note. It said, in the most distinguished handwriting I've ever seen:

Rand Hall

DEAR GLADYS,

I hope you will be as happy as I am about it.

Tonight we elected you a member of Spofford Club.

Our next meeting is at Libbey Forum Tuesday evening at seven o'clock.

Very cordially,
AMY V. BLAISDELL, SEC.

I had trouble getting the note back into the envelope. I could hear Ruth turning pages behind me. I put away my books and papers and went into the closet to get into my pajamas and Beacon blanket bathrobe. We have a very large closet this year; all our

clothes are hung across the back and there is plenty
of standing room in the front. Marvelous! We never
have to pull down shades, especially since our room is
on the back of the house looking into the side of
Mount David which is so steep that no one climbs it
there.

When I came out with my towel and soap and
headed toward the bathroom, Ruth said, "I guess you
aren't going to tell me what was in Amy's note, so I'd
better tell you that *she* told me; so I know. I don't see
why you want to keep it a secret, and I don't see how
you can."

I came back into the room and stood beside her
bed. She looked up at me and laughed.

"If you could only see your face! You look absolutely stunned!"

"I am. I'm double-stunned."

"Aren't you *pleased?* I am!"

"Oh, I'm pleased all right. But I don't know what
to think. All last year I was just trying with all my
might and main to stay here. Through the summer I
got up my courage to think I would spend the next
two years trying for the two things I hoped most to be
in my senior year — an English assistant and a member of Spofford. And here they've both happened already! I don't feel — old enough. I'm — not ready.
. . . I didn't think sophomores were ever English assistants, and I don't know as any sophomore was ever
elected to Spofford before."

"Dorothy Clarke is a sophomore."

"Yes, well — *Dorothy Clarke* . . ."

"So it won't make you feel any better to know that Dorothy was elected to Spofford tonight, too."

"Was she? Well, it doesn't make me feel *much* better, but I'm glad she was. If I was, she certainly ought to have been. And some other sophomores too."

"Two other sophomores were."

"Honestly? *Who?*"

"Erwin Canham and Kenneth Conner. So you see you don't have sole responsibility for carrying '25's literary torch."

Scholastically, Erwin Canham has about the same position among the men of our class as Dorothy Clarke has among the women. He is also a varsity debater already, and was one of the Bates team of three which in September, before an audience of over 2000 in Lewiston City Hall, met and defeated Oxford University in a debate on the subject "Resolved, That the United States should at once join the League of Nations." (The members of the Oxford team looked old enough to be the fathers of those on the Bates team, and were Edward Marjoribanks — pronounced Marchbanks — of Christ Church, K. M. Lindsay of Worcester College, and M. C. Hollis of Balliol College.) Kenneth Conner is Erwin's inseparable friend — they both live in Auburn, and so are Town Boys — and is as brilliantly creative as he is popular, which is to the nth degree. The two are often called the Damon and Pythias of our class; and people say, "Where Conner is there you will find Canham, and vice versa."

I shook my head.

"It's beyond me," I said. "I can't understand it.

. . . This is what I was going to work for. What am I going to work for now?"

"If you think it's beyond you," Ruth replied cheerfully, "work at catching up with it."

Ruth often says things Aunt Vinnie might have said.

The next week the story was in the *Lewiston Journal:*

BATES SOPHS TAKEN INTO SPOFFORD SOC.

The following members of the sophomore class of Bates College were initiated into the Spofford Literary society at its meeting in Libbey Forum Tuesday evening: Mr. Erwin Canham, Mr. Kenneth Conner, Miss Gladys Hasty, and Miss Dorothy Clarke. Two original poems and an original short story by Miss Amy Blaisdell, '23, were read and discussed, also an original short story by Miss Theodora Barentzen, '23. Mr. Herbert Carroll, '23, was appointed chairman of a committee to arrange for a camp supper on Friday the 20th.

It was also in the South Berwick *Independent* that week:

Miss Gladys Hasty has been honored at Bates College by being admitted to Spofford Club, a well-known literary club at Bates to which only those, and those including but fifteen members, whose literary ability is conspicuous are admitted. . . . Miss Hasty's ability in English composition has always been marked, and since her entrance to college her progress in this subject has been watched.

In the issue of October 27 my name appeared for the first time on the masthead of the *Bates Student* as an associate editor. The president of Spofford Club, Carl Purinton (brother of Mr. Arthur Purinton, English instructor, and son of Professor Purinton) is the editor in chief, and another Spofford member is the managing editor.

In that same issue there was a front page story of the Spofford camp supper:

Spofford's first social event of the year began with a long and mysterious motor trip. The cars, driven by Mr. Arthur Purinton and Erwin Canham, left Rand Hall at four o'clock. The roads were picturesque and the time of day the best for this season, so all were surprised when the journey ended and everyone discovered that Sabbath Day Lake was the destination. Pine cones and dry sticks soon burst into lively flames, and bacon sizzled, bread became golden-brown, coffee sang, and the sweet cider — ask Teddy Barentzen about that! Following supper the contributors were introduced by President Carl Purinton. The "literary benediction" was pronounced by Professor A. C. Baird. On the return trip, trouble with one of the machines prolonged the ride, but this was a pleasant delay except for the solicitous chaperones.

As my premonition had told me, my life is taking a new course. Or if not an altogether new one, a suddenly much accelerated and more definitely directed one. That is why I have written in such detail about these events of last month. They might seem insignificant to anyone else, and even to me in later years, but they are very important to me now. They are almost a promise that I can be a writer if I try hard enough.

But of course what happened to me last month had its beginning a long time ago.

It began when Aunt Vinnie taught me to make the letters of the alphabet with broken matches or toothpicks on the kitchen windowsill, and with all the books which were read to me before I could read for myself. . . . A few years later came the day when my brother gave me a half-used notebook and I decided to sit on the front stairs and write a story in it. . . . A few years more, and there was my district school teacher, Mrs. Knight, to tell me that each day I must place a new composition, at least a page long, on her desk before I could leave the schoolroom to go home. There was Auntie to encourage me to enter a story in a newspaper contest in which I was so fortunate as to win the prize. . . . At the Academy there was Mrs. Gray to respond warmly to my themes, urge me to go to college and to apply for a scholarship; and there was Mr. Townsend, the editor of the *Independent,* to publish and even to pay for my news columns. . . . Always, while I was growing up, there were my mother, grandmother, aunts, and uncles to read or listen to and praise whatever I wrote. My playmate, Bernice Dorr, two years younger than I, began listening to my stories when she was four years old and by the time *she* was six was writing stories too; we had our own exclusive literary society. . . . When I went to Bates there was Mr. Purinton to recommend me as an English assistant, and a senior English assistant to propose my name for Spofford and as an associate editor of the *Student.*

How lucky I have been!

I wonder if Dorothy and Erwin and Kenneth have had the interest and encouragement from their fam-

ilies that I have had from mine, and their Bernices,
their Mrs. Knights, Mrs. Grays, Mr. Townsends, Mr.
Purintons, and senior assistants. . . . I wonder if all
young people who find out what they can do best and
want more than anything to do better have had the
help I have had ever since I can remember. Or do
some of them do it after getting little or nothing from
their elders but mockery, criticism, and efforts to turn
them away from what they can do to something they
can't do? What if Mrs. Knight had said, "You write
well enough. This year you must concentrate on ana-
lyzing and diagramming sentences, which you do very
badly"? What if the Academy had required me to
spend the immense amount of time I should have had
to spend on science courses to pass them? What if
Bates had made me substitute mathematics for my
Latin, or for that writing course I am so looking forward to? I should have been so miserable and dis-
couraged that I think I should have given up completely long ago. If I had kept on despite such things,
what would I have had but misery to write about?

I must never, never forget what it means to me to
be where I am now, and how I was helped to get here.
When I have children I want to do for them what has
been done for me, and if I can I want to do it for
other children too. I don't believe there is anything
else so good for children (or for anyone else) as being
encouraged to do more and more and more of whatever they do best.

Before I go to bed I want to put the following from
this fall's *Students* into this book:

WE'RE BACK

Back? I'll say yes, with a 7:40 the very first morning!

Back? Sure thing! And isn't Birdie a dream in those knickers?

Back? Uh-huh — putting up curtains, tacking cretonne on the window seat.

Oh, don't, please, tell me telephone hours begin today — heavy date at two o'clock.

When do we eat?

BATES GETS 2 TO 1 DECISION OVER OXFORD
POLLISTER — YOUNG — CANHAM
AUDIENCE OF 2000 PACKS CITY HALL

We find Bates described in the *New York Times* for October 1 as "this little college of a few hundred students" which "by stern discipline in argumentative discussion has become the power center of college debating in America"! . . . The *Times* declares that "The Bates and Oxford men are ambassadors of a better understanding between the great English-speaking peoples." The *Boston Herald* says, "We should like to see these debates make sufficient impression on both the general public and the undergraduates to help a little toward a needed readjustment of values. Not that a debater who is not inerrant in his use of adjectives is likely to obtain the attention that a football player gets when he sprains his knee, but these wranglers ought to have greater recognition."

Bowdoin is good at the pole vault, and sometimes they
hurdle quite well,
Magee says they lack competition, and that's a good story
to tell.

U. of M. plays pretty good football, can beat us most any
old day;
And seems to me that they ought to with a thousand to
choose from, I'd say.
Colby is a surprise quite often and wins when her oppo-
nent feels sure,
Can often give competition when we expect her work to
be poor;
But when Oxford desires competition, where the head
does the work not the feet,
Were McGee's boys ready to enter, could they place in a
first trial heat?
Did Oxford know where U. of M. was? Had they heard of
that college at all?
And Colby, what about her boys? Did she receive any part
of a call?
Was it Harvard or Yale or Princeton, the elite of the
United States?
Oh, no, Oxford wished *competition;* so she challenged —
poor, wee, little Bates.

The study of science may soon predominate over the
study of the classics in our colleges. Although science may
displace the humanities, it can never replace them. . . .

A few of the boys had a mishap on their way to Orono,
but even the upsetting of their flivver couldn't keep them
from the game. . . .

Have you heard the good things Vice-President Coo-
lidge is saying about us? "The people must look to the
higher institutions of learning for the source of the ideals
which sustain the guarantees of freedom. Bates College is
one of the citadels of truth."

YEAR'S FIRST VESPER SERVICE HELD IN COLLEGE
CHAPEL; MISS FJERIL HESS GIVES IMPRESSIVE ADDRESS
ON NEEDS OF FOREIGN STUDENTS

BATES TRAMPLES ON BOWDOIN ELEVEN

CYK TAKES FIRST IN STATE CROSS-COUNTRY MEET

SOPHOMORES WALK AWAY WITH INTERCLASS
TRACK MEET

MILLION-DOLLAR DANCE SATURDAY NIGHT

YOUNG, CANHAM, AND H. MORRELL TO DEBATE YALE

Y.W. BAZAAR FRIDAY

CASTS ANNOUNCED FOR JUNIOR PLAYS

PROF. CARROLL AND NORMAN THOMAS MEET IN
HATHORN DEBATE

PRES. GRAY ANSWERS EDISON; CHALLENGES STATEMENT
THAT COLLEGE MEN ARE OPPOSED TO WORK

VOLUNTARY STUDY GROUPS ARE UNUSUALLY SUCCESSFUL

BATES-IN-CHINA DRIVE NEXT WEEK

SOPHOMORE DECS TO BE HELD TOMORROW

Monday, Tuesday, and Wednesday the eds and co-eds faced the firing line, brought their batteries into place, and fired their first volley of oratory. Wednesday evening Generalissimo Robinson announced the results of the first assault. The following Monday the thirty-one picked declaimers went over the top again. When the parting shot had been fired, General Robinson and eager news correspondents gathered in the German room and awaited the report of the senior judges. Gen. Robinson stated that he was glad he did not have to do the deciding as all the speaking was of such excellence that it would have taken him a month to choose twelve. At last the judges appeared and announced the names of those who had reached the front-line trenches. . . . The Prize Division will drop its final bombs on Saturday, Nov. 27, in the Little Theater. The twelve chosen are expert tongue-twisters and all loyal sophomores should rally to the colors and be on the scene of action at two sharp.

I was one of those twelve, again. I didn't win, again. But as I look through these *Students* I brought home, everything mentioned in them, including last Saturday's Sophomore Declamations, suddenly seems to have happened long ago to people I hardly know.

Perhaps I am tired.

ESTERDAY the hearse came back, and the undertaker and his helpers put a mourning spray on the
front door and brought the coffin into the parlor. Before he left he asked us to go in, and my father and
mother went, but I stayed in the sitting room with
Grammy. Aunt Annie Harriman, Grandpa's sister
who lives in Lawrence, Mass., had sent a spray of roses
and my mother said they were beautiful, but we all
remembered that Grandpa had said many times he
did not want *anybody* to send flowers for his funeral;
he didn't like flowers, and he thought the cost of hot-
house flowers was money thrown away. He said, "All
I want and all I'll need is a pine box and a few pine
branches."

Last night just before dark my father went down
in the pasture and came back with a cartload of pine

branches. He said the trees needed trimming, anyway, and would grow better for it. I helped him place branches along the wall behind the coffin and bank them in front to cover the metal frame it rested on. They smelled clean and good, and made my hands sticky with pitch; but other relatives at a distance had sent more flowers by then — carnations and lilies and snapdragons — and their strange heavy perfume soon mixed with the pine scent in a way I did not like.

This morning neighbors brought food, and I wished they wouldn't. Those who weren't coming back to the funeral went into the parlor and came out looking very solemn. Their faces did not look like their own faces.

Right after noon, Harold and Jennie came; and Aunt Hattie and my cousin Roland; and the undertaker and Elder Kent, who was going to conduct the service. We put on our coats, and the women their hats, and went and sat in the parlor. The undertaker brought some other relatives in there to sit with us, and the neighbors sat in the sitting room with Grammy. The four men who were going to be bearers sat in the front hall where Elder Kent stood and spoke so that everyone in both rooms could hear him.

I don't remember what he said. I don't think I heard him.

After he finished, the names of those in the sitting room were called, and they came into the parlor in single file and stopped by the coffin; then went out the front door, which was open now. It was very cold. I was glad we had put shawls around Grammy and left more for Grace to put over her if she needed them; Grace was sitting beside her.

Then the names of the relatives were called and they stood up, paused by the coffin, and went out.

The undertaker said, low, "Gladys and Roland."

Roland and I stood up, looked at each other, and went out. The sky was gray. There was no snow. The ground was frozen. Harold and Jennie came next and stood in front of us. Finally my father and mother and Aunt Hattie came together. I did not look at their faces. It was bitterly cold waiting there while the bearers brought out the closed coffin, and the undertaker and his helpers the flowers and pine branches.

They went ahead and we followed across the field and corner of the pasture into the cemetery, where an iron bar between two granite posts had been taken away to admit us.

Beside the open grave — which must have been very hard to dig — the bearers rested the coffin, and Elder Kent said a few more words.

> *Dust thou art, to dust returneth,*
> *Was not spoken of the soul . . .*

Oh, that's true. That is really true. So why were we there?

Dust to dust . . . The first time I had heard that — and the only time until today — I was five years old, and I thought the minister said, "Dusk to dusk." When I asked Aunt Vinnie what it meant she did not tell me that I had heard the words wrong. She answered my question. She told me what the words meant that I had heard.

Then we walked slowly back across the corner of
the pasture and through the field in the cruel wind
under the leaden sky.

And what was waiting for us to take us into its arms
and comfort us? The house George Hasty built! The
floors he laid, the rooms he lathed and plastered,
the mortared brick chimneys he raised to carry off
the smoke from the wood he cut and split to fill the
fireboxes!

The door had been closed long enough for the
house to get warm again. Grammy had laid off her
shawls. Grace had the big, nickel-plated teakettle
bubbling, tea steeping, coffee brewing.

We left our coats and hats in the parlor. All the
women began taking food from the oven, from the
pantry, from the cellarway. I brought plates and cups
and saucers from the sitting room cupboard. As many
men as could squeezed in around the table. Others
and some of the women carried their filled dishes into
the sitting room and sat by small stands, or at the leaf
of the desk, or at the sewing table Harold had brought
down from Auntie's room. The rest of us stood
around the kitchen stove or in the sinkroom, feeling
the hot drink reach the heart of the cold inside us,
and the good bread and meat, sponge cake, date cake
strengthen us, bring back our courage, remind us that
we had need of and use for strength, courage, and the
capacity to enjoy. I thought of the neighbors who had
brought the food and how it had looked to me then,
and realized that they were wiser than I. They had
known by experience that the time would soon come

when I, as well as the others, would be thankful for it. After this I, too, would know.

The talk quickened. Hands touched. There were smiles again. There was even soft laughter.

After a while people began to go.

Aunt Hattie asked my mother, "Shall we help you straighten up the parlor?"

My mother said, "No. We'll just leave the door closed for a while. Until after Harold and Verd can bring the stove back and set it up, and get the rest of the parlor furniture down from the shed chamber."

When Aunt Hattie and Roland went out to their car, I went with them to kiss Aunt Hattie good-bye. When they had gone I went to the front door to take down the mourning spray if it was still there, but it wasn't.

I drew a deep breath and the air smelled good. It was just at the edge of dark and there was one star out. I ran back into the house and my mother was lighting lamps. She took one into the sitting room where Jennie was talking with Grammy and we sat down and talked with them. My father and Harold had taken a lantern to the barn to milk by. When they came back they sat in the kitchen and talked together. My mother did not go out to strain and set away the milk for quite a while. I think she felt it would help my father to be alone with Harold as long as he could. There are times when a man can help another man more than any woman, as sometimes only a woman can help another woman.

But later we brought my grandmother out to the kitchen table. She is learning to use her new crutch quite well. We made fresh tea and had our supper, and quite soon after that Harold and Jennie put on their coats.

"Going back to Lewiston tomorrow, Spray?"

Jennie calls me Spray because that was my name in a play given by our church Young People's group two or three years ago. Harold had a part in it, too, and she coached it. I think that was when they began to fall in love.

I nodded.

"How soon will you be coming for Christmas?"

"In three weeks."

Harold glanced at my father.

"Why, she'll be back here almost before you know it." He kissed my mother and Grammy and shook hands with my father. "And Billie and I'll be over some evening the first of the week."

"That's right. Come as often as you can."

"You'll turn in early now, won't you? You need to catch up on your sleep."

"Think 's likely," my father answered. "Yes, chances are we will."

He went to their car with them. It had been gone some time before he came back. We did not ask where he had been.

He said, "Warming up a little. Feels like snow."

When the others had gone to bed, I thought I would write down just the events of the day; not how I felt about them, for I did not know how I felt about them. But now, as I read back, I see that quite a few feelings crept in. Not major feelings, maybe; just a

series of comparatively small ones. I am beginning to
think that in me emotional response is always bit by
bit and varied, never big-all-over-cataclysmic. I wonder if it isn't with most people — and deeper that
way? As for my mother there is more delight in a
good cup of tea taken in sips than in one hurriedly
drained. And conversely more bitterness in a grim
mixture tasted slowly by teaspoon than in one tossed
off in one draft. But for me today — as most days —
there has been some of both grim mixture and good
tea; and, as always so far, the flavor of the good tea is
what remains at the day's end.

My grandfather has been the head of this house
ever since he built it on a piece of land his father gave
him on his twenty-first birthday. Without him, life in
it will never again be the same. I think of him as he
was when I was three, and six, and ten, and twelve,
and I want him back; I want everything back just as
it was in those years before the war. But it can't be,
except in the part of my mind and heart where I keep
it. To stay as it was, it would have had to stop, and
whatever has stopped is not life. Living is going on
to the next thing, whatever it may be.

We all loved my grandfather, and respected him,
trusted him, depended on him, served him. I think all
of us except Aunt Vinnie and me also feared him.

I remember his voice as it was such a little while
ago, the night he talked so long with George Albert,
and I want so much to hear it again through his bedroom door that tears blind me and I swallow a sob in
my throat.

But he is not in his room, as he used to be, nor as he

was when I came home for Thanksgiving, nor as he was later that night. It is no longer his room. There is nothing in it now that ever belonged to him, except the walls he raised, the floor he laid, the ceiling he put up. The father of my father does not sleep there. The mother of my mother does. My father and mother sleep upstairs, in the chamber across from Aunt Vinnie's, which is unoccupied tonight.

I am alone, here in the sitting room, the only one awake in the house my grandfather built.

He is no longer its head. My father is.

The time has come at last for my father to be the head of his own house, as surely it should to every man. It came to my grandfather in his early twenties. My father was fifty-one years old last July. He has been a good son; my grandfather said so when he deeded the place to him soon after Aunt Vinnie died. My mother told me that, with tears in her eyes, last summer. The tears, I knew, were not only of sadness but of pride and of remembrance of past sacrifices. When a woman's husband is not the head of his house she does not have a home of her own.

My mother and father are not thinking of that tonight, but I am.

It is dark now and the sky is thick with clouds, but some day soon the sun will come out, and they will begin to see that my grandfather's going has left open doors. Grammy is already happier to have two rooms, one to sleep in and one to sit in, and the one she will sit in now is off the kitchen, closer to the center of all the household activity, and more convenient for my mother. By and by, the parlor stove will be set up

again, and my mother and father will for the first
time have a room always ready for their friends in the
evening or on a Sunday afternoon; a room, that is,
which no one else will need to pass through while
they are there. They have a guest chamber upstairs.
The parlor will no longer be a bedroom, cleared only
for a wedding or a funeral. And they can stay there,
talking and laughing, as late as they like, for Grammy
is never eager to go to bed early.

I remember evenings when she was here visiting my
mother and they sat late in the kitchen, close to the
cookstove, whispering their exchange of mother-and-
daughter confidences because once, as they talked
aloud there at night, my grandfather — tired from a
long day and knowing he would be up at dawn —
called out from his room, "You folks ever going to
bed?"

They did not blame him. My grandfather was a
man who worked, ate, and slept; a thinking man, but
a silent man. My father and all my mother's people
love to talk. They did not blame him, but they never
forgot it.

My parents are not thinking of the future yet, but
my grandmother is.

She said tonight as I was helping her get ready for
bed, "I should think your mother would have a telephone put in now. It would be handy in case of sickness, and company for us this winter when we're shut
in by storms."

In case of sickness . . . There is no sickness in
this house.

Tomorrow, before I go back, I'll put on my coat, go into that cold parlor, raise the shining cover of the piano Harold bought so that I could learn to play it, sit on the cold stool, and strike those icy keys. I'll make grand chords. Everybody in the house will hear them resound. I'll play hymns first because it will be Sunday and because there is a hymnbook with the Bible on the marble-topped table. But then I'll play something quick and merry, like "Dixie." I'll make the keys go fast, and if some of them stick, no matter. Auntie's table and red plush covered chairs are back in the parlor now. The rest of her things will be there soon. She will like that, if she notices.

I remember that when I was small, playing jig and reel records on the graphophone, if my father came in with pails of water or a basket of wood he would put down his load and "step it out." He said it was a jig he did. I don't know. But I loved to see him knock his cap back on his head, and the way his whole long, lean, strong body went loose like a much-cuddled rag doll, and how his feet in heavy boots flew in time to the music.

My mother, getting supper, would turn from the stove to watch him, a faint smile slowly spreading from her lips to her eyes.

At the end of the record, he would turn to her and hold out his hand.

"Come on. Step it out here, why don't you?"

"There, don't be foolish, Verd. You know I can't do that, and never could."

"Couldn't skate, either, seems like I remember."

She would look at me and say, "No. Only time I ever tried it with him, we cut a double spread-eagle on the ice."

But he would touch her on his way to hang up his cap and jacket, and either in words or with his eyes say, "I do my carrying-on with my feet. You do it with your smile and your voice." And I knew there was something fresh and sweet between them.

He did not "carry on" if my grandfather was there.

I see that I wrote, "Tomorrow, before I go back . . ." not "Tomorrow, before I leave . . ." There is that change in my thinking and feeling. I leave college to go home; I leave home to go *back* — back to my studies, back to the room I share with Ruth on the second floor of Frye Street House, back to the campus, back to those who are teaching me and those who are learning with me much that none of us has known before, back to more friends than I ever expected to have, back to all that is coming between me and the way of life which for so long was the only one I knew, and yet that — I hope — is not and will never be a wall but rather some sort of magic glass which will help me to see that way of life more clearly, to appreciate it more, and to understand how to share it with others who have not experienced it or, if they have, would like to find it caught and held in a book where they could relive it at will.

What a long sentence! If I find such a sentence in a freshman theme, how I shall break it up with blue pencil marks! But if the freshman is like me, he will not let blue pencil marks influence him against his own conviction as to what is the best way to say what he wants to say. . . . Must add I have no conviction about the necessity of the length of that sentence. I was writing too fast to consider style, clarity, or grammar. The oil is almost out of the lamp and the flame is sputtering.

HAT a Christmas! I think it began when the telephone was put in. My mother called me up that night, and had Grammy there to speak to me, and of course my father came and talked. They were all excited, and so was I. It was installed in the back entry, to muffle a little the sound of the bell. There is a great deal of ringing for we are the sixteenth family on the line. Everyone rings one long for Central, and the party numbers go from two through six (long ones), from eleven through sixteen (one long and so many shorts), and twenty-one through twenty-five (two long and so many shorts). Ours is twenty-five. The last family to come on before us had a choice between sixteen and twenty-five and we are pleased that they chose sixteen, but we don't understand why. We think two longs and five shorts are much easier to count than one long and six shorts. We have learned that if there are more than two longs we can stop counting, also if shorts begin after one long. Though unless we have something more interesting to do we count anyway, because we know who every number belongs to; and we have also now learned how different people ring, so we can usually figure out who is calling whom. Grammy is likely to say, "There's Em calling Em Nason. Listen in and see how they are. You know Em thought she had a cold coming on this morning." Or my mother will say, "That's Central ringing Pearl. Probably her brother calling from Fall River." And when thirteen is rung about nine o'clock at night we exchange knowing smiles, because that means —— (a young man) didn't go up the road to see —— (a girl) tonight and is calling her instead for one of their interminable conversations in code, which always sets many receivers to clicking up and down.

These are the first blanks I have put in this journal. There will be more, and those to come are by special request. I told the senior English assistant that I am keeping a journal.

He asked, "Do you put people's names in it?"

I said of course I did.

He said, "I wouldn't want my name in anybody's journal."

I replied airily, "I can't think of any reason why it would be in mine."

He said, "So I can take that as a guarantee that it won't be?"

Thus pressed, I declared that he certainly could. And I am a woman of my word. I am not sure whether he really meant he wouldn't want me to use his name, or secretly hoped I would. I'm not going to, anyway.

Now back to Christmas and the telephone. For us that telephone bell has joined sleigh bells and the chimes of Christmas records on the Victrola as the background music of this glorious season. For yes, my parents gave my grandmother a Victrola for Christmas, and Harold and Jennie and I and ever so many other people gave her records. She has McCormack records, Sousa records, Harry Lauder records, and several hymns. The one we all like most and play most is "The Holy City." We often wonder now how we used to get so much pleasure from the graphophone and the cylinder records. Christmas afternoon we played both machines, to compare, and the graphophone sounds so harsh, so tinny, it really isn't music at all. And what did we find so funny in "Uncle Jock"? Just the same, I miss that morning-glory horn on the old phonograph, and there is an excitement for me still in that familiar "Edi-*son Record,* Columbia Military *Band,*" with every syllable *snapped* out, that is equaled only by my excitement when I see a stage curtain going up. . . . Now the Victrola has banished the graphophone to the shed chamber, but we stored it carefully, the machine locked in its case, the records on their sides in their little round, covered boxes and strapped into a canvas valise, the horn and its stand inside an old flour barrel. I told my mother that I want to bring it downstairs and play it every Christmas.

She said I reminded her of the time she got up a Larkin order to buy me a big doll with real hair, my father made a doll's bed and spring, she made a featherbed, pillow, sheets, slips, a quilt, coverlet and matching canopy. They set the doll in her pretty clothes on the bed under the Christmas tree in the corner of the sitting room. When they opened the door to me Christmas morning I took one look, cried, "Where's my Margery? I want my Margery!" — and ran to get the doll I had had since I was two years old, and who had been dropped and broken and mended several times, whose elastic was sadly stretched, and who at the moment was wearing no clothes at all.

I told my mother I remembered that Christmas morning and knew why I had done that. It was because the new doll was so beautiful I wanted to run to her, but felt instantly that this would be disloyal to Margery and hurt her very much. I thought the new doll would not care yet whether I loved her or not; Margery was the one who would grieve unless convinced at the outset that I would never love another doll as I loved her.

"I was thinking only of dolls then," I told my mother. "I wasn't thinking of you . . . And of course it isn't the same with the machines. I know the old phonograph doesn't mind being in the shed chamber. And I certainly like listening to the Victrola much better. But, like Margery, the old phonograph has a place that nothing else can ever take."

Our tree this year is in the parlor for the first time. I rode into the woods on the horse sleds with my father to get it. It is the tallest and bushiest we have ever had. The top touches the ceiling. To decorate it we used not only all the old ornaments and the usual strings of popcorn and cranberries and gilded nuts but a dozen new ornaments and yards and yards of tinsel which we bought in Dover on our last shopping trip. How it shines and glitters! We had it decorated three days before Christmas. It sets in a pail of water (hidden by balsam branches) and we shall keep it up until New Year's. After the fire in the parlor stove goes out at night, it gets very cold; when we build the fire again the next morning the fragrance of the tree begins to spread through the house, and I remember the way the district schoolhouse used to smell on the nights of our Christmas parties.

Harold and Jennie came on Christmas Eve and had Auntie's room, so the house was full again for Christmas. After supper Harold sat — the way he likes to — a-straddle a chair in front of the open oven door with his folded arms resting on the back and talked with my father, who was smoking a cigar by the porch window (it was the first time I ever saw my father smoke in the house), while my mother, Jennie, and I cleared the table and did the dishes. I thought how fortunate it was that Harold had become a man before my grandfather went, and that he had brought us Jennie before Auntie went. There are as many Hasty men in our family as before, and as many Hasty women. It is only Hasty children we don't have now. And they will come.

Later on Christmas Eve Jennie and I sat on the sitting room floor with disc records in our laps, telling Grammy the names for her to choose among, and handing her choices to Harold, who put each on, wound up the machine, set the needle, turned the starter, then sat down next to Grammy and held her hand while her music played. My mother sat in her rocker with hands clasped in her lap, listening. My father, passing, bending down, spoke low in her ear. I saw his forehead touch the pinned-up blue-black coil of her hair, above the silver pompadour. She looked up at him and smiled and nodded. Until this Christmas, she has always been very pale and slight, but now suddenly her cheeks are filling out and there is a soft pink which never leaves them but sometimes, in heat or excitement, deepens to the color of wild strawberries. Her skin, as always, is so fine-textured, so translucent that the color glows and you are bound to think of rose petals. My father went on to the kitchen; between records we heard the clink of glasses, and he came back with Moxie for all of us and a plateful of Lizy Ann dropcakes, which are made by a very old recipe: big, soft, chewy spice cookies, with crumbled nuts and seeded raisins in them. The nuts are from trees on the abandoned farm where my mother and her mother lived with her grandparents after her father died. Harold goes up to get them for her every fall. She says no other nuts have the same flavor.

Since my grandfather is not here to build the fire in the cookstove in the early morning, my mother does it, but not at daybreak as he did. While my father is still sleeping, she slips out of bed and into a heavy bathrobe and slippers, and comes downstairs through the cold front hall to the sitting room, where in this weather there is still heat in the chunk stove. She opens the drafts in the funnel and below the door, puts in dry pine edgings and small applewood sticks, and the flames rumble until she closes the drafts partway and goes into the kitchen. Sometimes there are still red embers in the cookstove, too, for we are more prodigal with wood than we used to be. If not, she puts in kindling — chips and edgings — and sprinkles them well with kerosene oil; we are also more prodigal with oil now, as with eggs in cakes and cream for whipping. As soon as she can half-close the cookstove drafts and has the teakettle on, she comes back to the sitting room to bathe and dress, having left everything ready the night before, including a pan of water on the top of the chunk stove, which has an ornamental top on a hinge so that it can be turned back to leave a level surface.

I wake when she first opens the door of the chunk stove. As soon as she closes it she turns to see if my eyes are open.

This morning I whispered "Merry Christmas!" as she turned.

She whispered back, "Oh, no fair! I should have said it when I came into the room, but you were *so* sound asleep I couldn't bear to. I thought maybe your grandmother had a restless night."

"No. She didn't ring at all."

"I didn't hear the bell, I know. But somehow I don't when you're here. When you aren't, it seems as if I stay half-awake all night long, listening for it. Anyway, Merry Christmas to you, and many of them!"

"No need to whisper on my account," Grammy called. "I'm awake. Merry Christmas, you two!"

We called back Merry Christmases to her, and my mother went in and put up her shade, saying the sun was coming up in a sky as pink as May's.

"No need to whisper on anybody's account," my mother said, as she finished dressing. "Jump up quick. Hop up, jump up, pretty little yellow bird! I'm going to call Harold and Jennie now."

With the stove poker she reached up and opened the register in the ceiling above the stove.

"Merry Christmas, Harold! Jennie!" she called. "Warmth coming up! Gladie'll be at your door with hot water in about ten minutes. Ham and eggs and hot mince pie for breakfast!"

Jennie's "Merry Christmas, Mrs. Hasty!" came prompt and clear. Harold's "Merry Christmas, Muddie," was slow, slurred, and muffled.

My mother glanced at me and laughed.

"What sleepyheads our menfolks are!" she said. "When you go up, pour your father's hot water right into the washbowl and tell him it will be cool enough to use by the time he gets to it, as cold in five minutes as if it had come straight from the well. He won't shave until after breakfast anyway. But I suppose Harold always does nowadays."

He didn't today, though. And after breakfast we wouldn't let them because we didn't want to wait any longer to go in to the tree. I must say they didn't protest much. I think men feel most loved when their women accept them unshaven. So as they all sat around the finest Christmas tree we ever had and I passed out the fruit of it, my father's face had a ruddy-gold stubble and my brother's olive skin had darker shadows. . . . I think they were as eager to open the gifts or see them opened as we were. I remembered when we children had to be satisfied with the contents of our long, black Christmas stockings until my father and grandfather had come back from a trip with the sleds for a load of cordwood, and then had had their dinner; because I *would* not have the tree touched until we were all together. . . . Though I think now that the process of distribution was tedious for my grandfather, who made no gifts and cared to receive nothing except the essentials which might have been provided any day, and that it was embarrassing for my father and mother, who knew my grandfather sat there at best forbearing, at worst disapproving of Christmas indulgences.

No one was bored here today, and no one was disapproving, though we all gave and received more than we ever had before. All gifts were wrapped in bright paper which we folded carefully after opening, and tied with ribbons which we rolled smoothly into balls — as we have always kept twine — to be put away for use again next Christmas.

Afterward we had roast pork with apple sauce as well as roast chicken with cranberry sauce, for dinner, with mashed potatoes (beaten up with cream), squash and creamed onions, coffee, pumpkin pie with whipped cream on top (I really like it better without, so we left it off mine; I don't like butter either — no dairy products, really), and the prime sponge cake Jennie had brought, which we all say is the best cake we ever tasted.

After more music and more talk and more admiration of all we had which was new, Harold and Jennie went home just before dark. Our supper was whatever each of us (except Grammy who had a tray) wanted to take of what was left from dinner, under a cheesecloth cover, on the kitchen table. Why does everything taste better eaten from your hand when you are standing up?

Tonight the telephone has rung many times, with everyone up and down the road wanting to hear about their neighbors' Christmases and to tell about theirs. Everyone knew there could be no secrets tonight, so often there were five or six families on at the same time, joining in the revelations, exclamations, and exchange of thanks for cards or little gifts sent and received. Those who have children in school still have school Christmas parties, and now we know that those on The Line have telephone Christmas parties.

At last everyone else is asleep, and I am sleepy. Mine is the only light in sight except that of the stars. Some other night I'll write of the not-quite-three weeks between the Thanksgiving holidays and the beginning of Christmas vacation. Among my gifts was a pair of pajamas my mother made for me of white seersucker trimmed in black and white plaid gingham with red braid. I am going to get into them and lie in the dark and think about all that is new in my life lately. That is, I'll think about it as long as I can stay awake.

December 31, 1922

NEW Year's Eve! In an hour the kitchen clock will strike twelve — I shall be the only one to hear it — and when the clock has finished striking, it will be 1923! . . . It seems to me that my own New Year began last September, and that ever since Thanksgiving it has been building up to a crescendo.

I have been studying very hard, especially on Argumentation, since I want to do well in any course in the English department and argument is *not* natural to me. I have also been working as much as I could to earn the money for Christmas gifts. And there has been so much campus activity.

The *Student* says:

JUNIOR PLAYS GREAT SUCCESS

BATES-IN-CHINA DRIVE HAS GONE OVER THE TOP

———

BATES DEBATERS READY FOR YALE

Young, Canham, and Morrell, the Bates standard-bearers, are confidently looking forward to the debate. They will have a good-sized Bates audience in the home of Yale University as the engagement comes just as the Connecticut and New York Bates students are going home, and there will be a large gathering of loyal Bates grads now living in or near New Haven. Professor Robinson will be there on his way to New York, where he will spend the holidays with friends. Miss Elizabeth Chase, the President's secretary, will also be present. Here's to our debating team and may it chalk up its third consecutive victory over the Bull Dog of old Eli!

It did.

BIG STUDENT PARADE MARKS BEGINNING OF LOCAL CAMPAIGN DRIVE

The Million-Dollar Parade was a success. There is no doubt about it. Every class did its part, and did it well. Of course the girls made the best appearance; that was to be expected. . . . Around the head of each pretty Sophomore was a ribbon of black with a big white dollar sign emblazoned on the front.

Y.W. HOLDS BAZAAR IN CHASE HALL TOMORROW

Although we want and expect the town people to attend, the Bazaar is above all a college function. Of course every Bates man and woman will be there. With Christmas so near, everyone has shopping to do. At the Bazaar you can buy gifts for Mother and Dad and the other folks at home. These gifts are largely handmade and superior to those on sale in the stores. . . . Plan to come to the supper. The price is only thirty cents for oyster stew,

crackers, pickles, rolls, a choice of doughnuts, cake, or
cookies, and tea or coffee. Salads and sandwiches will be
ready for those who want to pay extra. This menu is an
agreeable change from prosaic pork and beans. Last week
we had cause to be very proud of our Junior Players.
Come to our entertainment and see another real show.

A selection from the headlines and columns of any
issue of our paper is an indication of how many campus activities there are which practically every student
participates in if only as a loyal supporter. In every
big undertaking we all feel we have a share, and help
to carry the responsibility for it. This is what it means
that we call ourselves "the Bates family."

Beside this, in lieu of fraternities and sororities,
there are dozens of clubs meeting at least once a week
in the evening, most of them associated more or less
closely with a major field of study but including social
activity, too, and leading to special friendships. There
is no one who does not belong to at least one of these
clubs, and the college places no limit on the number
which we may join. It expects us to know how many
are of value to us and how many we have time for. I
belong to several, but sometimes have to miss a meeting. When I do, it is not a meeting of Spofford.

One recent issue of the *Student* says:

Spofford had an interesting program Tuesday evening.
Erwin Canham read a humorous skit entitled, "The
Treasure of Coco's Island, or How We Got the Million
for Bates." It leaned decidedly away from the realistic
trend of the day. Herbert Carroll read a short story fea-

turing hypnotism and called, "When Mesmerism Met
Mesmerism."

Spofford is *always* interesting. Dot Clarke comes to
Frye Street House after dinner Tuesday nights and
we go over to Libbey Forum together. After the meeting the president of Spofford usually takes her home
and the senior assistant walks back to Frye Street
House with me. We feel very adventurous setting out
along the dim streets, each of us alone with a senior
man; and we meet before chapel Wednesday mornings to report on "how it went." We also pass notes in
classes, using symbols Dot selected. She and I are
represented as little sailboats bobbing about on a
rough sea. Within sight are an anchor lying on a
raft (which the D sailboat may or may not decide to
try to acquire and attach) and an island which the G
sailboat may or may not attempt to reach.

As freshmen we were permitted by our rules to
go downtown in the evening only if we were chap-
eroned by a senior girl, or by a faculty member or
a parent. As upperclassmen we may go with a companion of either sex if we are back on campus at
9:30 P.M.

One evening early this month I returned from a
movie date to find a note on my desk. It was from a
senior girl asking me to come to her room in Rand
the next evening immediately after dinner; it was
very important, she said, and I was to come alone.

"Did she bring this note?" I asked Ruth.

"She wrote it here. On a piece of my stationery

which she borrowed," Ruth answered. "She came
about eight o'clock, looking for you. When I told
her you weren't here, she asked where you were, and
then whom you went with." (Ruth DID say "whom."
She always speaks grammatically without the slightest
effort. One night she fell the whole length of the
stairs between the third floor and ours and when
someone called, on hearing the crash, "WHO's that?"
Ruth answered, "It's I.") "I really didn't see that it
was any of her business, but I couldn't quite say that
to a senior, so I told her what she wanted to know.
She seemed upset. And then she wrote that note. It
took her quite a while. She kept staring off into space
between sentences as if coming to momentous decisions."

I thought this was highly mysterious.

The next night after dinner, instead of going downstairs from the dining room with the other under-
classmen, I went upstairs with the seniors.

I had never been to this girl's room and had to
ask another senior which one it was. When I reached
it, the door was closed — unusual in a dormitory between dinner and study hours. I knocked.

I didn't understand why she had asked me to come
alone. I wished she hadn't. I wished I had asked Ruth
to follow me and wait in the hall. And I told myself
sternly that this was very silly, that probably I was
here to help plan a birthday surprise for someone —
perhaps for my senior sister.

When the door was opened, my hostess was a dark
shadow against a ruddy haze. I followed her in and
she closed the door. I searched for the source of the

faint light and saw that it was the usual light bulb
hanging from the ceiling, but encased in a Chinese
paper lantern. Below it two looped strands of clothesline were hung with pink and black silk objects which
my Aunt Mollie Goodwin calls "unmentionables,"
but we call them knickers, vests, and combinations.
In both dormitories where I have lived, though, we
have hung ours to dry only in the basement laundry.
And it is so hard to study even by a naked light bulb
that most of us have bought desk lamps; Ruth has
one which we both use.

The senior said softly, "Sit down, dear."

I looked around for a place to do so, but the only
chairs I could see were full of coats or books.

She sat on an unmade bed and patted the place
beside her. I sat down there and she put her arm
around me.

She said, low and regretfully, that she was very
sorry she had to tell me what she had to tell me, but
somebody must, and she was the only one now at
Bates who knew what danger I was in. She said she
had noticed that I was accepting attentions from the
senior assistant.

I said I had let him walk home with me from Spofford meetings, and I had been to the junior plays with
him, and also downtown to the movies a few times.

She said yes, well, she had been very much afraid
it would come to that ever since she had heard that
on the night of the Spofford Bacon Bat he had sat beside me on a log; and I must not see him again except in a group.

"Why?"

"Because, dear, he will break your heart. You are so young, and even if you weren't, how could you know unless I told you that he has done the same thing to other girls that he is doing to you? One of them was my dearest friend, who graduated last year."

"What did he do? Take her home from meetings, and to movies?"

"Made her think he thought a great deal of her, and led her to think a great deal of him, and then suddenly stopped seeing her, with no explanation whatever!"

I wished there were enough light so that I could see her face clearly. I wondered how a person would look saying that. Her voice was quite dramatic. It even trembled a little.

"Can you imagine, dear, how you would feel if that happened to you?"

I couldn't. Maybe it could happen to other people. It couldn't happen to me.

I shook my head.

"Well, I don't want you to find out — the way my friend did. She is much nearer his age than you are, and perhaps as brilliant as he is . . . but she almost had a nervous breakdown. She couldn't study. She cried night after night. We were afraid she might not graduate. . . . He is not trustworthy. That's why you shouldn't see him again."

I began to feel oddly annoyed. To escape her arm I got up and picked my way to the window.

"I know it must hurt you to hear this," she said, "but not as much as —"

"I'm not hurt," I said irritably. "None of this makes any sense to me. It's too bad about your friend, but I don't see why it was his fault if she thought he loved her when he didn't, or if she loved him when he didn't love her. Those were things she did herself. If he stops seeing me, I won't need any explanation; I wouldn't want any; I wouldn't *listen* to one."

She sighed tremulously.

"Oh, what a child you are! You don't know what love is! And I'm glad you don't, because that means you aren't emotionally involved yet. That will make it easier for you to stop seeing him."

I was really angry by then.

I said, "But I'm not going to. You haven't given me any reason why I should."

"Then you don't think you would ever love him?"

"I didn't say that."

"But I've told you what happens to a girl who does. My friend wasn't the only one. It has happened several times."

"I don't think it will happen to me. If it does, it will be my own fault." I groped toward the door. "I know you told me this as a friend, but —"

She was ahead of me. She had her hand on the doorknob.

"I did, dear," she said softly. "I should never have forgiven myself if I hadn't. Because if you keep on seeing him, you will think you love him. They all have, I don't know why."

"If I do, I may be the one he can love. And we'll be married."

I was pawing for the doorknob, but she held onto
it.

"No, dear," she whispered. "That can never be.
That is what I hoped I need not tell you. But you
could not marry him if you wanted to — even if he
asked you to!"

She had my attention now. I stood and stared at
her. Was she going to tell me that he had *married*
her friend and *deserted* her?

"Why not?" I demanded. But I have an idea my
own voice shook a little then.

"Because," she whispered, "he is not of your race!"

Not of my *race?*

"What do you mean?"

"I mean — haven't you noticed how dark his complexion is?"

Now I was furious.

I said, "He is no darker than my brother or my
mother. I *admire* dark complexions. If he is of any
other race than mine he will tell me so if there is any
need for me to know. I don't believe that is true. I
think you are just imagining it. Maybe it is something you thought up to make your friend feel better and now you have worked yourself around to be-
lieving it. I don't understand why you have done
this, and I think you should be ashamed of yourself."

I got hold of the knob and turned it, went out of
that ruddy haze, closed the door on it, and went
downstairs and out of Rand Hall as fast as I could.

When I reached my room, Ruth was not there.
This was too bad, for I needed her calming influence.

I felt as if I had just escaped from a ghoulish dungeon. I took what comfort I could from the familiar surroundings — our neatly made beds, her brown-and-green couch cover, my Indian blanket, my hooked rug and her Oriental, the Bates banner and the framed lines from Omar Khayyám on the walls.

A Jug of Wine, a Loaf of Bread — and Thou . . .
Oh, Wilderness were Paradise enow!

I stretched out on my bed and tried to study, but it was impossible to concentrate. I was beginning to see myself as the central figure of a life drama such as I had heard described as most desirable, if not essential, in the experience of those who produced literature. One girl in my class had told me that by way of preparation for greatness she was going to try to fall violently in love with a man in delicate health, struggle for about ten years to keep him alive — preferably on the shore of the Mediterranean — and then in agony of spirit fail, so that she would be a widow of complete emotional maturity and unlimited material early enough to write at least a dozen novels. Was I getting into a situation equally promising, if not more so? Ten years of nursing a hopeless case had no appeal for me, and it seemed too much to ask anyone to put up with my nursing that long and then die, just on the chance that it would make a writer of me. Possibly, I thought, I could manage to do all the suffering myself — which seemed fairer and would not put me so deeply in debt.

Of course it would not work unless I fell in love. Madly in love. That had to be the first step. As I had no idea how to go about this, I simply recognized the fact and set it aside for future consideration.

But once that was achieved, and my passion unrequited, I could then begin to suffer. He might forget me, but I would never forget him. I would follow him about the world, sometimes keeping my proximity secret — just catching glimpses of him, straining to hear his voice; and sometimes, unable to do this, driven to write him letters and give him my address, call him Long Distance, even appear at his office door or slip into the empty chair at the restaurant table where he was dining alone. (What if it *wasn't* empty? What if he *wasn't* alone? Ah, misery! Ah, that would be a night for walking the rain-drenched streets, the oil-slick trestle, the shrouded docks on the dark waterfront!)

When my imagination failed to convince me that it was *I* doing these things I reminded myself forcefully that being madly in love would supply the now missing chemical and so transform me into one of the Gish sisters with a strong strain of Theda Bara.

And why must I carry on this way? Not only because I loved him madly and he did not love me, which was tragic enough in all conscience; but also because he had to keep telling me that even if he did love me he could not marry me because he had grown up with the conviction that he must not marry a woman of another race, that this would be an insult to his ancestors, a crushing blow to his parents, and the first knot in an indissoluble tangle of social problems.

Here I encountered another difficult step in work-

ing out my plot. What *was* his race if not the same as
mine? Though dark, his features are every one rather
the reverse of those of the Negro boys on campus,
and though he has a fine, deep speaking-voice he
cannot sing a note. . . . Jewish? Possibly, I thought.
His nose is rather prominent. (But then, so is mine —
unlike the Gish sisters' and Theda Bara's.) He is as
brilliant as so many Jews are, goodness knows; last
June he won the Coe Scholarship, which goes to the
highest-ranking man in the Junior class. But if he is
Jewish, I thought, he must already have alienated the
Orthodox family he may have, since he has done student supply work in Protestant pulpits ever since he
came to Bates, preaches now every Sunday in the Con-
gregational Church in East Sumner and served last
summer as the seasonal pastor at churches in North
Shapleigh and Ross Corner.

What was left for him to be but a Hindu? And
how likely was a Hindu to have been born in Greenfield, Massachusetts, to a family named ——? But
for the purposes of my plot — which was fast becoming a movie script — I decided to let him be a Hindu.
He does look more like a Hindu, I *think*, than anything except a Scot. . . . Though if I ever love him
madly enough to pursue him over the highest mountains and back and forth across the seven seas, he is
going to have trouble putting an end to my travels
just by telling me that a Congregationalist born in
Greenfield, Massachusetts, to a family named ——
can't marry me because it would annoy his ancestors.

(Oh, no use! I can't go on with these blanks. If I
am going to mention him — and how can I not men-

tion him? — he has to have a name. Since I've vowed not to use his real name, I must give him another. Craig? I'd love to call him Craig secretly, but that belongs to Professor Baird. Wallace? Wally? Why not Wally? He does remind me of Wallace Reid, who played in the first movie I ever saw. But I can't use the whole name, of course; it is too well known. Wallace what, then? Wallace Fennelly? That sounds all right, I think. Wallace Fennelly he shall be, in this journal.)

Before Ruth came back from studying with Eleanor, he had called me up from Chase Hall where he was playing pool (which is what he plays when he isn't playing tennis or bridge) to ask me if I could go for a walk early the next afternoon before he had to leave for East Sumner, and I had said yes; and he had offered to help me correct my share of the themes when he got back Sunday night if I hadn't finished them — his were all done. He told me something funny his roommate had said, and I laughed and told him to get on with his pool because *I* had studying to do after wasting the whole evening. He asked how. I said never mind. He said he would have liked to help me waste it, if he had known I had it to waste. I said I had had help enough without his. He asked who was so helpful. I said that should be forever a secret. And so it will. At least for a while. It is too ridiculous to tell. Nobody would believe it.

Well, anyway . . . much as I love to be at home, I am looking forward to going back to Bates more than I ever have.

Wally called me up this morning from the depot in Dover. He was on his way back from Rowe (a little town in the Berkshires near Greenfield; that is where his parents live now) to hold a service in East Sumner tomorrow. He said his train was stopping in Dover for ten minutes. I think he hoped I would ask him to come to my house and take a later train, but of course I couldn't. He would have had to come on the train to Salmon Falls, and it would have been six miles for him to walk from there here, or for my father to drive Pony to meet him, and six miles back. I told him I wished we didn't live so far from Dover. He asked how far it was, and I said at least ten miles. He said that was just a good walk and I said, "Yes, except on a day like this with the thermometer hovering around zero and last night's snow blowing." He asked if Ruth lived nearer to the depot and I said, "Yes." He said maybe he would call her up, and I said, "Why don't you?" He said, "Happy New Year!" I said, "Same to you."

I wonder if it will be.

When I went back into the kitchen, my mother asked, "Was that Wally?"

"Yes. He got off the train in Dover to call me. He is on his way to East Sumner for a service there tomorrow."

She nodded and smiled. She and Grammy are very pleased that he is a preacher. They only wish he were preparing for the ministry, but he isn't. He wants to teach. In college, eventually. But before he can do that he will have to earn the money to do graduate work. He has been living away from his family, supporting himself, and paying for his own education since before he entered high school. That is one reason why he is older than most of the men in his class. The other is that he enlisted in the Army when we went into the war, and so was out of school for nearly three years. He was serving in the Medical Corps at the same time Harold was in the Signal Corps, and they were both sergeants. He is twenty-five years old now. Harold is twenty-six. I think they would like each other. They are different in many ways, and alike in some ways. I think maybe their work during the war should have been reversed. It is easier for me to imagine Harold as a wardmaster in a hospital and Wally standing on a ridge snapping out messages with flags; Harold is deliberate, gentle, and Wally is very quick. Still, maybe Harold was better with field telephones, etc. (Repairing them, I mean; Wally is not at all interested in mechanics.) And Wally was probably a wizard with prescriptions and remembering what was in the medical books.

Day after tomorrow! I wonder if he will call me up the first night I'm back. I would have been sure he would, if he hadn't called today. What if I sounded on the phone as if I didn't want to see him? But you aren't *supposed* to sound too eager.

Oh, dear . . . Happy New Year, Me!

I had better think about something else. I'll think about what has already happened, because I know how that turned out. Sad, is how most of it turned out, actually; but it was wonderful while it was going on.

When I was little, we had so much family to visit and be visited by.

There were my Grandfather Hasty's two sisters, Aunt Annie Harriman and Aunt Hattie Bragdon, who were widows and lived in Lawrence, Massachusetts, and his brother, Uncle Gran, who lived on the old Hasty place on York Road; now Aunt Annie is the only one still living of nine brothers and sisters.

There was my Grandmother Hasty's brother, Uncle Joe Brown, and his wife, Aunt Lou. Uncle Joe had been around the world three times after serving as a "soldier in blue," and set up steam shovels all over the country, and gone to the Klondike for gold. Found some, too, — enough to buy a hotel in Warren, Rhode Island. Uncle Joe's middle name was Warren (for his mother's people). By the time I first remember him he had sold the hotel, and he and Aunt Lou (her name is Lucia) had an apartment on Pinckney Street in Boston, but they lived there only winters; every late spring they came to set up a big tent on the old Brown place and stayed into the fall. They had a small wood building Uncle Joe called The Cookhouse which they could make quite warm with their wood stove, but they slept in the tent, for which they had what they called a "fly" as a second roof. The fly was perhaps ten feet longer than the tent, and the wooden floor of the tent extended the length of the fly to make a porch which Uncle Joe screened in. The screen was attached to white birch posts, and

Uncle Joe made a sofa, table, and chairs of white birch for this little sitting room. Aunt Lou made its braided rugs and chintz cushions. It was a fine place to sit and write stories while they were out berrying. (I never did like to pick berries.) They called it The Skeeterette, and the whole place Camp Happy-go-lucky. It was fairyland to me. But Uncle Joe died there one night three years ago, and then Aunt Lou went back to her own family near Boston.

There was my Grandfather Dow's brother, my mother's Uncle Will, who was an itinerant minister, a Seventh Day Adventist. He used to arrive unexpectedly, once or twice a year, to spend a week with us — an Ichabod Crane of a man in rusty black clothes, with the deepest, warmest voice I ever heard (until lately). He should have carried coffee with him for we never had coffee in the house and until someone could get to the village to get some he had a headache every forenoon. But he used to play checkers, dominoes, and fox-and-geese with me. I always read my stories to him and he said they were good. Once I read him a story of Harold's which had been much praised by Academy teachers. He said that was very good. I asked, "Is it better than mine?" He chuckled and said, "Now you're fishing."

He must have been about sixty years old the time he came in a car with his bride beside him and introduced her as our Aunt Susie. He was still very thin but he was wearing a new suit and looked happy. Aunt Susie was in her early twenties, quite stout, but pretty; she adored him, and had a beautiful voice to sing and could make Aunt Vinnie's parlor organ

sound like a pipe organ. That was while I was a student at the Academy. He wanted to show Aunt Susie
the village cemetery where his parents were buried
but was not sure he could find his way there so asked
my mother and me to ride down with them. It was
summer, and a bright, sweet-smelling day, which was
fortunate and unfortunate. Fortunate because Uncle
Will's car of earliest vintage either had never had a
top or had lost it. Unfortunate because most of my
schoolmates whom I had not seen since June and
would not see again until September were out enjoying the day as we rode down Portland Street, along
Main Street, and up Academy Street. To a girl — and
a boy! — every one stopped stock-still, staring, then
waved with a broad grin at tall, gaunt Uncle Will
bent over the frail, shuddering steering wheel, clutch-
ing it with both big, bony hands, at pretty, plump
Aunt Susie squeezed in beside him in fluttering white,
and at my mother and me perched on the high,
narrow seat behind them, even our knees higher
than the back of *their* seat, as exposed to the world
as if we had been riding on a float in a centennial
parade. By September my fellow students had not
forgotten it, and asked me, "*What* was that I saw you
riding on last summer?" But Uncle Will was proud
and happy, and so was Aunt Susie. They knelt and
thanked God every morning and every night for giving them each other and meeting all their earthly
needs. I could hear them, for both had carrying
voices and the partitions of our house are not thick.
They had come to us from northern Vermont, and
when they left us they felt a call to Canada. We

never saw them again. Aunt Susie wrote a year or so later that Uncle Will had been laid to rest.

There were my father's sister, Aunt Hattie, named Hattie Anna for Aunt Annie Harriman and Aunt Hattie Bragdon, though her older sister Vinnie was obviously the favorite of those aunts; and her husband, Uncle George Webber, and son Roland. It was always a great day when they came to spend it with us.

When I visited the Webbers Uncle George used to take me to Portsmouth on Saturday night. We rode from Eliot to Kittery with the horse and buggy, and went across the river on the ferryboat. In Portsmouth we usually saw a play. I saw *Everywoman* with Uncle George, and *A Knight for a Day*. In *A Knight for a Day* beautiful girls sat in swings made all of twinkling colored lights and swung right out over the audience. All I remember about *Everywoman* is the girl who played the part of Vice; she had flaming red eyes. After the play Uncle George took me to an ice-cream parlor before we went back to the ferryboat. At the far end of a room filled with round marble tables and metal chairs with heart-shaped backs he showed me a curtain-hung door. He said that if he should ever have to leave me alone for a minute and a man should ask me to go with him through a door like that I must not go but stay right where Uncle George had left me until he came back. I didn't ask why. I knew it was because there was something bad out there and I didn't want to know what it was. When I saw the curtain pulled aside for a girl to come out I turned my eyes away. It surprised me that when she came close she looked like a girl instead of Vice, and that when she had taken our order she went back out there. It worried me at first that that was where she then brought our ice cream from, but when Uncle George began to eat his I began to eat mine. Apparently what was beyond the curtain was safe for ice cream.

One summer while I was in the Academy, when I visited at Aunt Hattie's, Uncle George did not feel able to take me to Portsmouth. He had a very sore throat and lay on the couch all day every day. Aunt Hattie told me not to go close to him for fear I might catch what he had, but I sat in his Morris chair and read to him hours at a time. He died that fall.

My mother's sister, my Aunt Lula, died a few days after the birth of a little girl she named Helen, and the baby went to Boston to live.

You have to get used to changes.

We have been lucky late years that Grammy's brother, Uncle Than, lives within a stone's-throw of us. Uncle Than has made a kind of profession of operating farms. When I was small he ran the Hervey Wentworth place in North Berwick. This was a very big farm with a large stock, always from twenty to thirty head of cattle. After Aunt Nell died and the last of their children was married, he came to take care of Mrs. George's farm near us, and walked up to visit Grammy on Sundays and summer evenings.

Across the river which runs behind the Boston place is the Dorr farm. Will Dorr, my father's closest friend from boyhood, was born there, and married my mother's cousin, Grace. They had two sons, Leslie and Clyde, who used to be Harold's constant companions, and a daughter Bernice who was mine. Much later they had another son, Kenneth. Bernice and I helped to bring him up — or thought we did.

But the Dorrs don't live there now. You used to get to Dorr's by turning off the main road and through a gate. They owned a right-of-way across a neighbor's land to the river's edge and there they had a bridge by which they reached their own land. The bridge was about fifty years old but it was called the New Bridge because it had replaced an earlier one. My grandfather of course remembered that bridge-raising and "the great rinktum we had afterward" at the Dorr house, where the women folk gathered to serve a feast to the men who had been at the raising. In the evening somebody played a Jew's harp for singing and dancing, and Deacon Dorr did a hoedown. Deacon Dorr was Will's father, Charles. Will's mother was Olive. Charles and Olive have been gone some years now, and last fall their bridge went. A day or two after flood waters from a fall storm had receded, a man drove a two-horse team and a load of logs onto the New Bridge and just as they reached the center it went down. Fortunately neither the driver nor the horses were seriously hurt. But the bridge was gone. Bernice is now a junior at Berwick Academy, and word was brought to her at her desk in the Main Room that her bridge had "gone down with a team on it." She thought at once that it must have been her mother and Kenneth driving over, for she knew they had planned to go

to the village that morning. She knew there was no
one else at home, for her father was working away
at a sawmill. She did not know that anyone was
hauling logs from Nason's woodlot. She tried to telephone home but there was no answer. Grace and
Kenneth must have been out looking at the river,
now clogged with planks, piles, railings, wheels, logs
and perhaps still with men rescuing the horses. Bernice did not know what else to do but to run home,
and that is what she did. It was a long run. To go
home the usual way would have been nearly five
miles. With no bridge to cross by, the only way for
her to reach the Dorr place was to go five miles to
Knight's Pond and then take a woods road from
Brad Nowell's. It is at least a mile through the woods
from Brad Nowell's to Dorr's. It must have been a
great relief to her to see smoke coming out of the
Dorr chimney, and then to find her mother, her little
brother, and even the Dorr horse and wagon unhurt.
But it must have seemed very strange to get home —
to *be* home — knowing there was no way to leave, or
for her father to come, but through the woods.
They decided not to have the bridge rebuilt, at least
not until spring. The sawmill where Will is working for the winter is near Uncle Gran's place, and
Uncle Gran's daughter Ethel and her family, who live
there now, had more rooms than they needed. Ethel
was willing to rent the two big front rooms of the old
part of the house and the chambers to the Dorrs.
So that is where they live now, and we doubt that
they will come back, for a private bridge is costly to
build and to maintain, Grace is nearer to her mother

and brother and sister, and Kenneth is as near to Number Eleven school as he was here to Number Ten. So the Dorr farm is deserted and perhaps next year no one will cut the grass.

But how well I remember it as it used to be! The barn full of hay and cows; the shed full of wood and riggings, baskets of newborn kittens, a just-churned freezer of lemon ice cream, a rope swing from the rafters; the icehouse full of ice packed in damp red sawdust; a chicken house with a single, gently sloping roof to which Bernice and I used to climb to play dolls, read the colored "funnies" saved from Sunday newspapers, and write stories to read to each other. And the house! A side door went into what was called Grammy Olive's part, for the kitchen where she always sat was there, and her little sinkroom; also three bedrooms, one of them hers, one Bernice's, and one the boys'. The front door went into Grace's part — her big kitchen-dining room and the long pantry which was the passageway past the common guestroom-parlor to Grammy Olive's part. There are two upstairs finished chambers in that house, each with its own open chamber or attic and each with its own flight of stars. The one above Grammy Olive's part (which was the "new" section of the house) belonged to Grace and Will, and I don't think I ever went up those stairs. But the one above Grace's part was Granny Betsy's, because Grace's part was the old house, the original Dorr house, probably two hundred years old, where Charles Dorr's mother had been the last to reign supreme. (Grace did not reign supreme anywhere as long as

Grammy Olive lived.) Charles's mother, Will's grandmother, Bernice's great-grandmother, had been known to everyone as Granny Betsy, and though she had passed on long before my time and left to Grace the use of her big kitchen with the great fireplace and a share of "the best room," she seemed only to have gone up the narrow staircase beside the chimney with all her goods and chattels. Bernice and I never saw her up there, but we always assumed she was near, taking care of us while we played when we were little — and she never once told us to get off her bed, with its quilts pieced in intricate patterns and its heavy, strawberry-colored linsey-woolsey, or to keep out of her hide-covered trunks and domed-top wooden chests full of baby's swaddling clothes which just fitted our big dolls, and gowns and capes and bonnets and tiny, many-buttoned boots which just fitted us; or to stop reading her little old books, whirling her spinning wheel and her flax wheel, pretending to light candles in her pierced-tin lantern, setting a tipsy old table with her pink-luster dishes and the goblets with morning glories on them. We used to spend whole days alone there, taking up our dinner with us when we went in the morning; and when we were old enough we slept many nights there. It was our home. It belonged to us. Us and Granny Betsy. We liked it most on rainy days.

There were so many things to do at Bernice's! And nobody ever interfered with us there. When we went out nobody asked us where we were going or told us when we must come back. In the winter we might go out to the main road and spend the whole afternoon jumping off the fence posts into the snow; or we might slide for hours down the steep bank of the brook behind the house, spinning deliriously as our sleds struck the ice; or if the ice was clear of snow we might skate on the brook or on the river or on a little pond up in the woods. The only ice on which we did not skate was that which covered the Big Hole in the brook. The Big Hole was said to be bottomless. But in the summer we paddled back and forth across it in the canvas canoe which Harold had made and later sold to Clyde. (I mustn't forget the first summer Sunday after Harold finished that canoe. He took my mother and me to church in it. He held it close to the bank of the river, where it flows through the Old Joy field below us, and we in our thin, ruffled dresses, flowered hats, crocheted gloves, white stockings and black patent leather shoes stepped in with great care, were seated on cushions, and were paddled the winding way of the river through Lafayette's woods, behind Uncle America Warren's old black house, behind both Walker places and Mark Nason's, until we reached Emery's bridge, which is just behind the church. There we disembarked, shook out our skirts, and proceeded with great relief to the service. It would not matter so much if the canoe sprang a leak on the way home; though it might have mattered some, for neither my mother nor I could swim.)

I wonder why, when I decided to think about "something else," Aunt Annie, Aunt Hattie, Uncle Joe and Aunt Lou, Uncle Will and Aunt Susie, Aunt

Hattie and Uncle George, Aunt Lula and the Dorrs
were what I thought about.

I suppose because they, with my parents, grandparents, brother, Aunt Vinnie, and the few neighbors
we had were once my whole world. A world I am
sure I could never have moved out of as long as it
existed. But time and events gradually took more
and more of it away, and likewise gradually has
taken me more and more away. Until now I come
home only for vacation, and there are only my parents and Grammy left in this house; most of those
who used to visit us are now too far away to come,
and hardly anyone of my age still lives in the neighborhood. Most of those I used to go to school with
come home only on vacation, as I do. Even Bernice
to her new home at Uncle Gran's. In termtime she
lives in the village. She was at home for Christmas,
of course, but I have not seen her. It is two miles
from here to Uncle Gran's. This is the first Christmas
since I can remember that Bernice and I have not
been together to see each other's trees and gifts. She
is making new friends, as I am.

You have to get used to changes. You have to let
people go, if they must or if they want to. You have
to go yourself when it is time. Then nothing will be
the same as it was before. But when the old way is
gone, you can find a new way. What happens, I think,
is what was intended from the very beginning of
everything, what you do is what you were meant to
do, where you go is where you were meant to go, and
what you find is what has been waiting for you there.
There is a reason for it all, a purpose in it.

People say this is fatalism, but I don't think it is. To me, fate is chance, or luck; mindless. I don't believe at all in fate. I do believe in God and that when He made the world He knew exactly what was going to happen to everything on it as long as it lasts, and how it will end. This is a great comfort to me. I don't think He ever changes anything for anybody; I don't believe He can, in accordance with His plan, or that we really need for Him to, even though we may feel sometimes that we wish He would. I don't believe that it is right, at least for me, to pray for anything except to be better, wiser, braver, or stronger; and if I feel that I am, after prayer, I think it is because prayer has brought me that much closer to Him, and that this makes anyone better, wiser, braver, stronger, if he very much wants to be.

ERE I am at home again, where I hadn't expected to be until Easter! And ALL I have been through! I just don't know where to begin except at the beginning of this *extraordinary* New Year. To find my way back there through the maze I am lucky to have by me the letters I wrote to my family from the time I left after Christmas vacation.

Apparently the year started out *very* cold. In my first letter in 1923 I said, "I'm simply petrified though I have on practically every warm thing I am possessed of, and am standing on top of the radiator in the French room where La-La left us at the end of half an hour. I have to stay because I have another class on this floor next hour. . . . I went downtown to buy clothes yesterday, as you wanted me to. I didn't get the overshoes as they didn't have the new ones in, but did get the blue flannel middy and the camel's hair skirt. They're royal, as Harold says. The skirt had to be taken in at the waist (note I said IN) but they will send it up today, and *long!* — Oh, my goodness! But I like it rather. Funny how we always manage to like whatever is in style. . . . We are choosing courses for next semester and everybody is excited. There are three second-semester English courses offered to sophomores; anyone can take 4B, but 4A and 5 are restricted; 5 is Advanced Argumentation. 4A is imaginative writing, all forms; I asked Professor Baird if I might take it and he said, 'You may take any English you like, I'm sure, Miss Hasty,' so I was quite pleased. My next semester, then, will be English 4B, English 4A, History (European), Psychology, Latin, and Public Speaking. I'm not going to bother science until science bothers me — which will be next year because, if I *can* pass it, it would be wonderful to have one year that it wasn't hanging over me. . . . I wrote a crazy letter last time, didn't I, Mother?" (She must have burned that one. It isn't here.) "We hadn't really quarreled at all, but it was fun making up. I can't tell you about it in writing somehow; if I could see you maybe I could make you understand how much I liked everything he said. After a while I asked him if it was true that he wasn't studying as much as he had other years. (Those two senior girls who keep after me about him have been telling me that, along with everything else they can think of to make me feel I ought not to go out with him. *Why* do you suppose they do that? They can't seem to make up their minds whether he is going to

ruin me or I am going to ruin him if we keep on seeing each other.) He said maybe he wasn't, didn't think
he needed to, but that if I want him to he will see that
he gets all A's. Imagine it — *all* A's, when if *I* get
two I feel like a heroine! . . . I had too much studying to do to go to the movies any time this week, but
last night we went to George Ross's for ice cream.
Why, do you think? Well, I had finally told Dot
Clarke some of the things those senior girls had said
to me, and she had told Elwin Wilson (the junior
she goes with now), who told him. Not in any detail,
and maybe none of us should have repeated any of it,
but I can't help being glad we did. He said he had
known I would hear sometime about his friendship
with that girl who graduated last year, but didn't
suppose it would be so soon (he doesn't know yet *how*
soon I heard it after I met him) and hesitated to bring
it up, himself. Of course what he told me was absolutely different in every way from what they told me,
and I choose to believe him! When I told Ruth what
he told me, she said, 'Why didn't you tell him the
story the way you heard it? I should think you would
enjoy his sympathy.' Well, maybe I would, but I'm
not going to take it. . . . I always write a lot that
isn't very sensible, don't I? Please forgive me, Mother.
I'll do better sometime."

That was written on a Friday morning. Sunday
night I wrote:

"They say there is another big storm coming, and
since the last one there hasn't been a train through

between Boston and Lewiston for two days. This must be the kind of winter, as Grandpa used to say, to 'sit back in the corner and smoke old chaw.' He meant, didn't he, when the weather was so bad a man couldn't get to the village to buy tobacco and had to smoke what he had chewed? Sounds awful. But that kitchen stove would look fine to me right now, I can tell you. I hope you have a lot of dry wood in for the night. It doesn't seem possible that only two weeks ago I was there with you. . . . I led tonight for our Sunday Evening Sing at Rand Hall. Fauncy that! . . . Basketball practice has begun but we aren't under training rules yet. I can't imagine how I'm going to manage to get to bed at ten o'clock when we are, either . . . I told you about getting my middy and skirt, didn't I? Jiminy, I like them! Dot took snaps of me in them yesterday and if they come out I'll get some printed for you. The sun was so bright on the snow I'm sure my eyes were all squinnied up. Oh, yes, and I have my overshoes. Nice, thick, high, four-buckle ones. . . . I've had a perfectly wonderful weekend. Wally took a vacation because East Sumner is all snowed in. Last night he came over about quarter of eight and stayed until nine-thirty. Nobody played any tricks; they are too much in awe of him. He read the stories I wrote while I was home and chose the one for me to read at Spofford Tuesday night. This afternoon we went for a walk, and talked about everything from religion to Dot and Elwin — which isn't a great distance, I guess. I told you, didn't I, that Elwin is preparing for the ministry? He and Wally are great friends. We met Dean Niles coming in as we left Frye Street House and she really beamed at us. She knows Wally quite well, and drives him to East Sumner in her car if she is going that way any Saturday afternoon for the weekend. . . . I do wish we would have good weather long enough for your roads to get passable for the mailman. As it is, I'm not hearing from you, and probably my letters for you are cluttering up the South Berwick post office — unless they just lie in the Lewiston post office."

Wednesday

"After I write a half-dozen letters all dwelling on the one subject to such an extent that I am embarrassed to send them through the mail, I get word from you that you aren't hearing 'half enough about Wally'! I don't see how I could say much more and keep anything to myself at all. If the girls in the house knew a sixteenth of what I write to you, they would be amazed. I tell Dot Clarke quite a lot, and Ruth next most (she knows a lot without my telling her, anyway; she knows me well enough to read my expressions); to the rest I am very uncommunicative about personal matters. I have never liked the way so many girls talk about their interest in boys and I refuse to do likewise. I never repeat anything he says, or mention that he has asked me out. For instance, I didn't even tell Ruth that I was going to entertain him here last Saturday night. When she saw me putting on a different dress after dinner she asked, 'Where are you going?' I said, 'Nowhere at all.' She said, 'Why! Why, *Gladys!* Are you going to *entertain?*' I said yes. Ruth said, 'Why didn't you tell us?' I said

I didn't suppose anyone would be especially interested. Cookie was in the room and she said, 'Well, you
are the most reticent girl I ever met!' I echoed
blandly, 'Reticent?' She said, '*Yes*. Reticent. My
roommate and I were talking about it last night and
she said she didn't know how anybody in the world
could know whether you like Wally or not.' That
suits me perfectly! But I do think I've told *you* a
great deal and when I see you I can tell you all the little things — Oh, Mother! ! ! . . . I read my *Sentence
of a Soul* at Spofford last night. They liked the last
part especially. Gavie, the top critic of the group, says
my rural New England touch is best and urges me to
stick to what I know about and not try to fly too high
or dive too deep. I feel he is right. . . . Midyears
begin two weeks from today. . . . I'm glad the mails
are beginning to get through. Take good care of your-
selves. It is a bad time for colds and things. I never
felt better in my life. Tell Papa thanks a heap for giving me my own checking account and putting all that
money in it. I feel proud that he trusts me. Most of
the girls are on allowances."

Friday

"We had a cut in History this morning. Imagine a
cut in Pa Gould's History! I am almost sure he must
be sick. Dot and I went for a walk down College
Street. Now she is here reading my Psych book while
I write. It is such a wonderful morning! The sky has
a wide stream of rose-color and gold across it, and the
sun behind a heavy gray cloud has silvered its edges
. . . I have charge of the World Fellowship bulletin

board in the library. . . . Tonight the sophomore girls are inviting the freshman girls to a dance in the gym. The sophs have hired dress suits and will send flowers and call at the freshman dorms and take the freshmen home when it is over. All I've heard for two days is, 'Have you any dances left?' and 'Whom are you taking?' and 'Whose shirt are you going to wear?' and 'I told John to tell Arthur not to forget to remind Leon that he is going to give George his second-best cuff links to bring to me at English class tomorrow.' . . . We went to George Ross's last night. That is the best place we know for a good, long, quiet talk. (The ice cream is good, too. Homemade!) Wally always considers whatever I say worth thinking about and always decides the same way I think myself even though it isn't always what I *want* to think, and always understands what I mean that I don't say, and never asks me to tell him anything when I say I guess I'd better not, even though he knows that if he urged me I would. Sometimes I get to wishing I could help him a little the way he helps me when I'm all mixed up. But last night he began to say something and broke off with, 'I can't say it, but you know what I mean, don't you? You always have, and somehow I'm getting to expect it.' Then I just felt — oh, I can't explain *that,* either — but I was glad because he thought I did, and most of all because I *know* I DO. I'd like so much to see you, Mother."

Sunday

"Well! Here past the middle of the cruelest kind of January, the eaves are dripping, the snow is soft

and slumpy, the air is as stickily, foggily warm as if
it were April. It feels rather good, but I suppose it
isn't very good for us to have such sudden, complete
changes. Last night I slept the best ever because it
was warm enough to really stretch out. But Cookie
woke us before eight o'clock to have some of the ice
cream and cake she and her roommate had been out
to get for breakfast! After that we felt so lazy we were
almost late for church. I don't have much studying to
do because Dot and I worked hard yesterday. She
asked me down to her house for the afternoon and to
supper. We finished studying about seven-thirty and
then sat by the fire and talked until it was time for
me to catch the Figure Eight at nine. There are
plans for something perfectly marvelous tomorrow.
If it really happens I'll tell you about it in my next
letter. . . . Thanks so much, dear, for the beautiful
material and the money order to pay a dressmaker to
make it up. I don't really need a new dress, but of
course I'll be delighted to have one. Thanks, too,
for those dee-licious Lizy Ann dropcakes. You
mustn't try to send me food often, for it is too much
work and we aren't starved here by any means, but
if you should have a chance sometime you would be
sanctified by this dormitory if you sent us some cottage cheese. The girls who were at Milliken are all
forever reminiscing about that you sent me last year
and wondering if you are ever going to send some
more. . . . Our party in the gym was a great success, and Frye Street House cleared $26.15 for the
Million Dollar Drive."

Wednesday

"Well, it did happen! Early Monday afternoon Wally and I sorted themes at the library, and when Dot came from Greek class at 3:30 I had my bag packed and was signed out for the night at 159 Pine Street. On the way to her house we bought candy and nuts to make fudge but her mother said she would be glad to make it. She made three kinds while we were dressing! I wore my brown tricolette. Then Dot played the piano and we sang until the bell rang. It was Wally and Elwin but we made them wait while we put on our hats, coats, and gloves. Then we all left for dinner at the Royal. It was a nice walk. We had to go early as a dorm girl is not allowed in a downtown restaurant after six at night, without a chaperone. I had chicken chow mein (a Chinese dish) and all the fixings, and all the time the boys kept putting nickels in the slot to keep the player-piano going. When we finished the first course it was ten minutes of six, too late for dessert, so we went up to the Greek Candy Kitchen for college ices. That is a flowery, drapery sort of place. Then we went to the Empire to see *When Knighthood Was in Flower,* which is a splendid picture. When that was over, about nine o'clock, we went back to Dot's, where Mrs. Clarke had told us we could entertain until eleven — a whole hour and a half later than the rules permit in a dormitory! She had a warm coal fire burning for us in the parlor and a big dish of candy on the table, so we sat around the stove and ate and talked. My, but it was cozy! After the boys left, Dot and I talked almost all night — so we overslept in the morning and didn't get up to campus in time for chapel. I say 'boys' but that only makes it sound more *casual*. Elwin isn't a boy any more than Wally is. Dot likes him at least as much as I do Wally, so there should be many of these foursomes before this year is over. And don't you think we must have had a gorgeous time — dinner and theater and all? It was the wildest of my high school dreams to be part of something like that. (I say high school, because almost everyone here does. Only a few went to academies.) No classes tomorrow forenoon. The time is given to a chapel service. It is the Day of Prayer. I must recover from my dissipation. . . . Are you awfully cold at home? Pretty frosty again here."

Friday

"Doesn't it frighten you when you realize all the things that can happen like thunderbolts in a week, or a day, or an hour? At college you never have time to plan anything, you are so everlastingly busy dealing with what happens all of a sudden before you have even thought of it. Yesterday I came back from lunch in the blackest of black moods. I don't know why, I never do, but suddenly I felt as if I couldn't bear the sight of anybody. I just wanted to be alone and think myself out of myself. But a college dormitory is no place for such a feeling because people *will* stick around even though you look at them as if you would like to throw every book in the room square at their heads. I flopped on Ruth's

bed, turned my face to the wall, and squabbled inside
for an hour or more — until I got a telephone call
from Mr. Woodward asking me to come right over to
Hathorn to take a freshman English class for him. I
thought I'd rather die, but I put on my flannel middy
and camel's hair skirt and betook myself to the hall
of learning. You know how hard I've tried to keep
the freshman girls from knowing I had their papers, so when they came trooping in, you can imagine
their faces! Woodie told me to give them a twenty-
minute written, then have the papers exchanged and
corrected from the answers I would give them. Then
he left. As he had handed me question sheets (*and
answers!*), there was nothing to it really. The class was
meeting in Goosie's Greek room and I have *always*
wanted to sit tilted back in Goosie's chair. So as soon
as I had passed out the questions I mounted the platform, seated myself behind the desk, and tipped
back luxuriously against the blackboard — *way*
back! No sooner was I there than in popped Woodie
and *introduced* me to the class! I spent the whole
time he was doing it trying to get my feet back on the
floor! Before I did, he vanished again — only to
come back while we were discussing answers and take
a front seat and listen. That came near fazing me, especially when one student, wanting to know something about an assignment, said, 'May I ask Mr.
Woodward a question, Miss Hasty?' But really I enjoyed it all and it certainly got me out of my mood. At
dinner the freshman girls were shrieking, 'Say, I
think you gave me the only C I've had this year,' and
'I wonder if you gave me my A+,' and 'Is yours the

big red-yellow writing, or the little scraggly writing, or the nice round writing?' . . . And the other thing that has happened I scarcely know how to tell you; things look so bald in blue ink on yellow paper. But last night there was a union meeting of Y.M. and Y.W. in Chase Hall, and I went with Wally and he made the prayer and it was very good. Then we went down to George's, but we didn't go in for ice cream because we were having a very serious talk. He told me he wanted me to understand he isn't seeing me *only* for the good times we have, that he wants me to know him well enough to decide whether I want to see him sometimes after he finishes college, that he thinks he understands how I feel now and I needn't think about what he said except to feel sure that our friendship isn't a pastime with him. I think he does understand how I feel — at least, as well as I do myself, which isn't very well — and I am glad he will be patient. When I came back in I would have given worlds to be alone, but I couldn't — people, people everywhere, watching, curious, commenting. Oh, Mother, if you could know how *good* he is to me, how much I need him when things go wrong! What am I going to do? I need time and time and time. I'm going to bed where it's dark and nobody can see me think. I like the dreams I have. Oh, Mother, Mother, I wish I could see you!"

Sunday

"When I think of midyears beginning this very next Wednesday, I wonder where all my ambition has gone and if I'll get it back before the fatal days! It is

such cold, gray, bleak weather. Wouldn't I like to be
sitting right by the kitchen stove with my feet in the
oven! Do you play the Victrola much now? I was
thinking last night about Grammy's 'Alice, Where
Art Thou' and how pretty it is. Have you any new
records? 'The Daughter of Officer Kelly' is a very
catchy popular tune. . . . Prof. Baird has chosen
twelve girls from his Argumentation classes for a series of debates. Ruth and Eleanor and I are among
the twelve, and I wish I weren't. Argumentation is
the *last* line in which I have aspirations. I didn't like
debating even at the Academy. But here everybody
is *supposed* to like it. Wally does, so he is pleased
about this. He won the Sophomore Men's Prize Debate in '21, you know, and everyone says he would
be on the Varsity squad if he had the time to give to it.

"He was over last night. He asked me to go to
Chase Hall to the movies and dance but I had a little
cold and didn't feel like going out, so he came over
here. And he was so solicitous about that little speck
of cold, Mother — even worse than you! We talked
for two hours with no hint of anything he said the
last time we were together, except once. Then we
happened to be talking about the amount of deciding-
for-one's-self that one has to begin to do when he
leaves home for college; or, rather, that *she* has to
begin to do, for he said he could scarcely remember
when he hadn't done it.

"He said, 'Well, it's good for a girl, or for anyone,
to begin early to manage her own affairs, isn't it?'

"I said, 'Except that she has more time in which
to make mistakes.'

"He said, 'Only experience will teach her not to make them.'

"I said, 'Sometimes others than herself suffer in that experience.'

"He said, after a minute, 'A girl who knows herself and is true to herself won't make serious mistakes.'

"But how long does it take to get to know yourself? Do you know, or do you just think you know, or don't you even think you know? That is the three-horned dilemma!

"Ruth and I had breakfast in the room this morning; a nice one of ham and hot buttered toast and celery. She went downtown to dinner last night and brought all the breakfast things home in a perfectly beautiful new wastebasket — a wooden one painted garnet and white, with a big B on the side."

Wednesday

"Warning! Midyears are really on now, so if you don't get letters you will know it is really and truly because I don't have time to write them. I started off with a bang this morning — History. I don't think I flunked it, but it was a stiff proposition. French tomorrow, Psych Friday, Latin Saturday, and Monday I have both Argumentation and Public Speaking. Tuesday and Wednesday I won't have *anything* and can rest and have a good time. Until then, you'll understand if you don't hear, won't you? I'll be all right, and I won't study enough to hurt me; don't worry. If you're thinking about that cold, forget it. It's not nearly as bad as most people here have, and I'm practically over it. You should have seen the girls when that cheese came! The cookies were corking, too. All gone, everything. Now I must get into those French notes!!!!!"

Thursday

"I never would have believed I'd find time to write you tonight, but I seem to have a few minutes and know you will be glad to hear that I am through with the two first and presumably worst of my exams. This afternoon Cookie and I studied Psych industriously and then we had basketball practice. Tonight Wally and I went to George's for a little while. What a comfort he is at a time like this when sophomore girls get so excited! Last night while I was plugging away on French, A. and N. were fighting like all possessed, P. was on the verge of fainting, Ruth was cranky, M. was crying, and Cookie had a case of nerves. Then he called up and when I told him part of what was going on, he laughed — he has the *nicest* laugh — and said, 'Oh, just put two more hours on the French, go to bed and to sleep. Tomorrow night it will all be over and we'll go to George's!' Which I did, and we did, and I feel fine. Here is the snapshot Dot took of me in my new blouse and skirt. I'm going to stay down at her house tomorrow night to study for the Latin exam. Studying any subject with Dot is as good as studying it with the professor — and lots more fun. . . . I'm glad you're all free of these colds and hope you will stay as lucky. Mine is almost gone."

That is the *last* letter my mother had from me. The reason why was NOT that I did not have time to write. It makes quite a story. At least, it was quite a story to *live*.

As I had written I was going to, I signed out for 159 Pine Street Friday afternoon and went home with Dot to study for the Latin exam. We studied until midnight, got up Saturday morning and studied again. The exam was scheduled for the afternoon.

Now I think I should tell more than I have about the Clarke family. I have said Dot is an only child. Her father used to be a minister, but now he travels as a salesman for religious books and is at home perhaps one night out of three. Her mother takes all the responsibility for the house, for she wants Dot to concentrate on her college work. Of course they are very proud of Dot; they moved to Lewiston from Augusta to make a home for her, to see that she sleeps regularly, eats properly, and so on. Mrs. Clarke's sister Minnie boards with them and gives piano lessons. Aunt Minnie is tiny and very frail. I don't think Mrs. Clarke is strong but she is always busy and never complains. They rent the second and third floors of the house at 159 Pine. They have a kitchen, living room, parlor, bedroom, and bath on the second floor, and two bedrooms on the third floor. Dot sleeps on the second floor. One of the third-floor bedrooms is the Clarkes' and the other is Aunt Minnie's. Mrs. Clarke keeps all the rooms very clean, does all the washing and ironing, goes to the store for the groceries which she brings back up the long flight of stairs, bakes her own whole-grain bread. She never uses food from cans; all her vegetables and fruits are fresh-cooked to be more healthful; she does wonderful things with inexpensive cuts of meat. She doesn't even let anyone help her with the dishes, tells Dot and me to go on with our studying and Aunt Minnie to try to get a little rest or practice the music she will play in church next Sunday.

This is how it always is at Dot's when I am there, and how it was while we were studying for the Latin exam.

But on Saturday, just as we were closing our books before going out to the kitchen for lunch, the telephone rang. Mrs. Clarke answered, and called me. Dot and I exchanged dramatic looks. We thought of course it was Wally wanting to talk to me before he left for East Sumner.

But it was Ruth. She sounded the most excited I have ever heard Ruth sound, and I could hear dozens of other excited voices in the background.

"Gladys! Dean Niles told me to call you. You're not to come back to campus. We're all in quarantine! Somebody I never heard of, over on the men's side of campus — I don't know which dorm — has come down with scarlet fever, and two other cases — both men — are suspected. So the city Health Officer has clamped down on us. No more midyears. No more *anything*. Nobody who is on campus can leave, and nobody off campus can come on. Not only that, but we can't go into any buildings except our own dorm, and to Rand to eat. This is going to last at least a week."

A week! Anything happening to stop midyear examinations was too, too marvelous, but . . .

"Why can't I come back? I just left there last night. I'd walk. I'd even cross the street if I saw somebody coming. I *have* to come back. What else can I do?"

"You can go home, as far as we know. You don't realize how lucky you are. You couldn't see Wally. We can't get even within speaking distance of any man. I was telling you, this goes on for seven days after a case of scarlet fever is diagnosed. It is seven days from *now,* and if one of those suspected cases is found to *be* scarlet fever tomorrow, it will be seven days from tomorrow, and if six days from now somebody else gets scarlet fever, it will be seven days from *then;* and this may go on *all year!* We'd all give anything to be in your shoes, I can tell you."

"But I don't have any money, Ruth!"

"Borrow it from the Clarkes. You can send them a money order right back. For heaven's sake, write to me when you get there. Write every day. Tell everybody you see to write. *We* can't write to anybody. *We* can't do *anything!* We're prisoners!"

"Oh, dear," I said helplessly. "I never *heard* of anything like this. Yes, I suppose . . . yes, of course I'll write you every day."

I left the telephone in a state of confusion. Considering who was in the Bates prison I should have much preferred to be there, too, for seven days. But under the conditions maybe I wouldn't want to be there the rest of the year. Maybe I was lucky. I didn't know. Anyway, Dean Niles had said I was not to come back.

I told the Clarkes, and Mrs. Clarke said of course
she would lend me carfare, and Dot was beginning to
plan what she could do with a surprise vacation and
at the same time to wonder how long she could live
without seeing Elwin. I had my hand on the telephone to call the depot and ask when the next train
left for Boston, when it rang. I snatched off the re-
ceiver and said "Hello," thinking of course it was
Wally to tell me the awful news, and Dot dashed
across the room to my elbow in case it was Elwin
calling to tell her the awful news — but it was Dean
Niles calling Mrs. Clarke.

"Yes," said Mrs. Clarke. And, after some time,
"Yes, I understand. . . . Certainly. . . . Well, it is
hard for all of them. And for you, too. . . . Oh, it is
all right for them to go out as long as they keep away
from people? That will make it easier. . . . Certainly, Dean Niles. Good-bye."

We had a premonition of what she was going to
say when she turned to us.

"Dean Niles says the Board of Health has ruled
that all students who have been on campus during the
past week must stay wherever they are now, must
have no contact with anyone with whom they are not
in contact now for seven days, must use no public
transportation or enter any occupied building other
than the house in which they are living. So of course
you will have to spend the week with us, Gladys. We
shall be happy to have you, and you must try not to
be disappointed. You should telephone your parents
after the night rates go on."

I was ashamed of how homesick I suddenly felt.

Mrs. Clarke was so good — what an imposition for me to stay a week when I had been invited for one night! — but she wasn't my mother. Dot was one of my very best friends now, but I hadn't known her until this year; when I wasn't living with relatives I lived with Ruth; I was *used* to Ruth and she was used to me. The Clarkes shouldn't have to put up with me for a whole week; that was Ruth's job. I didn't feel right about staying so long at the Clarkes'. I was willing to go home. But what I really wanted — I was sure of it now! — was to go back to Frye Street House, prison or not. Only I couldn't. It was against the law.

"Well!" Dot said cheerily. "We can't have contact with anybody else, but we're certainly going to have plenty with each other. And there *is* the telephone, Sunny!"

So there was. But it wasn't ringing. And how we both wanted it to!

"Are *we* quarantined?" asked Aunt Minnie suddenly. "What about my pupils? I have eight coming in the course of the afternoon, the first one in half an hour."

"Oh, I don't think —" Mrs. Clarke, began, and then changed it to, "Well, we'd better make sure."

This started a long series of telephone calls. The Health Department said no, the house was not quarantined, as no one there had scarlet fever; adults there might come and go as usual. But on the problem of piano pupils? Hold the line, please. . . . Could the room where the lessons were given be closed off from the rest of the house, and had the

Bates students been in the room during the past twenty-four hours? The answers were yes; and no.

Dot poked me.

"I went in about ten o'clock this morning to get a dictionary," she whispered. "Should I take the stand and confess?"

"Is this how it feels to be a leper?" I whispered back.

The Health Department eventually ruled that, under these conditions, the parents of Aunt Minnie's pupils might decide as they saw fit. By that time a little girl was pulling the front doorbell frenziedly, so Aunt Minnie opened the door a crack to tell her to go home, whereupon Aunt Minnie called up the little girl's mother and seven other mothers. Some of them weren't at home and some of their lines were busy, but she persisted until she reached them all.

"Hello, Mrs. Whosis. Your little darling is to come for a piano lesson at so-and-so o'clock. I think you know that my niece Dorothy is a student at Bates College, and perhaps you have heard that Bates students are under general quarantine because of a case of scarlet fever. However, neither Dorothy nor the classmate who happened to be here when the quarantine was applied knows the young man who is ill, or has been in class with him, so we feel . . . and the Health Department feels . . . but if you don't feel . . . I can tell you that the room in which I give lessons is closed off from the rest of the house, and neither of the girls has been in it for the past twenty-four hours — "

Dot poked me again.

"What shall I *do,* Sunny? I don't think I was there long enough to *breathe.*"

But all the mothers decided that their children shouldn't come through the door of a house where two Bates students were. One would have been dangerous enough, but *two* — my goodness! A few asked if Aunt Minnie could come to their houses to give the lessons, so Mrs. Clarke helped her bundle up, and Dot and I watched her guiltily from the window as she picked her way down the icy street with the wind snapping at her scarf and veil and the skirt of her coat.

I turned and glared at the silent telephone.

"*Ring!*" I told it.

It rang.

It was Elwin calling Dorothy, but Wally was with him. Elwin had been trying off and on for hours to get through to 159 Pine, and so had Wally after finding out from Ruth that I was still there unless I had left for home. Word hadn't yet reached the campus that off-campus students were likewise imprisoned where found.

It was wonderful talking with them. It was also frustrating. They seemed to think it was great that they knew exactly where we were going to be for a week and they could call us up whenever the spirit moved. Otherwise, Elwin was delighted, it seemed, with this opportunity to catch up on his sleep, and Wally talked with unnecessary enthusiasm about the group he had lined up to play bridge all night long. They said they would call again in the evening. Dot told Elwin not to lose any sleep over it, and I told

Wally not to call after nine o'clock as I didn't want to disturb the family. We hung up.

Dot raised her eyebrows at me — she has very dark, expressive eyebrows — and I said I agreed with her. I called Ruth and she *still* thought I was lucky.

We ate supper. I called home and my mother was very pleased I was off-campus but concerned about the trouble I was making Mrs. Clarke, and kept telling me to watch for ways I could help her and try to return her kindness in any way I could. She talked to Mrs. Clarke and then she talked to me again and said she would send me some money to come home on if college didn't open in a week, also to pay for toll calls, and she hoped I would get a long sleep every night.

"She wants me to sleep," I told Dot.

"Sleep! Can't anybody think of anything but *sleep?* Let's play Flinch."

"Cards! Can't anybody think of anything but *cards?*"

"I suppose we can go play the piano."

"Why not? Nobody else is going to."

They called at eight-thirty. The crowd was gathering for bridge. Elwin was about to go to bed. They wanted to know what we were doing. We said they'd hate it if they knew and we wouldn't tell them. They laughed. We said *"Good night,"* with emphasis.

We went to bed. We got up and made cocoa. We went back to bed. We slept and woke up. We ate breakfast. Mr. Clarke had come home the night before. The three of them went off to church. We watched them go. We played and sang some hymns. We went

out and walked in the park. It was bitter cold. We
came back and ate dinner. Dot tried to read. I wouldn't
let her. They called up to tell us they had just waked
up. We heard the scores — the bridge score and the
sleep score. They said they would see us soon. We
said we didn't expect to live that long. They laughed.
They said they would see us *very* soon. We said they
couldn't. They said they were going to; nobody
would stop them from walking down Pine Street. We
said, Well, somebody would stop them from walking
in at 159 — the Clarke family and guest! They
said, Oh, they didn't expect to come in, but we
had a porch, didn't we? Dot said, Yes, about fifteen
feet above the ground. They said they didn't mind
stiff necks in a good cause. Wally quoted a few lines
from the balcony scene.

I said, *"Don't you dare!"*

He didn't say anything for a minute, and then, low
and gently, "We won't if you don't want us to."

Want them to!

I said, just as low, "We'll see."

We went right out to the kitchen and asked Mrs.
Clarke what she thought. She was making a pudding
and kept on stirring. Finally she said that she knew we
all needed something to look forward to; by Tuesday
afternoon the week would be almost half over; so
Tuesday afternoon, if the college allowed the boys to
be on the street, she saw no reason why they shouldn't
stop briefly below the porch, where we could go to
talk with them. But of course we must do it quietly,
and not for more than five minutes.

We both hugged and kissed her.

Five minutes! Tuesday afternoon! It was still only three o'clock of Sunday!

We talked of practically nothing else for forty-eight hours, by ourselves and on the telephone. How so much could be said about five future minutes of public conversation must remain unexplained. One of the good things about concentration on this topic, from our point of view, was that it shortened the bridge and sleep score reports we had to listen to. *We* didn't sleep much, though we stayed in Dot's big bed until lunchtime every day, with the shade down. Mrs. Clarke brought us our breakfast there on trays. I considered this the *height* of indulgence. Nobody had ever done this before for me unless they also brought medicine to be taken before and after — except Aunt Hattie Webber who, everyone agrees, always spoils me silly whenever I visit her; on my first visits alone to her, she used to spend two hours brushing out and braiding my heavy hair, to be sure she didn't hurt me the least little bit; this was a chore dispatched by either my mother or Aunt Vinnie in five minutes, including smoothing the end curls over a finger with a comb wet in a cup of water. . . . But I think it was easier for Mrs. Clarke than looking at and listening to us before noon. I hope so. She must have had enough of that the rest of the day.

Finally, it was 2:55 P.M. Tuesday; we went out on the porch because they were supposed to come at three; they were already there and Elwin had his watch out, and do you know how long five minutes last? Just exactly five minutes! We called down that they looked fine, and they certainly did. They called up so did we, and we ardently hoped so. What else was there to say that we hadn't already said on the telephone? They had already said more cases of scarlet fever had developed in the men's dorms, the latest that morning, which was far from encouraging; but none among the women. President Gray had been in Chicago all this time but was expected back on Friday, and it was rumored that if the girls were still all right then, they would be allowed to go home Saturday, also those men known to have had scarlet fever as children — which included Wally.

"If that's the way it goes," said Wally, face turned skyward, "I'll be first on the Boston train and save seats for you and Ruth and Eleanor."

It sounded heavenly, but we didn't say any more about it because Elwin would still be incarcerated and surely in *time* he would get tired of sleeping. And what would Dot be doing with herself? All her friends are Bates students. And she doesn't even enjoy not having to prepare for exams or classes! She *likes* to study, and she didn't even have all her textbooks there, much less access to the library!

Then they were gone. As soon as they rounded the corner of the house, we dashed through kitchen and living room to the bay window in the parlor. They went very slowly, and turned twice to wave; still they were soon out of sight. And *still* it was only Tuesday!

Tuesday . . . and *Wednesday* . . . and *Thursday* . . .

Of course I talked with Ruth several times every day, and then maybe Cookie would come on the line to tell Dot and me about the reams of poetry she was writing — we didn't see how she could! — and then Dot would ask to speak with Nellie Mae, Mary, Avis; and usually Ruth Marsh, Ruth Garner, Helen or Buddie or one of the Stanley sisters would come on. They were all as desperate as we were, in their own ways, having nothing happen but the mail, which was left in a heap on the porch; but there was a great deal of it, because almost everybody got a box from her mother almost every day, and lots of pitying letters. They could order ice cream from George's or The Qual, and it would be left on the porch, but they had to charge it.

"Everybody here is on everybody else's nerves," they all declared. "Let's hope nobody is murdered before Saturday. If Prexy knows what's good for him he'll get back here and get us *out* on that two o'clock train Saturday!"

He did. By noon Friday everybody was calling us to say that he was back and in conference with the City Health Department; and a little later that it was agreed — Bates girls and Bates men who had had scarlet fever years ago could leave for home Saturday afternoon.

"But no knowing *when* we can come back!" the girls wailed. "No winter carnival, of course! And probably no Easter vacation! What kind of a sophomore year is this?"

"I've had enough vacation to last me a year," I said. "The minute I get home I'm going to *work*. At *something*."

"Well," Ruth said, "at least we have stopped pressing our chests."

"What's pressing the chest? Same as beating the breast?"

"No. They told us if we saw any redness on our chest to press it with our thumb and if the white spot stayed white a long time we should report to Dean Niles or somebody. I thought I told you that. Seems as if we've all been sort of reddish, one time or another. If it stays white too long, that's the start of scarlet fever. Our chests are getting all black and blue, so we've stopped pressing. We don't think they can turn white anyway, and if they can we don't want to know it right here at the last minute."

"Lord, no! See you tomorrow!"

Elwin called to ask if he could come down at three Saturday to look at Dot on the porch, and Mrs. Clarke said Yes; also, since there would be only one of him, perhaps he might stay a few more than five minutes. This perked up Dot a little, and we decided to take her old sled out to the edge of town where there was a hilly field. It was bitter cold after melting a little the day before so we thought there would be a crust on the snow. We felt silly pulling that child's sled along street after street, but we had been feeling silly in various ways for nearly a week, so it didn't matter much. The sliding was fine when we got there, but the one who waited while the other slid was shaking with cold by the time she could climb on for her turn and then the rushing wind on the way down bit right through boots, suede jackets, sweaters, wool blouses, and all. We could feel our noses, cheeks, and chins congealing. If we opened our mouths, our teeth ached.

We stayed until almost sunset, though, and there was a magnificent one; all jewel colors, like pink and purple quartz and the white which is really pearl-gray. I was hoping there would be one just like it Sunday night when I would be seeing it at home. The sun sets over Rocky Hills here in winter, so the first place you see the colors is on the ice this side of them, the ice of White's Marsh which all those who have farms beside it own a share of. It is as if there were a sunset sky caught like a great torn balloon and spread out on the ground beyond the meadow. If my father notices it first he stands by the porch window and beckons to my mother or me, some-times both of us. He doesn't say anything, but we go, and he puts us between him and the window, a hand on the shoulder of whoever is in front of him. We feel him big and warm at our backs, looking over our heads. At first, before he knew I understood what to look for, he used to cup his hand under my chin to lift my eyes in the direction they should go. I can remember twisting to look at *him*, wanting to know why he did this but not using words because he wasn't speaking. (If trying to be like her father could make a boy out of a girl, I'd be a man now. But for all my trying I've just grown more different from him every year.) I remember how he smiled down at me and then nodded toward the sky. My mother always makes a soft little cry, like a moan of delight, and then says something like, "You'd think it was stained glass," or "It's all set in gold." These later years I answer her. "Look! It's rising. It's catching onto the top of Rocky Hills. Now the wind's caught it. It's spreading." But my father never says anything, at least until we all leave the window. Then he always beams down on us proudly, as if he had made this wonderful sight for us, or anyhow as if, except for him, we should certainly have missed it entirely. Usually he glances back at it once, as if to *nail* it, and sometimes he says, "Good *one!*" in the accent of French woodchoppers he knows.

When we got back to 159 Pine, Mrs. Clarke told us the telephone had been ringing for us for an hour, but it wasn't ringing then, and she said what people wanted to tell us was probably what we could read in the evening paper. She gave us the paper, and we practically crawled into the oven to read it. The front-page story, that is. Its headlines:

SCARLET FEVER CLOSES BATES COLLEGE DOORS

MAINE STUDENTS NOT AFFECTED MAY GO HOME

MEN WITH RELATIVES UNDER SIXTEEN HELD

HOCKEY TEAM FORCED TO ABANDON SEASON SCHEDULE

"Does that mean Elwin can go home?" Dot cried. "Are they free? Can he come here?"

We read on:

. . . President Gray returned from Chicago . . . to close the college for an indefinite period . . . Quarantine to be lifted tomorrow noon for women, faculty, and off-campus students . . . No new cases among women students for a week, therefore all may travel by afternoon trains . . . Men students have been examined daily during the week. After examination tomorrow morning all those free of symptoms, living in the State of Maine, except those who have been in contact with positive or suspected cases, may return home, provided there are no children in the family under 16, as soon as permission from the local health officer has been secured. However, they may not travel by railroad train, electric car, or other public carrier. Any student living in the state is permitted to take a friend home with him. Students remaining on campus will continue under quarantine. After the departure of all students, the buildings will be fumigated . . . It is expected that the usual Easter vacation will be abandoned this year. The Winter Carnival . . . given up altogether . . . The hockey team has been obliged to cancel all engagements.

Still shivering, Dot and I stared at each other, uncertain whether this was good or bad news for us, or which of us it would affect.

"It says nothing here about men who have *had* scarlet fever. That must make a difference."

"I don't *think* Elwin has anyone in his family under sixteen."

"Won't they let any Bates man into Massachusetts? Or on *any* train? Will he have to *stay* on campus?"

"Maybe he can go home with Elwin."

"Well — but how will they get there? Do they have to walk?"

Finally the telephone rang, and the news was bad for both of us. Yes, Elwin had to go home, and yes, he had to walk. At least, he had to *start* walking. They all did. And there was no exemption for Wally or anyone else who had had scarlet fever. He was not allowed to cross the Maine boundary. So he was going home with his roommate, Lloyd Hathaway, who lives at Bryant Pond. Lloyd already had the local permission. All the Maine men and those lucky enough to be their guests hoped to set out at noon sharp, to get as far as they could before dark. But presumably after Saturday noon we could all send mail from wherever we were. And of course Elwin and Wally would stop at 159 on their way. This would be before I left to take the train.

"Can you come in?" we asked plaintively, having passed the point of pride.

They didn't see why not. What did Mrs. Clarke think?

We asked Mrs. Clarke. She hesitated. She doubted that they were suppose to go in anywhere in the city, if they were not allowed on public carriers. She knew how we felt, and she wished she could say yes, but she probably shouldn't, especially considering Aunt Minnie's pupils and their parents. But when the boys came, we could talk with them from the porch for *ten* minutes even though there would be two of them.

We told the boys this, and we all knew it was reasonable. On the whole, Dot was quite pleased, but she sympathized with me because I wasn't going to have the train ride with Wally. We had supper, but we weren't very hungry and we were still cold. We hardly moved from the side of the stove except to the telephone. They called twice more, and then they were going to bed, so we did. Dot was soon asleep. (I suppose she was, anyway; she stopped talking.) I didn't go to sleep for quite a while. But in the morning we were both asleep when Mrs. Clarke brought in our breakfast trays at nine o'clock. We didn't let her put up the shades, thinking that if the room stayed dim we might go back to sleep after eating. We didn't want to be up more than an hour before noon. But we didn't go back to sleep. We talked awhile. Then Dot put on her robe and went through the kitchen into the bathroom.

A minute later I heard her shriek, "Mother . . . Mother!"

Mrs. Clarke called from upstairs, "What is it?"

"Come down here quick!"

I listened to Mrs. Clarke's footsteps on the stairs. The hall door opened. She crossed the kitchen.

"What," Dot asked incredulously, "is *the matter with my face?*"

After a minute Mrs. Clarke answered quietly, "I should say, Dorothy, that you have scarlet fever."

And I should say, Dear Diary, that that moment was one of the worst of my life. I had not the slightest doubt that whatever Mrs. Clarke would say was exactly what was so.

I got out of Dot's big bed, put on my sweater (I had not brought a bathrobe for the one night — so long ago — as they are so bulky) over my pajamas, and moved toward the bathroom as a friend of one who is missing must approach a morgue after an accident. I stood in the doorway and gazed upon the scene.

Dot was like a statue before the mirror. Her back

was to me but I saw her face as she was seeing it — a deep brick red and slightly swollen.

"Let me see your tongue," said Mrs. Clarke.

Dot put out her tongue and we all looked at it. It was a shade darker than her face.

Mrs. Clarke put her hand on Dot's forehead.

"Seems a little hot," she said. "How do you feel?"

"Dizzy. That's why I got up."

"Throat sore?"

"A little. Quite. . . . But how *could* I have scarlet fever? I don't even know any of those boys who have it, and besides it was a week yesterday afternoon since I was on campus — or *anywhere.*"

"It does seem strange. You haven't felt any of this until this morning?"

"Well, my throat did feel a little funny when I was out sliding yesterday, but I thought it was just from the cold. Besides, I don't even *know* —"

"Yes, Well, I'll call the doctor. You go back to bed."

I went into her room with her. We looked at each other, stricken.

"She'll never let me go out on the porch," Dot whispered.

"Isn't it awful?"

"But it *can't* be scarlet fever, Sunny!"

"If it is, what will I do?"

"Maybe you ought to leave right now."

"I don't believe your mother would let me."

"No, I guess she wouldn't."

"But if it is scarlet fever, you'll be quarantined *six weeks.* You and — all of us. I *can't* stay here six more weeks, Dot! And if *I* should get it! Why, what would your poor mother do?"

"Oh, isn't it *awful?* I'm getting dizzy again. And my head aches."

Mrs. Clarke came to the door with sheets over her arm.

"He'll be here as soon as he can, his wife says. He's out on calls now but she will try to reach him. I'm going to make up the daybed in the parlor for you. Then you can go in there while I give this room the cleaning it needs in case we're in for a long siege. How do you feel now?"

"My head aches."

"I'd better leave the shades low, then."

Dot turned over and lay face down with her forehead pressed into the pillow.

I took my blouse and skirt into the bathroom where the stockings and undies I washed out every night were hanging. When I was dressed, the clock struck eleven. I thought somebody ought to call the boys. I thought I ought to call my mother. I knew I had to call Ruth. If only the doctor had come!

But I called Ruth anyway, and told her if she didn't see me at the depot it would be because Dot was sick and I couldn't leave until we found out what she had; if it was scarlet fever, I probably couldn't leave for six weeks. My voice didn't sound like my own, even to me. When I stopped talking, there was no answer for a minute. I could hear Ruth breathing.

Then she said, "Good *lord*, Gladys!"

That was the only time I almost burst out crying.

"You going to call your mother?"

"Yes. Just as soon as I know for sure. Before time for my father to leave to meet the train anyway. If I'm not going to be on it."

"I'll tell everybody. We'll all write to you — 159 Pine Street, isn't it?"

"Yes."

"But maybe you'll find out it isn't — that. So even if you miss this train maybe you can come tomorrow."

"Maybe."

"I'll call your mother to find out what she's heard. Gracious, I *hope* —"

"I have to call Wally. He and Elwin were going to stop by here at noon."

"Oh, you poor thing! Is Dot very sick?"

"Not yet. . . . I never telephoned a men's dorm before."

"But this is an emergency."

"It sure is."

It seemed as if I couldn't let Ruth go. But I had to, to call Wally. And when I got him, it seemed as if I couldn't let him go. He kept saying he would tell Elwin and they would call up just before they left and maybe by then the doctor would have come and said all Dot had was tonsilitis or the grippe because how could she have scarlet fever after all this time when she hadn't even *seen* . . .

But, when they called, the doctor was there and had told Mrs. Clarke that Dot did have scarlet fever — she already had some rash — and a quarantine sign would have to be put on both doors. Nobody who was there could go out, and nobody else could come in. The doctor and Mrs. Clarke and Aunt Minnie were all in the parlor with Dot. Elwin was so distraught by not being able to find out exactly how Dot was that he said he wouldn't leave town until he had talked with her mother. But Wally had to go when Lloyd did, and Lloyd was ready to start now. He said he would call me from Bryant Pond that night.

I said faintly, "Be sure to, won't you?"

"Absolutely. Positively."

The doctor and Mrs. Clarke were coming out, so I hung up. After he had given her a long list of instructions about Dorothy's care, and how she would have to order her supplies by telephone and have them left at the door and Mr. Clarke would have to stay away for the duration unless he wanted to be quarantined too, he finally glanced at me and asked, "Who is this?"

I was glad I didn't have to answer, because I had practically forgotten. All I could think of to say was that I was "The Wept of Wish Ton-Wish" — which is a title I have always been fascinated by, though I have never read the book.

Mrs. Clarke was then for the first time that day justified in concentrating on me. She told the doctor my name, how I happened to be there, and where my home was to which I had expected to go that afternoon.

"She hasn't had scarlet fever?"

Mrs. Clarke said I hadn't.

He sighed and shook his head.

"They have been sleeping together?"

"Yes."

"They slept together last night?"

"Yes."

"Then she has been as thoroughly exposed as anyone could possibly be. You are almost certainly going to have two patients instead of one, Mrs. Clarke."

Mrs. Clarke is a wonderful and dauntless woman.

She said, "They will be company for each other." But her eyes looked tired.

"Let me see her throat."

I sent my throat an order: *Throat, be calm!*

He studied my throat. He put a thermometer in my mouth. He pressed his thumb against my chest. He put on his stethoscope and listened to my chest. He took off the stethoscope and read the thermometer.

"Nothing here yet," he told Mrs. Clarke, "but it must be in her system. Luckily she can't extend your quarantine more than a week at most. We'll do what we can to keep their cases from becoming severe. Routine cases will keep your hands full."

"Could I go home," I asked suddenly, "if someone came for me in a car?"

I was thinking of Harold. No, not Harold; he had never had scarlet fever. Maybe Uncle Ezra and Aunt Mollie would come — if they hadn't put up their car for the winter.

The doctor's reply was stern.

"Do you want to take scarlet fever to South Berwick?"

Of course I didn't. Flickering hope subsided.

"No point in keeping them apart, I suppose," said Mrs. Clarke, "until she does come down with it."

"No. Because she certainly will within the week. Until she does, she can be considerable help to you."

I certainly wanted to help Mrs. Clarke.

But — "But what if I *don't?*" I asked. "Even if I don't get it, do I have to stay six weeks?"

"Certainly. Being in contact, you —" He broke off and looked at Mrs. Clarke. "Well, if you have a room on another floor where you want her to stay and which she would not leave for any reason, and which no one else, not even you, would enter, when she had been there a week, if she still had no symptoms, she and her things could be fumigated and she could go. But such an arrangement may be impossible, or altogether undesirable from your point of view. And I am sure it would be effort wasted. The decision must be yours, Mrs. Clarke. I'll be back this evening to see Dorothy. I think you will find that the ice collar will relieve her throat. But remember — leave it on only twenty minutes of each hour."

He left and she went into the parlor to give Dorothy some medicine. I looked at the clock. It was twenty-five minutes of one.

She came out and got ice from the icebox. It was quite a small piece. She put it in a salt bag and began pounding it with the side of a hammer. When it was fine enough she poured it from the bag into a stocking, and went back into the parlor.

It was now quarter of one.

When she came out, she sat down in a chair by the kitchen table and smiled at me faintly.

"Well, now, Gladys," she said, "do you want to try it?"

"Do you want me to?"

"If you want to. If I were you, I think I would. As far as I can see, it would be as easy for me one way as the other. Dorothy is not going to need or be much company for the next few days. She will need care, and I am the one to give that. I shall sleep on the parlor daybed nights. You may have my room at the head of the hall stairs, if you want it. My sister's room is at the end of the hall, so she would hear you if you called her in the night. But you would have to keep your door closed. I would bring your meals as regularly as I could and leave them outside the door. I suppose you would be lonely. But it probably wouldn't be for more than a day or two — and then we would have the consolation of having tried, wouldn't we?"

I nodded. Hope was flickering again.

"You mean you want to do it?"

"Yes. Oh, yes, I *do*. I don't think I have scarlet fever, and I don't want to get it, and you shouldn't have to have me here six more weeks for nothing."

"Then I'll go and get my things out of my room. Before it's time to take off Dorothy's ice collar. Her Aunt Minnie is sitting with her. You'd better call your mother."

I called her. It was my last chance. I told her Papa needn't meet the train as I wouldn't be on it because Dot had scarlet fever, but I was fine. I just had to stay upstairs, separate from her, for a week. Then if

I was all right *next* Saturday — and I was sure I would be — I would be home on *that* train. I said I wouldn't be able to get to the telephone again, but I would ask Mrs. Clarke to call her up Friday night to let her know definitely that I was coming.

My poor mother! She was gasping from the shock. How could Dorothy have caught it? Hadn't I been sleeping with her? How was she? How was her mother? What in the world would we do if I caught it? Mrs. Clarke couldn't be expected to take care of me if I was sick. If I was, she — my mother — ought to come right down. Would there be room in the apartment for her? And she didn't know how she could plan for Grammy. Grace didn't have room for her at Uncle Gran's; maybe Harold and Jennie could take her — but they didn't have any bedroom on the first floor —

I kept saying we needn't cross all those bridges ahead of time, that unless Mrs. Clarke called her up before Friday night she would know no news was good news, that I felt fine and must go now because Mrs. Clarke had my room ready and the sooner I got into it the sooner I could leave it.

The clock struck one.

"But what will you do, dear? Have you any —" her voice was trembling — "any books to read?"

"What did you say? Any books to read?" I repeated.

"My room is full of books," said Mrs. Clarke, passing on her way to take off Dorothy's ice collar. "I left clean sheets on the bed. You can make it up."

"She says the room is full of books, Mama. I'm going up now. Write to me. I still can't mail letters, of course, but you write to me."

"Of course I will, Gladie. And I'll tell everybody —"

"Ruth is going to call you as soon as she gets home. Remind her she promised to write."

"Oh, I'm sure she will."

"I'm going up now. Good-bye, Mama. Give my love to everybody."

"Yes, dear."

"Good-bye."

"Good-bye, dear." She was crying.

I rubbed away tears with my wrist.

Mrs. Clarke came out of the parlor. I asked her if I could say good-bye to Dot. She said Dorothy was asleep.

"When she wakes up, I'll tell her where you are."

"I can write to her, can't I?"

"I don't see why not."

"I'm taking my loose-leaf notebook with me. It has lots of clean pages. I'll keep writing to her and pushing the letters under the door so that you will find them when you bring my tray."

"Don't write anything you don't want me to see." That was going to be hard. "I'll probably have to read them to her until her head and eyes clear up."

It was ten minutes past one.

"Do you want to stay down here for your lunch?"

"No, thanks. I'm not hungry."

Seven days from then I should be about ready to leave to catch the two o'clock train.

"You will be. I'll bring you something a little later."

I took my textbooks, sweater, and the little brown satchel which held my pajamas and toilet things, went out into the hall, and climbed the stairs. I had never climbed them before.

"The first door you come to," Mrs. Clarke called. "On the right as you reach the top. The door is open. Close it after you."

She closed the kitchen door.

Then there was no sound anywhere but that of my own movements. My footsteps on the upper stairs, crossing the upper hall, entering Mr. and Mrs. Clarke's chamber, the chamber door touching its frame, the latch falling into place.

I stood with my back to the door and looked around me.

It was a rather small room, but had two windows, one on each of the two outer walls. It had a double bed in one corner. Along one inner wall there was a bureau, a chair, and a commode. Between the two windows there were full bookcases from floor to ceiling. There was a straw matting on the floor, as there had been on the chamber floors of the village house from which Harold went to war.

The room was quite cool. I put on my sweater. The window shades were drawn three quarters of the way. I snapped them to the rolls. The bureau top had been cleared. I spread my few toilet things on it. I made my bed. Then I lay down on it with the book I had selected from the shelves. It was one which had been a favorite since I was a little girl: *Jane Eyre*. But the copy at home was the size of a magazine and had blue-paper covers. Mrs. Clarke's was cloth-bound.

When Mrs. Clarke brought my lunch I called through the door, "If anyone telephones to me, please tell them why I can't answer, and ask them to write."

She said she would, and after she had gone downstairs I took in my tray. When I had eaten, I put it outside on the hall floor and later she — or Aunt Minnie — came up to get it. At first I could not distinguish between their steps, but I soon learned to. I had no watch, but judged time by when my trays came. Sometimes when the dishes were picked up, I called out to ask the time. We nearly always had some exchange of words when either of them came, but only through the closed door. At night Mrs. Clarke brought me a pail of warm water, and another pail into which I could pour the water when I had used it. I spent some time deciding whether to bathe in it first, and then wash my clothes, or wash the clothes first and then bathe. Sometimes I did it one way and sometimes the other. I didn't like to listen to Mrs. Clarke climbing that long flight of stairs, carrying a half-filled pail, after her day of nursing and housekeeping. But it was wonderful to see and feel warm, soapy water.

On each breakfast tray and each supper tray I left, with my dishes, a letter to Dot in which I first reported my symptoms — or rather, lack of them — in case my mother should call and ask. ("Here I am again, right as rain. No sore throat. No redness on my chest. No dizziness. No headache. It's a wonder you don't hate me! I'm almost ashamed to feel so well when you're so miserable. But you have one consolation. If I do get what you have, you will be over it long before I shall. . . . Do you like *Wuthering Heights* as much as *Jane Eyre?* I know I should but I can't, and this is the third time I've read it. But I know *Jane Eyre* almost by heart. I hope I'm not in love with Mr. Rochester. I don't think it would be normal to love a man like that, do you? But poor Jane! Who else did she ever see?")

It is a real strain on the equilibrium to stay even twenty-four hours completely alone in a closed room with everybody you know waiting to find out whether you are going to get sick or not. I told myself I wasn't. I did all my praying for strength and courage. I didn't bother about trying to be good for I didn't see what else I could be, under these conditions.

I knew I was expected to know at once if I had any symptoms. Sometimes my throat felt sore, but I thought that was from swallowing so much to see if it was; it always felt all right after I ate. Sometimes my chest looked a little red, but after I pressed it with my thumb the color came back quickly (or I thought it was quick); I smiled grimly during this procedure, thinking, "Just as Ruth stopped pressing hers I started pressing mine!" Sometimes my head ached a little, but not if I stopped reading and kept my eyes closed for a while.

I had been in solitary twenty-four hours when I finished my Sunday dinner. . . . Monday I had a scribbled note from Wally, who had mailed it on his way out of the city Saturday. I knew he and Lloyd had been given a ride on a truck almost as soon as they passed the city limits and were at Bryant Pond by three in the afternoon; he told Mrs. Clarke that, by telephone, when he called Saturday evening, and that he would call again Friday evening, and in the meantime would write to me, and to Dot, too, every day . . . Tuesday I got slews of letters, — from Wally; from my mother and Grammy and Harold and Bernice and Aunt Em and Pearl (who lives on the next farm to ours) and her daughter Dorothy who is still going to district school; and from Ruth and Cookie and Ruth Marsh; also a very funny one from Elwin. Wednesday I heard from most of them again, also from several people I used to know at the Baptist church in the village and whom I have kept on writing to even though I hardly ever see them now.

I read my letters over and over, and how I wanted to answer them! But the only person I could write to was Dot. I did do some practice writing on stories and play-scenes, but, knowing I couldn't keep them, I didn't feel much inspired. I like to keep what I write, and especially now I like for Wally to read it, even if it isn't good. But Mrs. Clarke had told me the doctor said all papers and magazines would have to be burned. Books could be fumigated, but papers couldn't. After I heard that, I spent a good deal of time studying my notes and praying to be helped to remember them until I got back to college—if ever.

In a way, the worst part of those days was knowing

that the college was closed and not knowing when it would open. I can't say why. Except that I should think if you were alone on a tiny, barren island which you couldn't get away from and which nobody could get to, it would be a great comfort if you could see the lights of your house on the mainland, or even to know that the only reason you couldn't see them was the fog. But if somehow it were possible for you to see the house at night and it was all dark, and it stayed dark night after night, wouldn't you begin to feel you had no place even to long to go back to, and wouldn't it be impossible even to imagine yourself there, safe and warm and happy and *talking,* the way you used to be? I thought a great deal about home for I knew my parents and Grammy were there, fires were burning in the stove, my mother was lighting the lamp, filling the red sugar bowl, heating irons, playing records, and my father was coming up the shed stairs with the milk. But home was so far way. Bates was close by. I could walk there in fifteen minutes. I could run there in ten. I was only *downtown.* But the doors were locked. The windows were dark. The campus was deserted. In the rooms of the dormitories the cots had been stripped to their thin, bumpy mattresses, the desks were all neat, the closets were half-empty, no bells were ringing, there was no running in the halls and no splashing in the bathrooms. And it was *not* vacation time!

Even if I could go there, Bates could not take me in.

I tried not to think about it.

It was Thursday . . . It was Friday . . . It was

really Friday . . . It was Friday night and when Mrs. Clarke brought up the water she told me through the door that my mother had called and said my father would meet the train the next afternoon; also that Wally had called and said he would leave Bryant Pond for East Sumner by way of Lewiston the next day and would be at the depot to ride into Portland with me. And she told me what must be done the next morning before I could go.

It sounded like a beautiful dream. But I was still waiting. I took nothing for granted. A week ago that night I was to have taken the train with Wally the next day, on my way home. And *that* Saturday morning Dot had called: "Mother! . . . What's the *matter with my face?"*

I prayed for strength, and I prayed for courage.

That night I left all my clothes outside the door, except the pajamas I was wearing; also my other few possessions, even my toothbrush. When I took in my breakfast tray the next morning they were gone.

A little later Mrs. Clarke called, "It's nine o'clock. You may come down now, and bring your tray."

It was a very strange feeling to go through the door. My knees buckled as I went down the stairs. I knocked on the kitchen door but there was no answer. After a minute I opened it, went in and put my tray on the counter by the sink. I felt guilty, as if I were breaking and entering, for there was no one in the room and all its doors were closed.

I knew which door I was supposed to open. It was the bathroom door. I opened it, and closed it behind me.

There was a rosy glow from some sort of lamp or little stove in the semi-darkness, and from it came an odor of disinfectant which was almost overpowering. My clothes and books were draped and laid out open around it. I supposed it had been burning all night. My toothbrush was soaking in a pan of solution, my hairbrush and comb in another. I had been told to rinse and use the toothbrush and then put it back into the solution; I did so. Next, I washed my hair with soap the Health Department had provided, drying it as well as I could, then braiding it and pinning the braids around my head. By then I was so dizzy I could scarcely see, my throat hurt, and I was red all over. But I drew water in the tub, poured in the contents of the bottle on its rim, got in, scrubbed with the Health Department soap, got out, dried myself, and put on my clothes.

Finally, I gathered up all that belonged to me and staggered out into the kitchen — *the* most evil-smelling collection of flesh, rags, bones, hair, books, and brushes that a human being could become!

I was almost ready to give up then. I wanted to drop everything I was carrying, fall into the rocking-chair by the window, have Mrs. Clarke come and see how sick I was and put me to bed beside Dot to stay for at least six weeks and maybe forever. It was almost certainly going to come to that in an hour or two when the doctor examined me, so why make the awful effort to climb those stairs? But no, I told myself; you may be down but you're not out—yet.

I left the kitchen. I clutched the railing and pulled myself up the stairs, having rather more strength in my arms than in my legs. I got back into the room, dropped my burden on the bed, unbraided and shook out my hair, and sat down in front of the sunny window.

I don't think I was more than half-conscious. I know I didn't even try to read. The smell was absolutely revolting. I didn't dare to open a window on all that wet hair. If I had, I think the smell would have cast a pall over both the Twin Cities. I just sat there, my heart going like a triphammer—whatever that is.

I was sitting there when the doctor came upstairs and knocked at the door.

I said, "Come in."

I must have looked like the Witch of Endor. I know I smelled like her vilest brew.

He said cheerfully, "Well, how do you feel this morning?"

I told him honestly, "I don't know. All I can think of is how I smell."

He laughed.

"Our stuff not only kills old germs," he said. "It scares newcomers away."

He looked at my chest. He listened to it. He looked at my throat. He took my temperature.

Then he looked at me, and I looked at him.

What was he going to say?

My poor child, you not only have scarlet fever well advanced. It is complicated by the black plague, and . . .

He said, "Well, you have certainly surprised *me.* Either you had scarlet fever in infancy or you are immune. You are a very lucky girl. Looks as if the worst is over for Mrs. Clarke. Dorothy's temperature is normal this morning, and she is beginning to peel."

He tucked his stethoscope, his little flat stick, and his little thermometer into his black satchel, and went out, leaving the door open.

I sat watching him go. I felt numb.

He glanced back from the head of the stairs and smiled.

"Guess you'll be glad to see your folks tonight. Likely they'll be glad to see you, too."

He went on down the stairs.

I was dismissed! I was going home!

I got up slowly and felt of my hair. It was dry. I began brushing it out. I thought I would *never* get it clear of tangles. I stood in front of the bureau pushing waves into the top, retangling the sides to make puffs, putting pins into the back coil for the first time in a week.

I used up some of the small stock of courage I had left to look into the mirror. How I looked was scared-to-death.

How do people who have been imprisoned for years dare to leave the place where they have been kept? I had been under guard only two weeks, in solitary confinement only one week, and it seemed to me I *could not* step out into the street alone, face strangers, go up to a ticket window, get on a train. The distance between me and home looked absolutely uncrossable, like a vast desert without roads.

I sat on the bed, pushing my books and toilet things into my bag, stuffing into my coat pocket the fumigated bills my mother had sent in a letter, and I thought, "I have to stay with this bed, these two windows, this bureau and commode and chair and straw matting. I *can't* go where people are! What will they think?"

Then, for the first time that day, I remembered.

People! *People?* . . . If I ever got to the depot, there would be Wally to ride into Portland with me. With this fumigated, prison-pale, oddly attired, half-witted menace to society!

I wanted to cry. But I hadn't before when I wanted to, and now I couldn't.

"Shall I bring you some lunch?" called Mrs. Clarke from the kitchen door.

"No, thank you. I'm not hungry. I'm almost ready to leave. I'm — writing a letter to Dot."

I did write a short letter to Dot, and a longer one to Mrs. Clarke thanking her for all her kindness to me at such a difficult time, promising to write again as soon as I got home. I took my sheet off the bed, folded the blankets, and put the letters on the pile of blankets.

Then I put on my reeking cap and jacket and gloves and overshoes, picked up my bag, went down the stairs, passed the kitchen door and went down another flight of stairs to the sidewalk. I don't know how I ever did it, but I did. There I stopped and looked up at the kitchen windows. Mrs. Clarke was there and waved and smiled and nodded encouragingly at me. I'll never forget that. I'll always love her for it.

I waved back, even blew her a kiss, and started on down the street.

Everyone I met looked at me curiously — or I thought they did. But it would be quite a long walk to the depot and there was a good wind blowing. I told myself most of the smell might go, quickly, out here.

I turned the first corner — and there was Wally!

"Well, hello!" he said. "I took a chance you would come this way. Thought Mrs. Clarke might not approve of a stage-door Johnny. Let me take your bag. So you fooled them all, didn't you? I knew you would. How does it feel to be back in circulation?"

And suddenly, right that minute, everything began to be glorious. Glorious, and miraculous, and funny. There he was, dressed to preach a sermon, and there was fumigated me in campus clothes, sauntering together along Lisbon Street in February with the college closed down. He was asking me if I was hungry and all of a sudden I was ravenous, but neither of us was sure that I was supposed to go into a restaurant; so I waited outside while he went in and brought out sandwiches and cup cakes wrapped in wax paper. While he was gone I saw a little gilt box being blown along the street and it looked to me as if it were dancing. We went on to the depot, and it smelled the way depots do and *that* was a change. It was still quite a while to traintime, so we sat in a corner and ate our sandwiches and cupcakes, talking as fast as we could because there was so *much* to tell and we had been able to get only a fraction of it into telephone calls

2

4

and letters. He was fascinated to hear all I could tell him about my reactions to a week of being completely alone, and said he hoped I would write it down before I forgot it, so I have tried to, as much as I could in a reasonable space. All of it would make a book! I never knew anyone who was so alertly interested as he is in the feelings and thoughts other people have. He makes them seem so *important,* and you feel as if you are living it all over again when you tell it to him, and as if he is living it with you.

Just before traintime he bought our tickets — but I made him use my money for mine; I don't think a girl should let a man pay for anything she does unless he invited her to do it.

I guess he would be interested to hear if I could and would tell how it felt to me to be sitting beside him on the train, and how it seemed to me when we started that it was a journey which wouldn't end, and what a shock it was when the conductor called "Portland! Portland!" and I knew he had to get off while I went on alone, not knowing when I would see him again; but I can't, and I wouldn't if I could. Some things are *really* "beyond words" (which we say at college of other people's evening gowns, meaning they're gorgeous, other people's hats, meaning they're ghastly, professor's reading assignments, meaning they're long, and a game, meaning we were behind all the way and came up to win in the last minute of play).

But I will say that I found I was still happy after he left. I didn't feel alone even though I had the whole seat to myself. I sort of curled up, thought of all that had happened in the first six weeks of 1923 and how lucky I was, and I'm sure I must have been smiling, which probably looked pretty silly if anyone noticed.

Now I have been at home three days and everything is still glorious. I had a long, long letter from him today. He is staying on at East Sumner, with some wonderful friends, the Eastman family. He says he wants me to meet them someday.

Come to think of it, it is quite a while since I "met" anybody, or even saw, near to, anyone I knew except him and my parents and Grammy. Everybody around calls me up since I came home, but they don't come in or ask me to their houses. Ruth and I talk every day and she says it is the same with her. She says she guesses they think there is a chance we are carriers.

"Oh, well," we say, "any day now we'll be back on campus with the rest of the Scarlet Fever Marys and Scarlet Fever Joes. Finishing those exams, no doubt. Can you remember *anything?*"

We can't. So we go skating. Or we read letters and write letters, write letters and read letters. At least, I did. Until I began to have an uneasy feeling that it was safer to go skating. Or to write for my own eyes only. A pen does something to me. I may have said more than I meant to say to him. I am almost sure I was at least implying quite a bit more than I would if he and I were together. I mean, I am more reserved in person than I am on paper. Luckily, what I write is honest — more honest, actually, than the way I act. But in some cases it is best not to tell the whole truth. And I certainly didn't! The question is, how *much* of the truth did I tell him?

$\mathscr{I}$ T is over. My whole sophomore year is over. It is already difficult for me to remember what my world was like — what *I* was like — when it began. Even the letters I have here, written to my mother during the last three months, look to me as if someone else had written them. Someone years younger than I.

I went back to college on a Monday.

Tuesday morning I wrote home:

"It did seem so good to see everybody last night, tired as I was. . . . But I suppose *you* want to know about Portland! Well, he was there. At first we didn't get a seat together on the Lewiston train. Then we did. The train took about an hour and a half to come in, and we were a little over half an hour walking up. He is coming over tonight if he can, but he had quite a cold and may not be able to. He wasn't in chapel this morning. More later!"

Wednesday night

"It has really begun! I rejoice every move I make! Sitting down at a table in the dining room, waking up in my own bed in the morning, straightening up the closet, hearing the old tinpanny piano, answering the telephone, doing *anything* that is normal again makes me beam and marvel! I can't even come into the dorm without getting a real, honest-to-goodness thrill! . . . No studying yet. Three classes tomorrow, but no assignments for them. . . . Carnival begins tomorrow afternoon and lasts afternoons and evenings the rest of the week. . . . I went away out into the country with Wally this afternoon. We were walking from a little before two until a little after five."

Thursday night

"It has happened. Somehow I guess I knew it would. Maybe it wouldn't have yet except for my next-to-the-last letter to him. . . . But I told you I would make no promises until you know him, and I meant it. He has agreed that there won't be another talk of this kind for a month anyway. How soon do you think I can bring him home?"

Saturday morning

"Cookie won the mile snowshoe race for the women yesterday afternoon. We're all so proud of her. Webster came up from Bowdoin to take her to the Carnival Hop last night and Ted came to take Ruth. Ruth hadn't known Ted was coming. He called up in the afternoon. The proctor said there was a call for Ruth and she was out, so I answered.

" 'Hello. You were calling Ruth?' "

"A minute's silence, and then, 'I wish to speak to *Miss Nutter,* please!' "

" 'She isn't here right now. Is this Ted?' "

"Another minute's silence, and, 'This is Ted Miller, yes.' "

" 'Indeed! Well, this is Gladys Hasty, yes. Will your honor condescend to leave a message with me for *Miss Nutter?*' "

" 'Oh! This is Gladys? Why, sure. Where *is* Ruth?' "

" 'At the carnival. I just left. She wasn't as cold as I was. She'll probably be there another hour. Come up and you can find her, maybe.' "

" 'Where are the events?' "

" 'The athletic field. Today.' "

" 'Okay. I'll come up. If I don't find her, I'll come over and see you.' "

" 'What fun! I love threesomes!' "

"Thank goodness, he found her. I was listening to *The Ancient Mariner* being recited to me while I sewed. Honestly, Wally knows every word of it by heart! I'm making a dress I chopped out last night. Didn't even have a pattern! . . . Your letter has just come. Don't for goodness' sake, worry about diphtheria. There are only two cases, both in Parker Hall, and both are nearly over it. Nobody here thinks of it. It is of no account at all."

French class (cut)

"Such a storm! And day before yesterday I thought April had come a month ahead of time! It is a perfectly wretched day, the snow just *whistling* through the air. La-La must have been scared. He put on his coat and sailed home right after chapel, saying we would have the same lesson next time. . . . Last night we had our Spofford sleighride. Left Rand Hall at 5:30 in a long, low hayrack half full of hay with dozens of big blankets, drawn by two big horses. Dean Niles and Birdie were the chaperones. We were out two hours, and at 7:30 arrived back at our president's house where his parents — Prof. and Mrs. Purinton — had the dinner table set for all fifteen of us. Steak, baked potatoes, peas, molded salad, hot apple pie and ice cream, and coffee with the after-dinner speeches. But those speeches! ! ! Especially Alice Jessamine's! It was all about Wally and me, and I appeared to be the *only* person at the table who didn't thoroughly enjoy it! . . . Later we discussed the two original plays we are to give April 20. They are a one-act by Teddy Barentzen and a two-act by Erwin Canham and Ken Conner. . . . Mrs. Purinton had red candles with red shades for the table, and masses of red carnations between. She gave me the flowers to take down and leave on Dot's doorstep, but Wally said he would take them when he went downtown to tend furnaces this morning. He does that every morning before breakfast, you know. . . . I hear grades for last semester are coming out soon. I don't like to think about it. I can't imagine what mine will be."

Psychology class
(*Not a cut — just a broad-shouldered fellow in front*)
"I suppose you are in receipt of my grades. Isn't it

great? The best yet — and in the very semester when I was having the best times I ever had in my life, too! . . . Ruth got an A in French — the only A in the class, I believe. Of course Wally had four A's. But he did get one B. Only in the course he has to cut every Monday morning, though. Don't remonstrate with me on my late hours. I'd never keep them if I didn't have to, because Wally can always tell the next day and then I take more remonstrances than you could think of in a week. Thanks, Mother, for the advice, but I can't take it."

Sunday afternoon

"It seemed so good to talk with you last night! I knew it must be the storms which had held up your letter, so I wasn't really worried, but I did *so* want to hear your voice. It was worth it, wasn't it? . . . I'm enclosing a bit of the cloth I made my dress of. It is very full and long-waisted with an elastic at the waist and a narrow ribbon sash. The slits at the neck and tops of the sleeves are drawn together with bows of the same ribbon. The sleeves are gathered to puff, and bound. When I told you last night that the girls said my dress was a peach and even Mr. Fennelly liked it, I was thinking that if I said it that way nobody on the line would suspect 'Mr. Fennelly' was a student. Actually they added, 'Or so we should judge by the frequency of his appearances.' But I didn't think it best to add that over the wire! . . . Now away to lighter things! If you still think of those diphtheria cases, don't, for that scare is all over. One of the men who had it is back at classes, and the

other two are nearly well. You might concern yourself now — if you must concern yourself — with the
one case of mumps and the two of measles which
have lately appeared in our midst. Isn't it *too* funny?
Prexy must be looking forward hopefully to the days
when his brood shall have successfully passed through
all their little ailments!"

Wednesday

"I hadn't any idea you were sending food so didn't
hurry to open my laundry case until Ruth urged me
to look and 'make sure.' The pie was divine. We ate
it all last night, and there are only a few cookies left.
. . . Mother, I don't *want* to wait until June before
I bring Wally home! I need to know how you like
each other. The changes you are going to make in
the house this spring will be very nice, no doubt, but
I want him to see it the way it has always been. . . .
Poor Dot is so disgusted! She is completely well now,
but the health officer is too busy to come to examine
her and fumigate. She has stood confinement just
about as long as she can, I judge from our telephone
conversations."

Friday

"Another snowstorm! I suppose this means that I
don't get any mail for another week or so. And just
yesterday when we went to walk the sun and winds
were summery over all the snow, the sky was the blu-
est of blues, and Wally said, 'A few more days of
this, and it's good-bye to the snow, hello to the fields
and the riverbank!' But before we can say 'Good-
bye' to snow, we get more to say 'Hello' to! Mother,

do you really want me to get a new suit and hat?
You said so when I was home but I want to be sure
before I actually go shopping. Of course I want them.
Easter is two weeks from this coming Sunday."

Monday

"Rain for a change! You ought to save my last
few letters as an official report on March weather in
1923. . . . We had the best time Friday night! Eleanor had asked the proctors for the reception room, to
entertain Allen in, so — with great trepidation — I
asked Dean Niles if I might use her private sitting
room. She said, 'Why, yes, Gladys, I'd be glad to
have you. If you would like to build a fire in the fireplace, get some wood downstairs.' Of course I was
delighted. Ruth, Eleanor, and I built a wonderful
fire, and when Nellie Mae came in to see it she looked
all around the room in a mysterious way and then
whispered to me, 'I prophesy that this is going to be a
memorable evening.' The boys came together and at
first we all sat around the fire and toasted marshmallows. Then the others went into the next room to
play cards, and Wally and I sat on before the fire that
was now a bed of glowing coals, and talked and talked
and talked. I *must* bring him home soon, Mother!"

Wednesday

"A friend of Wally's died in Farmington Falls, and
Wally had to go to assist at the service today. This
friend was about his age and had been married only
two years. Last night was the first time I have gone to
Spofford when Wally didn't, and Gavie walked home

with me — just to talk about my writing. He wants
me to put more and *more* and *more* Maine into it,
and leave out everything else. He certainly is a genius
— in writing, in criticism, in acting, in singing, in
aesthetic dancing. I've told you, haven't I, that he is
Birdie's assistant and corrects my English papers? So
he sees all the writing I do, both in my two English
courses and for Spofford. . . . The Eastmans of East
Sumner have asked Wally and me to come up there
for a weekend the first of May. I received my invita-
tion today. They have also invited Mr. and Mrs. Arthur Purinton (you know he was my freshman English
instructor), and they will be our chaperones; we can
ride up with them in their car. Won't it be fun? . . .
Do you suppose you can have us some weekend before
that?"

March 24

"You remember my writing you b.s.f. (that's 'before scarlet fever') that Ruth, Eleanor, and I were
three of twelve chosen to try out for the Sophomore
Women's Prize Debate, and I didn't want to? Well,
Fate was with me. When the day for the tryout came
I had such a cold that I honestly couldn't speak a
word! Ruth and Eleanor were among the six selected
and they are assigned to the same team. I'm so
pleased for them — and glad I don't have to do it.
Cookie and I are going downtown this afternoon to
look at spring hats. . . ."

Much, of course, was not getting into my letters
home.

The front page of the *Bates Student* on March 23 had these headlines:

WOODCOCK'S RADIO COURSE VERY POPULAR; CLASS
HELD ON TUESDAY AND THURSDAY

UNCLE JOHNNY'S BOOK COLLECTION OPEN TO STU-
DENTS; 3000 VOLUMES PRESENTED TO COLLEGE

LET'S BOOST SWIMMING AS A BATES SPORT

OUR LITTLE THEATER MOVEMENT

. . . Bates is the pioneer college in the State of Maine in establishing a little theater group — the members of which are encouraged to write, produce, and act in their own plays. . . . As an organization of students interested in the newer forms of the drama, the English 4A Players are the outgrowth of a class in the writing and appreciation of drama given by Professor A. Craig Baird. Bates may well feel that she is making one more contribution to the intellectual and moral life of the community, the State, and the nation."

Is my dream of last summer beginning to come true?

The lead editorial of that issue quoted from one in the *New York Herald:*

There are things a small college can give that a larger institution cannot. A more intimate contact between students and faculty is possible, and when a college can command the services of men of high character and ability that contact is a privilege which youth later estimates at its true value.

March 25

"Did I tell you that everybody here is playing 'Mr. Gallagher and Mr. Shean' and 'The Parade of the Wooden Soldiers'? . . . Cookie and I did go shopping. I bought a coat, a hat, and a dress! The first two you said I could have, you know, and the dress I paid for out of my second check from the English Dept. The hat is brown Milan with brown ribbon streamers on the side, a ribbon medallion on the crown, and a knot of vari-colored flowers. The coat is dark brown, too, with a blouse back and quite a lot of embroidery, fastens low in the front with big dark pearl buttons. The dress is dark brown French serge, made with the new tight, long waist, and the full circular skirt longer at the sides, and a bright bead girdle. I just love them all and can hardly wait for you to see them! By the way, how soon are you going to invite us up? I'll tell him the house is to undergo repairs before summer. For goodness' sake — he won't even *see* the house!"

Wednesday

"I went shopping again Monday. Bought some brown oxfords with dark stitching, good brown silk stockings, and brown silk knickers to wear in place of an underskirt. My checking account still has a balance of $85 but my checkbook is empty. Please ask Papa to get me another."

Friday

"Oh, mother, you should have seen me when I opened your letter at the beginning of Latin class.

When I saw 'the 18*th*' I almost sprang right out of my seat. I must have looked as if I had just been left a fortune, for Dot Clarke who sits near me gasped, 'What in the world . . . ?' But I didn't tell her. I'm not going to tell anybody but Ruth until the last minute. It makes me so happy that you are willing to have us, and that soon! And so long — Wednesday night until Monday morning! Of course I showed Wally the first page of your letter as soon as I could and he said, 'Your mother's wonderful, isn't she?' And I said, 'Oh, wait until you know *how* wonderful!' You needn't worry about what we'll *do*. We have more planned already than we'll ever have time for. . . . Don't forget to tell Papa I need a checkbook. . . . You know that gold Phi Beta Kappa key that Jennie has? Well, Wally is going to have one, too. It was announced at chapel yesterday. I'm so proud! . . . Something rather embarrassing happened this morning. Prof. Baird asked several of us to give talks on subjects we had just written essays on. When I finished mine, he said to the class, 'Miss Hasty's sentence structure and choice of words was remarkable for an extemporaneous speech. It would almost seem that she had memorized her essay, but of course that was impossible. She didn't even know she was to be asked to give a speech on it.' But it *was* memorized. That is, I remember what I have written. After I have written anything as well as I can, I can't think of any other way to say it. I felt as if I should tell him so, but I didn't because I really don't know how to explain it. Should I have tried?"

Sunday

"After church today, where do you suppose I had my Easter dinner? At the Royal. Mrs. Nutter sent Ruth five dollars to take herself and four friends to dinner. Ruth invited Ruth Marsh, Eleanor, Dott Hoyt and me. (Cookie is spending the weekend off-campus.) We had oxtail soup, turkey with dressing, mashed potatoes, peas, cranberry jelly, celery, olives, hot rolls, strawberry ice cream and sponge cake. Then we came home and ate chocolates! Ruth's father sent her a box and her grandfather sent her another, and her mother sent her a huge bunch of red, pink, and white carnations. . . . Mother, dear, *don't* worry about the wallpaper, for Wally won't know whether it is one or ten years old! By the way, what does Papa say about our plans? I hope he treats the idea with dignity. It would be just like him to take it as a joke! Have you impressed on him that Wally is almost twenty-six years old, a veteran of the World War, the managing editor of the college paper, the highest-ranking man in his class, and a self-made man at that? And *is* he impressed? I am, anyhow!"

Wednesday

"Gym Meet last night, and we sophomores won. (We won last year as freshmen, too.) Each girl chosen to participate was entitled to a ticket for a friend. I hadn't any idea that Wally would want to come. I'd always thought the men who came did it from a sense of duty and were bored stiff. But yesterday afternoon he asked rather disconsolately why I didn't want him to come. So I provided him with a ticket, he came with the other fellows, spent two hours and a half in the balcony watching us perform, had a ten-minute walk home with me (I was so tired I could hardly stand up) and claimed he had enjoyed himself. . . . I'm so glad you are enjoying the plans for the middle of the month. I hoped that was the way it would be. I think it's going to be fun; I'm the only one who doesn't have to get acquainted with somebody; I can just sit back and watch the rest of you! I say that, but I'll be heartbroken if you don't all like each other. You will, though. None of you can help it."

Friday

"Just think — two weeks from now! . . . Ruth has gone home for the weekend. Ted is going to meet her in Portland when she comes back."

Sunday

"Such a melee as I'm writing in! Practically everyone in the house is dieting to reduce, and it is a continuous series of 'Gee, I'm so hungry!' . . . 'Hey, what did you eat this noon?' . . . 'May I just *smell* that hot chocolate?' . . . 'Now, let's do our exercises.' . . . 'Oh, joy — oh, bliss — oh, rapture! I've lost a tenth of a pound!' . . . 'When do we start hiking?' . . . 'Look, can you see I'm a little thinner?' . . . 'How much did you weigh today?' . . . 'No use; I can't stand it; I have to eat!' . . . At times it is funny. Occasionally it is pitiable. Most of the time it is just plain ridiculous. . . . You remember my speaking of Freddie Knapp, our Latin professor, don't you? Dear, romantic old Freddie with the adorable little impediment in his speech? He has just passed his fiftieth birthday and is still an ardent devotee of his wife and their only child, a daughter, Rachel, who was graduated from here two years ago and married the day after her Commencement. Well, two or three weeks ago Mrs. Knapp went out to New York to visit Rachel, leaving Freddie alone and very lonely, as he frankly admits. But a few mornings ago he came snail-like across campus, bent over a gnarly cane and greeting everyone with a cracked 'Good morning.' It was his unique way of announcing that he is a grandfather! And, boy, is he proud! Yesterday in class we were translating something about a nearest relative, and he beamed and said: 'Speaking of a nearest relative necessarily makes a man think of his *newest* relative! Let me assure you now that, *if I can live until next Saturday,* you will get a cut!' So I suppose Freddie will then be on his way out to New York to beam on his descendants, and to bring his adored little wife safely back to Lewiston. They say Rachel has named her baby Crete for the classmate who was her closest friend here. It is a lovely gesture, and fine if your best friend has a distinguished name like Crete, but Ruth and I have warned each other that *we* shall not name any daughters for each other. We agree that our names should not outlast our generation. They have been all too frequent in this one! . . . I must tell you that Wally may be teaching in Illinois next fall. Even without graduate work, he is being considered for a position as head of the Argumentation and Public Speaking Department at James Milliken University in Decatur. Professor Baird has recommended him. James Milliken has 1500 students (three times the size of Bates) and the starting salary would be $1600. . . ."

Tuesday

"I have just been talking with you and feel much better now that you have been reassured about that smallpox case. I was sure you would hear of it, because Mrs. Nutter did. She has just called up for the second time today to urge Ruth to come right back home. Of course Ruth thinks that is foolish, but I know it worries her that her mother feels that way. . . . The past two days have been so busy I couldn't write. Yesterday I had play rehearsals whenever I wasn't in class or at meals, until 10:00 P.M., and then all my studying to do. Today I was up early to do a little more polishing for a written, went to class, saw Wally for an hour, had another class, went to lunch, came home to study — but the telephone was ringing constantly (parents calling up about the smallpox scare), and there were committee meetings and more rehearsals. Besides, I had to stand in line in the gym for vaccination — know it won't take, but the precaution was compulsory — went to dinner, and then another play rehearsal. . . . Now you won't worry about that one case of smallpox, will you? As I told you, it is extremely light and the doctors say there is practically no danger of its spreading now that they've completed their flurry of vaccinations . . ."

Sunday

"Only three more days! We went to the Royal for supper tonight and to church afterward. All we talked about was 'going home.' He says he looks forward to it more than he has to anything since he can remember. He even knows the number of *hours* before we go! He is holding Sunday services now in a church in Freeport. At his second service (today) the congregation was increased by 50 per cent. The people are giving him practically a unanimous call to come there in June as their full-time pastor, but he insists it is not his work. I'm sure he is going to be a completely dedicated teacher. . . . See you soon, *soon,* SOON!"

Yes, much was left out of these letters home. They mention cuts but not classes, grades but not courses, though English 4A with Professor Baird and European History with Professor Gould were the most enjoyable and the most challenging I have ever had, and I loved reading Horace with Freddie. They sound as if sophomore girls in a college dormitory think of little but food, clothes, and romance when the fact is that most of us are very serious, conscientious about our responsibilities, study hard, spend hours every day on outside reading in the library, share what we learn with those majoring in other fields, worry a good deal about the philosophies of Spinoza, Nietzsche, and John Stuart Mill, the educational theories of Dewey, the economic and political ideas of Marx, and try to answer them with quota-

tions from the Bible, with the evidence of our own
school experience, with the facts of American history, and, in general, with the principles by which
our parents have lived and brought us up. There are
references, again and again, to the number of hours
Wally and I talked, but they do not say what we
talked about. He says he is an Emersonian, and he
usually took a collection of the *Essays* in his pocket
when we went for a walk. But there is not time during a college year to write home what you have
learned, nor is there time during vacations to put it
into a journal. Even if there were time, you would
not know how to organize it. You are not sure even of
what you have, much less of what you will choose to
keep and what you will throw away. You feel certain only that you are making the acquaintance of a
collection of what men and women before you, singly
or in groups of varying sizes, have felt were of great
value, and that gradually you will be able to sort it all
out and to recognize easily, as you sort, what you will
cherish, what you will live by, what belongs to you
— and what you will oppose for the rest of your days.

At the same time that you are learning what
men and women have thought in the past, you are
acquiring skills, you are living, and you are growing
older. You would be doing the last three, at our
age, and doing them all the time, if you were not
in college. In college you are also doing them all
the time, plus studying and reporting the results
of your study the greater part of every day. It is all
exciting. It is very strenuous. It leaves less and less
time for sleep, particularly if one has thinking he

wants and needs to do which is intensely personal. And I did a great deal of that between mid-February and mid-April, though there is little mention of it in my letters.

I thought I had to decide whether or not what I felt for Wallace Fennelly was love.

I spent many hours comparing it with the way I had felt about Chase, Ted, and the two Freds; the way I had felt about Henry and about Paul; the way I felt about Ruth; the way I felt about various members of my family. The conclusion in every case was, "Different." But then the way I felt about each of the others was different, too. Was what I felt for him *more* than what I felt for any of the others? It was certainly far more than I felt or had ever felt for Ted, Chase, either of the Freds, Henry, or Paul — but was that enough? I could not say that I "loved" him more than I loved my parents or Harold, or Ruth who was my college family. There has never been any question in my mind but that I belonged with them, to them. He was a Newcomer, an Outsider; and if I loved him I would, in a sense, have to leave them. But there he was!

Away from him, I tried to analyze exactly how I felt when I was with him, but this was difficult to do. I was never sure that I was doing it accurately; perhaps my imagination was leading me astray. I only knew that I wanted to see him again as soon as I could, that when I did I would not want to leave him, and, when I had, the whole circle of vain attempts at analysis and the longing to see him would begin again. Was this love? If so, why wasn't

mine like his? I wanted to be as sure as he was. Why
wasn't I? Was this a typical difference between a
man and a woman? I listened to other girls talk,
and the answer seemed to be No. I hid in the library
stacks and read Russian novels, French plays, Elizabeth Barrett Browning, the love letters of famous
women; the answer still seemed to be No. Man or
woman, if you were in love, you knew it. But how did
you? When you felt something brand-new to you,
how did you know what name should be given to
the feeling? Or that the feeling — whatever it was —
would last? I knew that if it was love it would last,
and if it wasn't it wouldn't. But also that if you wait
a lifetime to *find out* if it lasted you are a silly
woman, for it didn't.

Increasingly, I felt that I must see my mother.
Not to ask for help in making my decision (she had
already written to the effect that if I had any doubt
about being in love I wasn't, and that I must not
try to convince myself that I was; almost certainly
I was too young — she had been twenty-two before
she cared for anyone in that way; and she had advised me not to associate so exclusively with one
friend but to give more time to cultivating the
friendship of several; to which last I had replied,
"Thanks, Mother, for your advice, but I can't take
it"). But just to see her . . . Especially to see her
with my father. For they not only love each other.
They are lovers; and this I have known as long as I
can remember.

Increasingly, also, I felt Wally must be there with
me. This seemed an entirely separate necessity, and

I judged it to be a practical one, a matter of ethics.
I must know whether my parents liked him. If I came
to the considered conclusion that what I was was "in
love," of course I would marry him anyway; but if I
were to promise to marry a man my parents did not
like, I should know that I was doing so.

Thus on Wednesday, April 18, the day before Pa-
triot's Day, and with plans to cut our Saturday and
Monday classes, we left the campus and took an
afternoon train for home.

It was dusk when we came down the train steps at
Salmon Falls. A spring dusk, but chilly. My father
stood on the platform, smoking a cigar. He was
wearing a brown checked topcoat I had never seen
before, and a brown felt hat tipped a little over one
eye. It was a new hat worn as he had worn his old
one. I ran to him as I always had. He hugged and
kissed me, and then I heard him say over my head,
"You're Wallace Fennelly, I guess. Glad to see you.
We'll get these bags into the back of the wagon.
Horse blanket there to cover them over and keep
off any mud that splashes. Road's pretty soft in
places."

I had turned in time to see their handclasp, hear
Wally say, "How do you do, Mr. Hasty," see warmth
exchanged between blue eyes and brown.

Then my father picked up a valise — it wasn't
mine — and we went toward where Pony waited in
the shadows. I talked to Pony and stroked his nose
while the bags were settled. Then Wally came to
speak to him, and he and my father talked about the

kind of horse that Pony is — a square-built Western horse, dappled gray and brown, with short, thick legs, so-many hands high and weighing so-many hundred pounds.

"Well," my father said, "we'd better be getting along to where the woodbine twineth. It's a bit of a fur piece, as Uncle Columby used to say, and supper'll be ready at the end of it."

I climbed into the wagon and Wally followed. My father climbed in on the other side of me and picked up the reins from the dashboard.

As we rode down the hill toward the bridge my father was explaining to Wally that the Salmon Falls River is the boundary line between New Hampshire and Maine, that when we had crossed the bridge we were back in "the Grand Old State, as Uncle Joe Brown always used to say when he got back to his old stamping-ground from foreign ports or from setting up steam shovels in Texas," and that in the old days our folks had been surveyors and gone up this river to record its course before there was any State of Maine and we were part of the Commonwealth of Massachusetts.

Wally said his father had been a surveyor, too, and had worked out in Michigan when it was mostly a wilderness and he had both wolves and wild Indians to contend with. But after he was married he had stayed in Massachusetts. Worked on the railroad until he lost his arm, coupling cars. After that he was one of the men in charge of building the Hoosac Tunnel & Wilmington narrow-gauge railroad.

"Built railroads, your father did?" my father asked. "Shouldn't wonder if he and Uncle Joe met up somewhere along the way."

We had come through the village, under the street lights, past the brick-fronted stores and the Jewett House. Now Pony was plodding up Portland Street. Cars passed us, and we met some, but Pony stolidly held his ground. He was headed home. Back where the woodbine twineth.

I was in the middle of the wagon seat as I had always been when we were three; protected on both sides.

Where the woodbine twineth . . .

My father likes that phrase and uses it often, in various ways. I think it was a line of a song. I remember his saying one day when I was a child and had been searching the yard a long time for a lost toy — perhaps a marble or a doll's-size saucer — "I guess it's gone where the woodbine twineth. Never mind. It'll turn up again someday." After that, for quite a while, whenever I crossed the porch to the kitchen door, I looked up at the woodbine which clung to the roof and ran down to wind itself around the posts, trying to spy out my toy held safe and snug in the tiny, strong tendrils which were its thousand hands.

But "where the woodbine twineth" is also his name for home. And that was where we were going, through the dark, the wheels lurching in the muddy places and cutting through to scrape on rock.

They were talking now about roads, and finding

that their fathers, highway builders both, had agreed on the importance of stone foundations, clean culverts, and ditches.

I reached out and found a responsive hand on each side of me.

" 'Don't start with a solid bed," one slow, low voice said into the dark, "nothing you put on top will last, no matter how good 'tis. Bottom goes out; whatever's on top goes with it. And running water in time will eat through anything, even solid rock. Have to channel it off to where it's needed, or anyway won't do any harm."

"It's the same with everything, Mr. Hasty," the other quick, deep, positive voice responded.

I knew he was thinking of education, of motivation, of a philosophy of life, of the choice of a profession, and how all can be riddled in time by the unchanneled waters of impatience, of discontent, of self-distrust, of disillusionment, of outside influence and opposition.

"Why, yes," my father agreed. "Take a piece of land. If it's run out and you don't dig deep down to bring it back, it'll come up to wolf grass and then juniper. Take a paint job. 'Don't start by scraping clean down to the bare wood, new paint'll flake off in a year or so and you're worse off than before. Take a building. Have to put it where you can anchor it and have a dry cellar and dry sills; have to put up a frame stout enough to hold against any wind that blows; have to keep a tight roof on it. Old ones used to say, *Dry sills and a tight roof, house'll stand forever.*"

Their minds, using different materials, worked together.

We had crossed the railroad track, the bridges, Goodwin's hill and Nason's hill, passed Dorr's gate, the Boston place, the Min Joy cellarhole; had come between the high banks of the lane, and turned into the yard lighted only by the lamplight from the kitchen and sitting room windows.

My father pulled up on the reins.

"You go right in," he said. "Your mother's been waiting for you. I'll just put up the horse."

Your mother. . . . Whose mother? *Our* mother.

I ran up the walk and across the porch. She opened the door, stood in a rectangle of lamplight.

"We're home," I cried.

"Well, high time! Your train was late. We heard the whistle. And your father must have let Pony dawdle worse than usual. Thought you'd never get here. Come in, come in."

She called Wally by his first name. They could not shake hands until he had put down the two valises. The table was set for supper with a white cloth and the red and clear glass sugarbowl. The stove was covered with steaming kettles.

They were smiling at each other and did not stop.

"Put your coats in the front hall closet, Gladie. Take this lamp and show Wally the way to his room. He'll have your Aunt Vinnie's. There's water in the pitcher for him to wash. And as soon as you're ready, Wally, come right down to supper."

As we went through the sitting room I hugged and kissed Grammy and introduced Wally to her. It was the first introduction I had been given a chance to make. Grammy sat high in her platform rocker with her lamp on the windowsill, peered up through her new, gold-rimmed spectacles, and held out her tiny hand. He bent over it. I thought for an instant he was going to kiss it. I have always thought that one day someone would. . . . But not, I suppose, anyone *in the family.*

I passed the parlor door and went up the stairs, carrying the lamp. He followed me with his valise. The air was cool and fresh there. I knew my mother had had the front door open until sundown. But Auntie's room was warm, for the heat of Grammy's woodfire was coming up through the open register, along with the glow from her lamp which laid a rosy lace medallion on the ceiling.

I set the lamp into an iron bracket above the washstand and turned to go.

"Hurry up, won't you?" I said. "I'm starved. I smell steak. And I saw a lemon pie."

He was standing in the middle of the room with his hands in his pockets.

"What a smell!" he said. "What a kitchen! What a place to sleep! What a house! I never felt so at home anywhere in my life!"

"That's probably because you are."

"And your father and mother! I don't know which one I like more —"

"I never have, either."

"I feel as if I'd always known them. And your grandmother — she's a — a little queen —"

"Little Queen Louise of Dunnybrook! That's my Grammy!"

I was in the half-dark at the head of the stairs, laughing back at him, as he stood in Auntie's lamplit room, hands in pockets, laughing through the open door at me. It was a soft, radiant kind of laughter running in and out, back and forth, brightening all the dim corners, warming every spot the heat from the register did not quite reach. Something I had not realized I needed was happening. He was filling spaces I had not known were there. He was not Aunt Vinnie, he was not Uncle Joe, he was not my grandfather. He was *instead of them*. But they looked down and loved him. They were glad he had come. He was One of Us. More than that, and best of all, he was himself, and he was mine. Now I understood what I had had to wait for — the assurance, the evidence of *continuity*.

I ran downstairs.

I caught Little Queen Louise into my arms and whispered in her ear, "Do you like him, Grammy? Do you?"

She smoothed her starched white apron.

"He has a good face," she said judicially. "And nice manners. If further acquaintance bears out the first impression he makes —"

"Oh, it does, Grammy! You'll see!"

I ran out into the kitchen where my mother had just taken a pan of biscuits from the oven. Her

cheeks were flushed from the heat of the stove. I
pressed my cool one against her hot one.

"You like him, don't you, Mama?"

"I don't see how anybody could help it."

"I don't either. I love him, Mama."

"Well, if you love him, I love him."

My father was coming through the shedroom. I
met him in the pantry and threw myself against him.

"I can tell you like him, Papa!"

"Like him? Yes. Why wouldn't I like him?"

"And I'm so glad. Because I'm going to marry
him."

My father's low chuckle came down from above my
head. My face was hidden against his new overcoat.
His gloved hands enclosed my wrists as I stretched to
reach his shoulders.

"Thought's likely," he said. "I thought, As like as
not . . ."

I don't know how long Wally had known I was
going to marry him. He says he had never doubted
it since before the first time he asked me to; which
must be why he did not find it so difficult as I
had thought he must be finding it to wait until I
knew it too. Even when I knew it, I waited until the
next day to tell him so because I had in mind exactly
where I wanted to do it. There is a place I had been
many, many times alone but had never before been
with anyone. It is down beyond the pasture hill
where granite posts and iron bars protect the white
stones on which are cut the names of GEORGE, SA-
RAH JANE, and VINNIE HASTY; beyond the wooded

ridge where I used to pick ivory pips and plums to
bring home to my mother; through the grove of pines
which used to be no taller than I but which now reach
into the sky. At their edge the White's Marsh brook
runs below a steep bank, and there grows the ancient
patriarch of all our pines, surrounded by flood waters
in spring and fall, spreading shade and fragrance in
the heat of summer, creaking stoutly in winter winds,
and scattering its seed calmly year after year, generation after generation. Its sprawling old roots make the
back and arms of a wide seat. It allows no other trees
to grow near it, only soft grass, patches of moss, and a
few wildflowers. . . . April nineteenth was a warm
day for the season, and the sun filtered down through
a pearly haze as it always does in April if it shines at
all.

During the next few days we made many plans, deciding that I would finish my college course and we
would be married at my Commencement; that,
wherever he was teaching during the next two years,
he would be in Maine for Christmas and in the summers; that whenever we were separated we would
write to each other every day . . . and that no one
except my family, his family, and Ruth — *no one*
— was to be told of our engagement until summer,
when he would have his degree and I should have
my ring.

Whenever we wanted to be by ourselves, we were
by ourselves. We took long walks to see all my favorite places. Long after everyone else was asleep
at night we sat on in the kitchen, keeping a fire in the
wood stove.

But often we wanted to be with the others. We inspected the barn and tramped all over the farm with my father; we played records and demonstrated the latest dance steps for my grandmother; we sat on the front doorstep with my mother one mild evening, listening to her sing, and Wally, who at my urging had brought along his cornet, went up on the hill in the dark and played bugle calls for us, ending with "Taps." Harold and Jennie came to celebrate his birthday and we went over to the pond and rowed around. We were thirsty and Harold made a birchbark cup for us to drink from. Drifting drowsily in the boat, Harold and Wally talked of Army life, Wally and Jennie and I of college courses and the personalities of favorite professors. Harold and I promised to bring them back for lilies in July.

Everything was so peaceful that sunny April morning!

Everything has been peaceful ever since. Exciting, busy, but still wonderfully peaceful. It is as if all the strands of my life have been braided smoothly and sewn together to make a warm rug for my feet.

We went back to college on Monday. On Wednesday Ruth and Eleanor won the Sophomore Women's debate. Friday night we gave the Spofford plays — the original one-act by Teddy and the original two-act by Erwin and Ken — and Wally and I had parts in both. I wrote my mother:

"They held the attention of a college audience every minute, which is quite a remarkable feat. . . . When the curtain was drawn for the last time,

Birdie *leaped* from the audience into the midst of us, rubbed his hands, hugged the fellows, saying, 'Great work! Great work! This show ought to go on the road! You acted like a bunch of professionals!' In Erwin's play I was Miss Harkness, the reformer. I do wish you could have seen me, Mother. Eleanor did my hair — curled it, coiled it high, and powdered it. I had elderly make-up, wore black satin, jet earrings, and colonial slippers. People say I made a handsome lady. Isn't it wonderful what paint and powder would always do for me? . . . Mrs. Nutter sent Ruth a big box of the pinkest mayflowers I ever saw. We do so hope that next weekend will be pleasant and that this heavy rain won't make the roads so muddy that Mr. Purinton won't dare drive his car. (That's when we're going to East Sumner, you know.) I saw him in the bookstore yesterday and he greeted me with, 'I hear very bad accounts of you, Miss Hasty, very bad accounts. Five whole days away from the campus, and now a weekend house party off in a little town with insufficient chaperones!' . . . Mother, darling, I'll never forget how good you were to us last week. Only yesterday, speaking about another couple, Wally said, 'I think her mother is trying to run their affairs. If only she would trust them, as your mother does us!' . . . I've had my baronet skirt lengthened, cleaned, and pressed, and Ruth Marsh has knit me a tan silk-and-wool sweater with a white angora roll collar."

On Saturday afternoon we went to see Bates win a track meet against New Hampshire State, and then were off with the Purintons for East Sumner, where Postmaster Eastman and his sweet wife had five young couples to supper and to toast marshmallows and sing and play games until midnight. After which, I wrote my mother:

"Augusta and I talked in bed until 1:00, and I was up at 5:30 to walk with Wally until 8:00. The country up there is beautiful. All hills, and hills beyond hills, and mountains beyond them. After breakfast Roger Eastman drove Wally and me to Hartford Center. The road winds through deep woods, and a violent little brook splashes over the rocks alongside. We were back just in time for church, and Arthur (Mr. Purinton, but everybody else was calling him Arthur, so I did) conducted the service, so Wally and I sat together, with the Eastmans. Afterward Wally stayed for Sunday School, and Arthur, Burtra (that's his wife) and I went mayflowering. Have I told you that Arthur is the Bates tennis coach? When he was in college he was a New England tennis champion. After Sunday dinner we climbed the Pinnacle — which is really quite a climb. Arthur almost had to carry Burtra up. But Wally and I were sitting on top when the rest reached it. . . . It had been given out that the evening service was the last Wally could lead there, and there were over fifty in the congregation, most of them young people. His text was 'So run that ye may obtain.' How I wish you and Grammy and Aunt Em and Harold could have heard him! But sometime you will. He has such fire and personality in speaking, and such absolute sincerity! After the service, they all swarmed around him to say good-bye, and some of the elderly people cried. . . . Then we went back to the East-mans to get out things, and they were all so sweet to us. I think Mrs. Eastman *suspects*. She is the dearest lady! She told him, 'Mr. Fennelly, I've decided that she is just right for you.' As we were leaving, Augusta said, 'We can't let Gladys go.' Whereupon Wally said promptly, 'Sorry, Arthur, I can't go back with you tonight, then.' Oh, we had the best time! On the ride back Arthur was sighing over my youth, but said perhaps I made up for it by being intelligent enough to get A's from him. He and Burtra were ideal chaperones — pretended to be very officious, but really left us quite to ourselves. I almost for-got they were faculty!

"I know of nothing else in which you would be especially interested — except that Wally has been appointed head of the Argumentation Department at Milliken University and will leave for Decatur, Illinois, the second week of September. Oh, Mother!"

I worried about Ruth, who had hurt her back in the Gym Meet and strained it again in an interclass soccer game (we lost the game, too!) so that she could not climb stairs, and when I brought her din-ner on a tray she told me to put it on her bed, and she knelt beside the bed to eat it. But then she was called home by her grandmother's illness. I packed her suitcase, Wally and I helped her onto the Figure Eight, and we walked down to the railroad sta-tion, he carrying her suitcase, to buy her ticket and help her onto the train. I worried all the way down about how she would get off the Figure Eight, and wished we could have ridden with her, but we couldn't afford the fare. She managed. The motorman helped her. And Dr. Nutter met her in Salmon Falls.

We were always going on picnics:

"It was warm, blue-skied, sunny. We set off for Pole Hill. Man and maid beneath whispering pines, going over his lines in *Medea* (Commencement play). Curtain begins to fall (coal-black cloud). Raindrops patter. Instant confusion. Next scene: Crumbling springhouse covering an icy spring with a stone wall around it; one side wholly open to the weather, three sides partly boarded. Maid, now heavily coated, huddled under side of roof covered by man's raincoat. Cueing goes on. Finally hunger takes over, so a fire is built. Where? In a drinking cup, of pine needles and a few twigs. Eventually two wieners are *smutted* and consumed between two bedraggled rolls. Finally, rain slackens as darkness falls and man and maid emerge, splash romantically offstage. And we never even sneezed, either of us!"

"This afternoon we went up the river to the dam, about eight miles. It was a rough walk. We forded streams, and blazed trails, and had a perfectly lovely time. We can have the best times doing *anything*, and I'm getting happier and happier by the minute. The sunset was beautiful on the river. I had visions of you out driving around Dover in the twilight."

Great changes were taking place at home. Not only was the house getting painted outside and painted and papered inside, and roof windows being put in to enlarge the east chamber, bring light and ventilation for the first time into the alcove at the head of the back stairs, and provide the first step toward a bathroom, but my father had promised to buy a car if my mother could learn to drive it — and *she was learning!*

"Carpenters are here all day," she wrote, "and as soon as they are out of one room I go in after them to tear off the rest of the paper; then your father and I start painting. He is putting doors on all the open pantry shelves. New windows are in now all over the house, except in your Aunt Vinnie's room. I remembered you said you wished we would leave the old, small-paned one there, but I still don't see why. The new ones have only one pane below and two above. They let in much more light, and are so easy to wash! Besides, they're *tight,* and we'll appreciate that next winter. . . . We have supper as soon as the carpenters go, and then usually Fred England comes. Fred sells the Willys-Knight and, on the chance that that is what your father will buy, he is teaching me to drive. First we practiced in the yard, then we went as far as the Junction several times. Last night I drove right through the village and up Academy Street. He says I am about ready to try Dover traffic. Your father thinks I do fine. He goes along in the back seat. Your grandmother doesn't mind being left. She is looking ahead to going to ride, when you are here to help me get her into a car. We always get back before it is really dark. I don't like to leave her with a lamp burning, unless Uncle Than comes up to sit with her. He makes great sport of the idea of my being behind the wheel, but I tell him when I have my license and set off for the beach he will be glad enough to go with me."

It still seems miraculous to me that my mother is able, all of a sudden, to do all these things with such zest. Until lately she was always frail, and it was a Great Occasion when she went farther from the house than the clothesline unless someone was in dreadful trouble. She never used to begin to paper a room unless Aunt Vinnie was there to help her. Now she is growing younger and stronger by the week.

On Memorial Day we went again to East Sumner with the Purintons, for a picnic with the Eastmans and their friends at New Concord Lake, and came back with a carful of apple blossoms and lilacs, which are my favorite flowers. . . .

I wrote home:

"I'm afraid our secret may get out. The girls are beginning to hint. We haven't told *anyone* here but Ruth. I tell her almost as much as I tell you. Even Wally's roommate doesn't know. He can't understand why, when Wally works out a budget for next year, he insists on allowing $100 for coming East at Christmas. . . . I do hope you will have a Willys-Knight since you both like them so much. I haven't the ghost of an idea what one *is*. It sounds like a

Rolls-Royce, but maybe the similarity is all in the hyphen. Is a Willys-Knight really as good as a Buick?"

Mother replied: "A Willys-Knight is five hundred dollars better than a Buick, if that means anything. And we have ordered one! A lovely dark red. . . ."
I wrote her:

"I hope it comes before I get home. Will you teach me to drive this summer? Did you decide to put on a front piazza? Are we going to have a couch hammock? I must go downtown some day this week and look at evening gowns. Finals begin Thursday. Oh, Mother, these last few days! They seem so beautiful to me — the last times we can walk to class together after chapel, the last few telephone calls, the last times he will ring my bell downstairs with that quick *Ding-ding ding-ding ding-ding! Di-i-ing!* of his. Everything, *last!* Sometimes I feel as if my college life were ending, too."

As finals were beginning, Wally received the wonderful news that a sister who lives in Ohio was driving East with her husband, who is a professor at Western Reserve, and that they would reach Massachusetts in time to bring his mother to Commencement. She is quite elderly and not at all well and her eyesight is very poor, so she had not felt she could travel so far by train. His father is not able to travel at all, but another sister had promised to stay with him. There are six sisters and two brothers. Imagine

growing up in a family that size! Seven of them
were born after their father lost his left arm! What
courage that couple had! All but two of their children are married now, with lots of children of
their own, and one even has a grandchild. I can
hardly wait to meet them all, but I was, to tell the
truth, relieved that I could begin with his mother, a
sister and her husband, and no more than two others at most, as the car is a five-passenger one. (I
asked its size as tactfully as I could, as soon as I
could.)

Ruth's grandmother died and I could sympathize
with her without saying anything, as she had with
me when Aunt Vinnie went. I don't see how she
knew how to do it for me, for at that time nobody
close to her had gone. I think it was because we were
not only college friends, but the bit of home which
we had brought with us. I have needed that many
times, and this was one of the times she did. I wonder
if I should have stayed at college if she had not gone
with me. It certainly would have been an altogether
different place. I know I couldn't go back next fall
without her.

My mother wrote me that the dark red Willys-
Knight had been delivered, that she had her license,
and that I was to telephone her if I needed more on
my checking account to buy what I should have for
Commencement. She thought I might like a different
evening gown for each of the two dances, and asked
if I could use my Academy Graduation dress for
Commencement or Class Day or the Greek Play.

I answered that I could make what I had on my account do; that I had bought one evening gown (my first), and "Oh, Mother, I love it! It's crepe de chine, kind of blue and a little green — mostly blue, I guess — with a bodice and long, very long skirt that is all ruffles and puffed out on the sides"; but the first dance would be informal, and for that I had bought a dress from Cookie for seven dollars — a thin black China silk with a wide bertha collar of ecru Irish lace. "You asked about my graduation dress. Well, dear, I did an awful deed. It had yellowed; so I had it dyed black, and have made it a skirt with an attached camisole. I wear it with my pongee blouse and everyone likes it. For dancing I have some black satin pumps with adorably high heels and cross-straps, and bead embroidery that sparkles in the light."

I took my last sophomore examination and was almost sorry when it was over. I went back to Frye Street and found some of the girls already leaving. We reminded each other of how when we said good-bye at the end of freshman year we had cried; we laughed at that, winking back this year's tears. The rooms seemed to have nothing in them but trunks and suitcases, looked cold and impersonal. But that afternoon Wally took Ruth and me for a hike and a picnic supper in the woods. I wrote my mother, "They like each other, and I think so much of both of them that I love to see them together and listen to them talk."

Something else pleasant happened that day, too.
When I passed in my blue books after the final,
Birdie returned my last two stories. One was marked
A and the other A+. As I took them he said, "I
suppose you're going to read papers for Mr. Woodward again next year." I said I hoped so, but he
hadn't definitely asked me. He said, "Oh, he will
ask you, but I wish he wouldn't." I was startled, and
asked, "W-why?" He said, "Because I'd like to have
you with me for sophomore English." How I should
love to read papers for Birdie!

The next day Ruth went home; Frye Street House
was cleared to be the headquarters for an alumni
class reunion; and I went to Cheney House, where
undergraduate girls are assigned if they are staying
over Commencement either as the guests of seniors
or to work. There were six there from my class
and we all had cots in one small third-floor room.
We were under the same rules as during the year except that of course we had no study hours. It was
fun, but I missed Ruth whenever I was in the room.

The North Shapleigh church, where Wally is to
be the summer pastor, sent him his June salary that
day, which was a great help to him financially at that
point, so he asked me if I would like to go out to Lake
Auburn. That is about a half-hour ride on the street-
car from Lewiston, and of course out of town, where I
could not go without permission from Dean Niles.

When I asked her, she looked at me across her
desk, gently and thoughtfully, for a minute before
she answered.

Then she said, "Ordinarily we never allow under-
classmen to take that trip without a chaperone. But
you are almost a junior, and are here now as the
guest of a senior. Yes, I think it will be perfectly all
right."

I thanked her and turned to go. Then she said,
"Now, about the rest of the week. I don't want you
to have to come here for permission for every little
thing. You know what reasonable hours are, and you
are quite capable of choosing proper places for your
good times. So this week do just as you think best."

I wrote my mother:

"See? You brought me up so that I could, while
living a year in the same house with the Dean of
Women, meet, be almost constantly with, and become engaged to a senior man — and at the end of it
be told I'm capable of making and following my
own rules! Of course part of the credit has to go to
Dean Niles; she is a wonderful woman. And to Bates
for having confidence in its students and in the wisdom of a dean like her."

There is no possibility of my ever forgetting my
first college Commencement.

Not quite nineteen, secretly engaged, making my
own rules of conduct without advice for the first time
in my life, separated from close friends of my own
age, I felt the earth move beneath my feet as my
little world underwent a transformation like that of
a small country taken over by a larger one.

The campus grass was suddenly shaven as close

as I imagine English lawns to be. Summer heat beat down. Familiar crisp green borders burst into extravagant bloom, disappeared under masses of great soft pink and wax-white flowers which filled the air with intoxicating fragrance. A professor became a man in shirt sleeves, with collar unbuttoned, sauntering off to buy a newspaper, or an ice-cream cone for a child he had by the hand; I hardly recognized him. The dormitories and walks were crowded with strangers of all ages except college age — little boys chasing each other; little girls running with balloons; pale young mothers sitting on the library steps singing lullabies to babes-in-arms; handsome young fathers parking strollers in front of Chase Hall and leading toddlers into the bookstore; teen-agers being introduced by their parents and looking as if they wished the ground would open and swallow them up.

Still, *most* of the strangers were middle-aged or older.

Some were the families of seniors. These were easy to identify because they were all dressed for travel, all wore hats, spoke little and low, and unless surrounding a senior looked uneasy and lost.

The rest were alumni, and the older they were the younger they seemed to feel, despite all odds. None of them wore hats, and most were white-haired or bald. They were coatless, in short sleeves, regardless of their dimensions. They shouted, perhaps because many of them were deaf.

Oversized women lumbered along eagerly after wrinkled little ones, and if they caught up there were glad cries of *"Aren't* you Emma Travers?" "Oh

— oh — don't tell me! Let me guess! You're —
you're — why, *Lizzie Paul!*" Then, amid great hug-
gings and kissings, spang in the middle of the walk
or in front of the chapel, or while someone held a
door so that it wouldn't crash into them, they declared neither had changed a bit since '89 and they
would have known each other anywhere.

Lame men hobbled up Hathorn steps to shake
hands with fat men who had stopped on the first
landing to catch their breath; and, grinning, huffing
and puffing, they debated their chances of ever getting to the top floor. If Hathorn bell then began to
ring — it was always ringing at unlikely times for no
reason I could see except to give them the pleasure
of hearing it — they turned up their old faces toward the tower with half-happy, half-sad expressions, as if receiving invitations to a wonderful party
they were not at all sure they could go to.

A tall, thin man, leaning against a pillar, smoking
a pipe, watched a short plump woman in a flowered dress and thick glasses coming his way. When
she was near enough, he took his pipe from his
mouth, looked down at her with extraordinary ten-
derness, and said, *"Flossie. . . . Little Flossie Bea!*
Bless my soul!" She stared up, leaving her ringed
hand in his, almost whispering, "John. . . . John
— dear!"

They sat stiffly on dormitory porches talking,
laughing, singing. They crowded the dining halls,
men and women together, always looking a little in-
credulous, as if their time sense had escaped them
— was this Now or Then? — and saying over and

over and over, "I'll never forget . . . ," asking over and over and over, "Who else remembers . . . ?" They swarmed into Chase Hall to watch the dancing; some of them danced, and here and there one of the oldest professors appeared like a ghost and danced with them. . . . The night of the Greek Play they came from all directions out of the dusk into the area before Coram Library and filled the rows of teetery folding chairs under the moth-encircled, multicolored lights strung like a giant web among the tree branches. They watched the shrouded figures of the Chorus of Corinthian Women swaying in a long line between the great white pillars, and listened to Medea, Jason, Creon, Aegeus and the others saying old words they had learned to know and appreciate under Goosie, or with Goosie under Uncle Johnny. Who could guess their thoughts as they sat there that June night? Or the next day when a band played and they paraded in firemen's hats or with big paper sunflowers to the Commencement Dinner, served at noon in a huge tent where they sat on long, narrow, wooden benches at long, narrow wooden tables in the steaming heat a canvas-top creates, and ate a Thanksgiving menu? After the dessert of strawberries and melted vanilla ice cream they listened to speeches, rose by classes to cheer, and rose all together to sing the Alma Mater.

In the front of our menu cards was printed in garnet letters on white:

GATHER THE CRUMBS OF HAPPINESS AND THEY WILL MAKE YOU A LOAF OF CONTENTMENT.

It was the college's fifty-seventh Commencement weekend, and my first.

I don't think I could have endured staying with it constantly from Sunday through Wednesday. Whenever I came back to it (from a picnic with Wally, from watching him in *Medea,* from meeting his family, from the Class Day exercises in front of Hathorn which were attended only by seniors and their friends, from a dreamy waltz with Wally, I was bewildered and swept by something very like despair. Was this what all the Ruths and the Dots and Cookie and Caroline and I were coming to? Was this what lay ahead for Wally and Lloyd and Elwin and Erwin, and Kenneth and Pete and Frank? Euterpe, Lucy, Ursula; the Helens, the Bernices, the Alices, the Evelyns, the Graces, the Elsies, the Hazels, the Marys; the Stanley sisters; Eleanor, Connie, Marion, Betty; Rubie, Kay, Aletha, Ellen; Annabel, Avis, Nellie Mae; Eloise, and Priscilla? Okie, Tom, Hap, Scotty, George, Chet, Ike, Doug, Mel, Ev, Ralph; the Reds, the Carls, the Jerrys; Herb, Tracy, Naga, Jonah, Pop; Fuji, Don, Peanut, Mike, Al, Charlie, Johnny; Bob, Clarence, Ham, Cal, Roger, and Archie? Was what I could see here all there was? Then I would never come back. Never again after my own Commencement. None of us should ever come back, for the crumbs of this happiness we have now will never content us. . . . But part of my despair grew out of a strong feeling not only that there ought to be more, there must be more, but that there *was* more, here, now, for these strangers; only I could not find it, could not see or feel it. Now, long after, I think I should not have tried, should not have spied on them, should not have eavesdropped, for they were where they belonged. I wasn't.

I was happy with Wally. I was happy with his mother. She is tiny; not even as tall as I am. And such a little lady in her black satin dress and black lace hat! Her name used to be Allen and her father was a druggist, but her mother died before she can remember, and when she ran away at sixteen to marry the big, blue-eyed young man who had lately come back from surveying in Michigan, her father disowned her. She missed her lovely home, where the library was filled with leather-bound books and the walls of the dining room were painted with woodland scenes from floor to ceiling; but with her big, blue-eyed surveyor she made other homes and brought nine of their ten children to man- and womanhood, all of them now nearer his size than hers. She is over sixty years old and has not a gray hair. She is dark like Wally, and talks rapidly, as he does. We were proud of him together, as we sat side by side in the chapel Wednesday morning, watched him come down the aisle, read our programs where his name was printed under *Honors in Language and Literature,* and saw him receive his degree. When he came back up the aisle he smiled at us. I blinked back my tears, but she took a little white embroidered handkerchief from her bag to dry hers. It smelled of sweet lavender.

After the Commencement exercises his family started home. Most of the alumni had already gone. He and I had a quiet supper together. That evening we danced once more in Chase Hall, with the other

graduates of the day and their partners. It was the
Senior Prom. We had dance orders, with tiny pencils
attached to them by gold cords. The guests of honor
were President and Mrs. Gray, the patrons and patronesses Dean Niles, Professor Robinson, Dean and
Mrs. Pomeroy, Professor and Mrs. Gould, Coach and
Mrs. Jenkins. The first three and the last two dances
were ours, also the last before and the first after in-
termission. The rest I danced with the men who had
come with the girls in his class whom he liked best —
Teddy Barentzen, Dorothy Wheet, Marcia Walling-
ford, and others. I watched them across my partner's
shoulder and wondered what it was like to know
you were saying good-bye to people you knew well
and whom you might never see again, and that even
if you did, everything would be different. I had done
it at our Senior Dance at the Academy but without
fully realizing it. Now I realize. (I never saw Ralph
again after that night. He died during his freshman
year at Northeastern.)

It was all beautiful, but the beauty trembled with
sadness. It was in the eyes and smiles of the patrons
and patronesses seated along the wall, and in the
figures and movements of the dancers. I thought it
was also in the face of President Chase over the fireplace. Everyone was tired. Even President Chase was
tired. It seemed to me he was saying, in the words
and voice of his son, our Greek professor, "You have
done well. Very well. All of you" — and that he
added, "I have helped you where I could. It is over
now. The year is ending. Another class is going out.
My constant concern for you has been exhausting for

an old man like me, one whose time was unlike your time. It is late. I must rest now. Good night. God bless you. . . . Good night. . . . Good night."

Thursday morning the campus was deserted and all the buildings closed except the few dormitories, from which new graduates and some of their families were carrying out trunks, suitcases, blankets, pillows, snowshoes, skis, and loading them into taxicabs or family cars, setting forth on the Great Safari.

Wally had already sent his trunk to the depot. We had only a small suitcase apiece. He was going home with me for a few days, but must be at North Shapleigh for the Sunday morning service. We left the suitcases on the sidewalk and crossed College Street to try the chapel door. It was locked. But two years from then, we told each other, almost to the day, the door would be open and we would be married there. We picked up the suitcases and walked on down College Street, Sabattus and Main and Bates Streets, to the depot. His undergraduate days were over. When next he walked on a college campus it would be as a member of the faculty. When I came back, he would not be here.

We were rather quiet all the way to Salmon Falls. We did not want to talk of what had been and it was too soon to speak much of what would be.

Then suddenly the conductor was calling out the home station, the train was stopping, we were running down the steps into the sunshine with our suitcases — and there was the shining, dark-red Willys-

Knight, with my mother alone in it, *stalled* halfway up the steep little hill between the street and the brown depot.

We waved and called.

"Hi, Mother! Hi! It's a beauty!"

She waved and called back.

"Hi! I'll be there in a minute. Just as soon as I get this thing —"

The sound of the engine increased, but the automobile rolled back several feet and jerked to a stop.

"Are you all right, Mother?"

"I'm all right. I just can't get this thing —"

She started up and rolled back quite a way. She was almost down to the street now, where other cars were coming and going.

"Is she all right?" I asked Wally.

"She is if that's her emergency brake she has on and she'll use some power as she takes it off."

"But those cars in the street —"

"Don't worry about them. They'll stop. They're stopping —"

At that instant there came a terrific roar; the shining red Willys-Knight with my mother at the wheel came rushing up the hill at a great rate, straight at us. We froze, and the wheels stopped with a wild scream of brakes just as the tires touched the platform.

My mother, scrubbed, powdered, starched, white-pompadoured, with twin red flags billowing in her cheeks, took one hand off the wheel to wave, smiled gaily, and called, "Didn't hit anything, did I?"

"No. No, Mother, you didn't!"

"Lucky your father isn't here. He says *never* to drive faster than fifteen miles an hour even on a straightaway, and ten around curves. I must have been going at least twenty then. But I don't see any other way to get a thing as big as this up a hill from a standing start, do you?"

I didn't. I thought she had done splendidly. I climbed in beside her and after Wally put the suitcases into the back seat with the groceries he got in beside me. My mother backed up a little, started ahead and hit the platform (but only lightly), backed up again, turned around, pressed both slender feet against pedals — "If you throw in the clutch going downhill," she told us happily, "you save gas and wear-and-tear on the brakes" — and we inched slowly down the hill. At its foot we waited awhile until there were no other cars in sight, and then rode grandly out into the street, across the bridge, and along lower Main Street into the village square.

"You can be thankful you're not riding with Henry Warren," my mother said. "Henry's just got him a car. The first Sunday he had it, he says, he took it into his head to go to the beach. So he put a daisy into his hatband, and rode down through York Woods well enough, but when he got to Route One there was a long line of cars coming by him both ways. He waited for them to thin out until his patience was exhausted, and he decided to *go*. Go he did, he says, right into the middle of them, and we should have seen the cars fly in all directions and traffic pile up as far as the eye could reach. I don't doubt the story. Sounds just like Henry."

We were already up Portland Street, passing the Soldiers' Monument.

"You watch the speedometer for me, Wally," my mother said. "I don't *mean* to go over fifteen, but one thing that bothers me is watching the speedometer and driving at the same time. When your father's with me, he always watches it."

"I'll watch it, Mrs. Hasty," Wally assured her.

So he watched the speedometer and my mother drove, and I looked around me at the familiar places flashing past, and at the chariot in which we three sat, with the feeling that this was the tryout of a brand-new play which I had not rehearsed and for which I could not remember one of my lines. Still, I had no doubt that it was a marvelous play and that what I was supposed to do and say in it would be clear when the time came.

We rode up the lane, almost brushing the sweet-fern on its banks, and turned in beside the bell-flower tree, stopped under the maples. My mother's slim fingers pulled on a long lever beside her until it snapped. She turned off a key in the dashboard and took it out, dropping it smartly into her handbag.

"Matter of habit," she said. "Your father says if I *always* take it with me, there'll be no chance of somebody driving the car off while I'm gone. We're using your father's old carriage shop for a garage, but I don't put the car in until dark. You'll want to look it over, I expect."

My father was coming, all smiles, down the steps from the porch. He kissed me and shook hands with Wally and they began looking over the car. They looked under the hood, at the tools under the cushion of the front seat, into the rectangular steel box which was the trunk on the back.

"I had to pay extra for the trunk," my father said, "but you have to have a place for things you can't carry on the seat without wearing out the upholstery. I'd never put up with the racks so many fasten on the running boards."

I was looking at the house. It has two new dormer windows on the back and one on the front. Where the front door used to open onto three wooden steps, there is now a broad, screened-in piazza which covers half the old croquet ground.

"Isn't it lovely?" my mother asked. "See the couch hammock you wanted? And we don't have to worry about mosquitoes any more."

I noticed the swing-chairs hadn't been repainted and set up between the ash tree and the maples as every early June before they had been.

"It's *elegant*," I said. "But I miss the swing-chairs."

" 'Where's my Margery? I want my Margery!' " my mother quoted me, laughing. "The swing-chairs are in a horse stall in the barn. Your father and Wally can get them out and set them up if you want them. But I doubt if you'll use them much. Now come see the *inside* of the house!"

My father and Wally were still looking over the Willys-Knight, but she and I went in. There is a brown enamel cookstove, heated by oil, where the black wood stove used to be. (But there is still a black wood stove in the shedroom.) There is a white enamel sink in the pantry. (The black iron one we used to clean with vinegar is a drinking-trough for the chickens.) There is a new dinner set, complete, with all the pieces matching; new stemmed glass-ware; and silver in place of the bone-handled knives and forks. The once open shelves have doors with amber glass knobs, and are dust-free. The ceilings have been whitened, the floors have been stained and waxed, there is linoleum in the kitchen, new wall-papers and new shades and curtains everywhere.

"It's — it's just beautiful," I said. "Oh, Grammy! I'm glad you haven't been turned in for a new model!"

"I'm one thing they can't improve," said Grammy smugly.

"Come up the backstairs," Mother urged me. "See all the light and air in the alcove now? It's my little sewing room. I've always wanted one. . . . And look at our chamber! With the roof window it's twice again as big, and we have cross-ventilation at last! (But see? We left the old window with the small panes in Vinnie's room.) Here at the head of the front stairs is where we'll put the bathroom as soon as your father settles on a generator to make the electric power to get the water up. When we have that, we'll put in electric lights, of course. We may not get them before next spring, but we'll certainly have a furnace in the cellar by this fall. Think, Gladie, what a dif-ference all that will make in my work — and our comfort. Remember that cold winter when your father had to get me a pair of boy's felt boots to wear right here in the house, because so much cold came up through the floor that I thought my toes would freeze? Your Aunt Vinnie said it must be my circulation was poor; she didn't mind it. Now come down and see the parlor."

The flowered ingrain carpet has been taken up and replaced by a taupe art square. Auntie's little red plush sofa, and the armchairs with the finger carving, or grapes and roses on the backs, and the marble-topped table have been covered with old sheets and stored again in the shed chamber with the graphophone. Now we have a long, deep brown sofa with no wood showing, all deep cushions; and chairs to match, except that one of them is covered in yellow velour and the other in figured green. There are new bookcases with glass doors, end tables, and a long, low coffee table before the sofa. The old wallpaper was striped red and green with a kind of gold lace all over it; the new is what my mother calls "oatmeal paper" — plain tan, and rough, with little brown grains in it. She says it is a much better background for pictures. But there are only a few small watercolors there, all signed by Wallace Nutting. She has taken down Saint Cecilia, and my Great-grandmother Brown in charcoal, and the castle with the mother-of-pearl windows, and she says she may use their frames for pictures she is going to paint. She has not had time to paint a picture since early in her marriage, only rosebuds or clover on sateen aprons and yellow daisies on mirror corners.

I am still slow to accept change. It is still difficult for me. But as I look back I am glad that after that one remark about the swing-chairs and my mother's reminder of Margery-I-want-my-Margery I took myself in hand that first day at home and followed her lead.

"See the sun streaming in?" cried my mother. "The art square and upholstery are guaranteed not to fade."

"Isn't that wonderful?" I exclaimed. "I remember when this room was always dim. Auntie even closed the blinds in the daytime in summer."

Though being dim was part of The Parlor.

But this house belongs to my mother and father now. For the first time they have it — or are getting it — just as they want it. And I know it is pleasanter to live in, and easier to care for, this way. Ever so much pleasanter. Ever so much easier. They are good to keep the graphophone, the swing-chairs, and the small-paned window for me to come back to. Because that is what I do now, and probably shall always do — go away, and come back, and go away again. Two years from now I shall have another home. I wonder where it will be. In Decatur, Illinois, probably. . . . And, so far, the only states of the Union I have been in are Maine and New Hampshire, except for one brief visit to Aunt Annie Harriman in Lawrence, Massachusetts. That was when I was ten years old. Aunt Vinnie was visiting Aunt Annie, and I went with Harold while they selected his suit for graduation from the Academy.

Those few days before Wally left for North Shapleigh were gala days. My mother was so happy with the house and the car, and to have us to enjoy them with her; whenever she was by herself for a few minutes she was singing. She looks so *well* now. Not ethereal, as she used to, but sturdy, healthy, gay. And my father is so proud of the car, that it is so beautiful and that he bought it for my mother (he says he will never drive it; Pony is good enough for him) and of Wally, because when they went into the woods Wally could estimate the number of feet of lumber in a tree as closely as Papa could himself. We went for a ride every day, and twice Grammy went with us — each time saying, "I'll have this to think about next winter." My father and Pony brought Wally's trunk home in the democrat wagon and it is stored here until September.

Now he has gone and we are quieter, but very busy. I am learning to cook many things I have never cooked before. I am also learning to drive the car, and my teacher is not my mother. She explained the process to me, but when she sat beside me I could feel her tension as soon as I turned the key and moved the spark lever on the steering wheel. So one morning when the car was out in front of the shop and she was giving Grammy a bath, I went into the yard and slid in behind the wheel.

My father finished pumping a pailful of water, set it on the curb, and came slowly toward me.

"Where you going?" he asked. "Gonic?"

That is where he always says he is going when someone asks him and he doesn't want to tell.

"Just getting the feel of it," I said.

He rested his folded arms on the door opposite me and studied the dashboard.

"What's that?" he asked curiously, pointing. "The key I told your mother to keep with her?"

"Yes. She did. I just got it out of her handbag."

"What does it do? Turn the engine on?"

"Yes."

"Then what do you do? To go?"

"Move up the spark and the gas. Press this button."

"Then 'she starts, she moves, she seems to feel the thrill of life beneath her keel'?"

"I guess so. If I take my foot off the brake. If I don't stall."

He opened the door and got in beside me. The only adjective I can think of to describe the expression on his face is mischievous.

"What's this?"

"The emergency brake."

"Well, what say I lay to this and you try her out, easy? Don't see what harm we can do."

So I did. But too easy. The engine stalled.

"Must need a mite more gas," he said.

The engine roared, the car leaped forward, he pulled up the brake, we stopped so suddenly that his head almost went into the windshield. We looked at each other and burst out laughing.

"Don't they build any happy medium into these contraptions?" he asked. "With all this horse power, ought to have some horse sense."

I tried again. That time we moved forward slowly for perhaps twenty feet, and I stopped with the use of the foot brake and only a slight jerk.

"Well, now, what's the matter with that?" demanded my father, delighted. "You started her and you stopped her. What else does anybody have to do but steer? You could always steer a sled. No reason why you can't steer this."

"Sometimes you have to back up."

"Nobody ought to start backing up until they've done a good deal of going ahead," declared my father. "Figure it right, might never have to back up. Next trip, why don't we turn left as if we were going into the barn, but then turn left again around the ash tree, between that and the pump, and right back in front of the shop, headed out?"

"I may hit the well curb and knock over your pail of water."

"Do, go back into the well again, and we can pump it out."

But I didn't hit anything. I kept coming up in front of the shop and stopping, then starting up and making the circle again. My mother came out on the back porch and watched, clapping her hands as we passed her.

I had already sent for my license, and it came the next day. Then my father and I ventured down the lane and up and down the road. I can turn in Aunt Em's driveway or at Nason's pump or at the fork of the roads beyond the Junction bridge without backing. I haven't tried backing yet.

I see another reason now why Wally and my father are such good friends. Both have the qualities of great teachers.

I think this will be the last entry in my journal. The kind of thing I have been writing in it I now write in long, daily letters to Wally and shall be for the next two years. Beside his letters and those I write home, I need my time and thought for imaginative writing. I want to do a great deal, and it can't be in connection with my courses as it has been the past two years, for Bates offers only literature courses to English majors in the junior and senior years. I must do a great deal of reading, too, on my own, for none of our courses are on American writers, and I want to read all I can of them. Not only Hawthorne, Cooper, Bret Harte, and Mark Twain, but several who are writing now — Sherwood Anderson, Sinclair Lewis, Esther Forbes, Zona Gale, Willa Cather. I think especially Zona Gale, because her characters seem more like people I know than any of the others. I may decide to write my senior thesis on Zona Gale's work. I like her understatement, though that may be the reason why she isn't properly appreciated. I had never heard of her until I read her play *Trifles*. How I should love to take the part of the poor woman whose little singing bird was killed! I want to read not only American novelists, but American playwrights and American poets. Especially Robert Frost. Carl Sandburg is exciting, and Vachel Lindsay makes my heart ache. But I love Robert Frost. The New England I know is in every line he writes.

And this summer I am going to reread all the

books by Sarah Orne Jewett which Grandmother Hasty had and get the rest from the Academy library. Because Miss Jewett was our own. The two houses, side by side, where she lived, are the very center of our village: I know the color and fragrance of her lilac bushes, have sat by her hearth fire and in the thatched-roof cottage in her garden.

Her sister, Miss Mary, has been very kind to me.

Last winter when I was doing a paper on Sarah Orne Jewett I wrote to Miss Mary asking for whatever she could tell me about her sister.

She replied:

Jan. 24th, 1923

DEAR MISS GLADYS:

I am sending you herewith some very random notes about my sister in answer to your wish. I am very glad to do it for you and only hope you will find it useful and that you will not hesitate to write me if I can be of any further help. . . . I wish you all manner of success, not only in this special case but throughout your college life and always.

Very sincerely yours,
MARY R. JEWETT

These are the "notes" she sent me:

"S. O. J.'s childhood was an imaginative one. A shy little girl with dark eyes which seemed to look beyond the things that other children saw. Her great joy was to get away from the village streets and wander through the woods and fields, often disappearing for an hour or two in a way which was rather trying to her mother, but always coming home safely, usually with some playmate who had gone with her, and bringing some flower or plant in her little hands to show. She never had robust health as a child, and so never went to school steadily. In fact the schoolroom was looked upon more as imprisonment than anything else and so was avoided on any reasonable pretext, and long drives with her busy father were substituted as he went his daily rounds among his patients hither and yon. She always looked back to those early days with deep pleasure and all her life spoke with gratitude of what it had meant to her to learn from her father's wide knowledge of the trees and plants and birds of the region, and the many things he taught her besides as they drove along the pleasant roads of the town she loved so well. Very early she began to love books and read eagerly those that would seem to have been beyond a child of her age. One would find her curled up in a big armchair hour after hour heeding little of what might be going on about her, but reading some poem or story so eagerly as to take her whole attention. In this way she laid the foundation for her lifework and as the years went by reaped the reward of her efforts. She began to tell little stories to her older sister when she was still very young and write little attempts at verses from time to time. All very simple and childish efforts of course but with a steady growth towards better things as time went by. She never had what one might call a conventional education, for her delicate health prevented that in great measure, but probably gained from her intimate companionship with the best authors far more than with her nature she could ever have received from the regular school curriculum of her day. She never had set times for writing, but would work when the spirit moved her, oftentimes almost too long for her strength. I think she carefully framed her story before putting pen to paper. Except possibly a few notes as her only preparation and then worked it through to a finish. I think she often and perhaps nearly always laid the story away for a little while to ripen as it were before she was satisfied to let it go out of her hands. And only once did she ever consent to let a serial story be published until it was entirely finished before it went to the publisher. That was the only time that she was obliged to work steadily day after day on any piece of writing, and she was much broken down by the effort for a time. She would never have undertaken to do it but for wishing to help a friend. Like every other literary worker one would suppose that discouraging moments came in her work, when it would be put away to wait for better ideas or progress, but she has left behind very few half-finished pieces of work, singularly few when one thinks of all the long years she was writing. I do not think she ever wrote simply because she seemed to have time to do it, but the best things were done because the impulse was strong upon her to say the things she had been thinking about. So strong that the impulse could not be denied. Then she would often write many hours in succession until she felt it was safe to leave the unfinished story for another time. Probably the *Tory Lover* was the most difficult piece of writing

that she did, for the adapting of certain historical
facts to the course of her story was anything but an
easy task, for one had to watch constantly lest the
one overstepped the boundary of the other and
caused confusion. The last years of her life were sad-
dened because an accident prevented her from carrying on her beloved work to the end, but her interest in books and music and the best things of earth
never wavered until the end came. In the published
volume of her letters, you will find on p. 247 (I
think) some advice that she gave to a young friend
who was beginning to write, and in whose success she
was greatly interested. I hope these hastily written
suggestions of mine may prove to be helpful to you.
Any further questions I shall be delighted to answer
if I can at any time."

(That letter on page 247 was written to Willa
Cather.)

At this same time Jennie sent me a poem Sarah
Orne Jewett had written and given to her friend,
Miss Kate Sanborn, who was Jennie's aunt.

At Home from Church

The lilacs life in generous bloom
  Their plumes of dear old-fashioned flowers —
Their fragrance fills the still old house
  Where left alone I count the hours.

High in the apple trees the bees
  Are humming, busy in the sun —
An idle robin cries for rain
  But once or twice and then is done.

The Sunday morning quiet holds
    In heavy slumber all the street
While from the church, just out of sight
    Behind the elms, comes slow and sweet

The organ's drone, the voices faint
    That sing the quaint long-meter hymn —
I somehow feel as if shut out
    From some mysterious temple, dim

And beautiful with blue and red
    And golden lights from windows high,
Where angels in the shadows stand
And earth seems very near the sky.

The daydream fades — and so I try
    Again to catch the tune that brings
No thought of people, nor of priest,
    But only of a voice that sings.

This poem is on a piece of stationery, in Sarah Orne Jewett's handwriting. I don't know whether it was ever published.

Her world was the village and the coast of Maine. Mine is the inland farms to which she used to ride out with her father, the doctor. She respected and loved farming people, but she was not one of them as I have been and as I hope always to be, however far away I go. I want to learn to write of them in such a way that if Sarah Orne Jewett could read what I say she would imagine herself one of them, at least until she closed the book. Perhaps I can never do it, but I can try.

What difference will it make, I wonder, that I shall

be writing — if at all — in a different century than hers? That she was a Jewett and I am a Hasty? That I shall graduate from college, and she didn't? That I shall be married, and she wasn't? That I shall — I hope — be a mother?

In every way, so far, our lives have been unlike and will be more so; except that we grew up in the same town, a little Maine town, settled and developed by people we admire, people both strong and gentle, who respected themselves and their neighbors, and who built for the glory of God. We had the same sky, too, the same hills, the same roads, the same rivers; sang the same hymns, and honored the same flag.

Whether I can ever put it in a book or not, I feel very close to Sarah Orne Jewett because I *want* to put it in a book, as she did.

This is the place, at the head of tidewater, to which shipbuilders, shipowners, sea captains, sailors, fishermen, farmers, surveyors and their women came, from across the sea, almost three hundred years ago, to make a town together. It was from here they rounded the Horn, sailed to the Orient, rode by bridle path to Boston Town. When every green pine needle is encased in ice and glitters in the sunshine, our children cry, "Come see the icy-jane!" because their great-grandmothers said, "Look out the window at the icy jade." . . . From here young men went out to throw off the yoke of kingly rule; later, young men — and older ones — went south to save the Union and free the slaves; and still later, their grandsons went back across the sea to fight a European ty-

rant in his stronghold. We are against tyranny in all
its forms. We live — and when necesary die — in freedom.

This is the place where a carpenter led his people
to God . . . where all one long summer a doctor
drove his horse and buggy eight miles every day to
see an old woman, dying of tuberculosis, who had no
money to pay for his calls, and brought her a pint of
ice cream each time he came . . . where district
schoolteachers told their pupils, "Do as much as you
can each day of whatever you can do best."

This is the place where the woodbine twineth.